THE
MEMORIES AND WRITINGS
OF A
LONDON RAILWAYMAN

A Tribute to
HAROLD VERNON BORLEY (1895–1989)
edited by Alan A. Jackson

RAILWAY & CANAL HISTORICAL SOCIETY

First published in 1993
by the Railway & Canal Historical Society
Registered office: Fron Fawnog, Hafod Road, Gwernymynydd, Mold, Clwyd CH7 5JS
Registered charity no.256047

ISBN 0 901461 16 4

Designed and typeset by
Malcolm Preskett and Carol Davie
Printed in England by
Hobbs the Printers of Southampton

FRONT COVER
A North London Railway train entering Broad
Street station about 1910. Broad Street No. 1 Signal
Box is in the background and to its left are NLR
Loco Department coal wagons at the loco coaling
stage. This specially-commissioned painting by
Richard Downe was presented to H.V. Borley by
the Railway Club upon his retirement as Trustee
and Chairman of the Committee in 1984 and
remains in the possession of his family.

Contents

1. H. V. Borley crossing the bridge at Verney Junction
on the occasion of a Railway Club visit, 27 June 1964.
Alan A. Jackson 5279

Editor's foreword

I FIRST MET 'Borley', as he was generally known, in the late 1950s after Edwin Course had pointed him out to me at Liverpool Street station as 'the man anyone interested in London's railways must know'. I was left in no doubt that he was the leading authority on the subject. Soon afterwards I encountered him in the Railway Club and at Club events and we began a regular correspondence which was to last some 30 years. Towards the end, he could no longer type a letter, but until a week or so before he died, he was still telephoning me to talk of railway events and history and would set me complicated questions to answer in writing. Over the years, as well as discussing railways, he regaled me with information on foreign currencies and measurements, French slang, the 24-hour clock, and London social life in the early decades of the 20th century. Into his 93rd year he was still questing elusive facts. When thinking of him, I am reminded of Dr Johnson's statement, 'A generous and elevated mind is distinguished by nothing more certainly than an eminent degree of curiosity'.

It was therefore with considerable pleasure that I accepted from the Publications Committee of the Railway & Canal Historical Society the task of editing a compilation which would present the major part of Borley's published work (other than his books), introducing it with the recorded interview of 1983. In editing this material, the objective has been not only to collect and place on permanent record his knowledge of the many subjects covered, but also to give the flavour of the man, and to produce a suitable and lasting tribute to one who made a substantial contribution to railway history, particularly London railway history.

Except where stated, everything in PART THREE, the main part of this book, was written by him. Each item is noted to show the type of contribution and the original place and date of publication.* Editing has been confined to slight alteration of some of the original headings (or inserting headings where none existed) and deleting introductory sentences which merely refer to earlier matter in the same periodical. Apart from this, and the correction of two or three printing errors, all is as originally published. Any addenda and corrigenda by HVB appear as separate items at the end, or as footnotes.

Although some pieces repeat facts given in other contributions (he was always anxious to ram the correct data home) I have reproduced them here in all cases where they are accompanied by additional material or where the alternative version helps to increase understanding.

Thus whilst no claim is made that PART THREE is comprehensive, the only items consciously omitted are those which either wholly repeat information which appears in pieces printed here, or short statements of minor or ephemeral interest. Borley's corrections to books which have subsequently appeared in new editions have also been left out, on the charitable assumption that the texts have been suitably amended.

The idea of this book originated from Grahame Boyes and I wish to record my thanks to him and to Harry Paar and Peter Davis for welcome assistance which rendered the editorial task easier. Mrs Doreen Castell, HVB's daughter, graciously agreed to publication in this form; the Editor of the *Railway Magazine* kindly allowed reproduction of text and maps originally published in that periodical; and John L. Brown cheerfully undertook the chore of providing a transcript of the interview. Finally mention should be made of Nick Howell for gathering in the illustrations, Richard Dean for preparing a map, and Tony Jervis, Michael Messenger, John Nestor, Malcolm Preskett and Sylvia Rymell, who undertook the donkey work of processing the raw text that I supplied.

Alan A. Jackson
Dorking, June 1993.

* For example: '(A) *JRCHS* 3, 6, pp.105–107 (11/1957)' means an article in the *Journal of the Railway & Canal Historical Society*, volume 3, part 6, pages 105–107, published in November 1957; *and* '(L) *UN* 256, p.86 (4/1983)' means a letter to the Editor, *Underground News*, serial 256, page 86, published in April 1983.

Introduction

AROLD VERNON BORLEY (1895–1989) was a Londoner who worked on the railway from the time of leaving school in 1910 until he retired in 1960. He was first employed by the London & North Western Railway and subsequently by its successors, the London Midland & Scottish Railway and the London Midland Region of British Railways, working first as booking clerk and latterly in a clerical capacity. An intelligent man, blessed with a long and clear memory, he took a minute interest in all aspects of his work and in the history of railways, notably those of north London. In particular, he pursued the precise dating of events, searching relentlessly through timetables, contemporary newspapers and (when they became available for study in the 1950s) the original railway company records. He began early: his copy of *The Railway Year Book* for 1914, bought when he was barely 19, contains a loose sheet recording over 30 errors and omissions he had detected. The principal product of his scholarship was his *Chronology of London Railways*, compiled when he was in his mid-80s and published by the R&CHS in 1982, but the columns of the journals of the R&CHS and the London Underground Railway Society and to a lesser extent *The Railway Magazine*, contain numerous letters and contributions by him. His last was written in November 1988, within weeks of his 93rd birthday.

After serving in the Army's Railway Operating Division in France and Italy in World War 1, he set up home in Letchworth from 1919 to 1946, travelling to work in London daily (hence the interest in the Great Northern lines). In the latter year, he moved to Ruislip, renewing acquaintance with London Transport railways and their history. After his retirement, he used the Piccadilly Line into London regularly, travelling twice a week or more to the Railway Club. His final years,

2. H. V. Borley in South Acton Junction signal box, 9 December 1961. *Anon*

from 1984, were spent at Bexhill and in 1985, at the age of 89, he made his last visit to London, journeying on his beloved North London line from Richmond to North Woolwich and paying his last respects to the doomed Broad Street station.

Like many of his generation, he continued his good but limited education by reading and travel. He explored most European countries, enjoying the intricacies of the lesser-known languages, currencies and measurements as well as the railway systems. Country walking, coins, and tickets also featured in his leisure interests. An enthusiastic member of several railway societies, he joined the Railway Club in 1920, becoming Hon. Assistant Secretary in 1939, Chairman of the Committee in 1947, Trustee in 1958 and Honorary Librarian in 1962. Except for Librarian, which he relinquished in 1981, these offices were retained until his move to Bexhill, when he was made an Honorary Member of the Club. He was one of the earliest members of the Railway & Canal Historical Society, joining soon after its formation in

1954. In recognition of his scholarship and the assistance he had given to many other members in their researches, he was elected a Vice President of the Society in 1983. He became Vice President of the London Underground Railway Society for 1966–67 and served as its President for 1967–68.

His somewhat gruff and brusque manner overlaid a compassionate and generous nature. He did not waste words in castigating others but was content to correct errors and omissions of railway historical fact when they appeared in print. He always responded willingly to those prudent enough to ask for his help in good time and their subsequent publications were invariably improved by such intervention, since he had a great fund of research and experience to bring to bear. Although a high priest of accuracy in his specialist field, he had a puckish sense of humour which made him a most entertaining companion for those who developed a closer acquaintance. His accents were those of the educated Cockney, brought up in a London harder in many respects than the one we know today. Of a generation to which Christian names did not come easily to the tongue outside the family circle, we do not recall that he was ever addressed other than as 'Mr Borley', or (by those who knew him very well) as 'Borley'. He reciprocated in the same style, and in correspondence his greatest concession to intimacy was to use one's surname prefaced by 'My dear'.

In 1983, at the age of 87, his recollections were recorded on audio tape by three R&CHS members and the complete transcript of that interview opens this book. With typical thoroughness, he brought along a typed supporting memorandum and, although there is some duplication, both with the interview and with some of his written work for periodicals, we have chosen to reproduce this in full as well as the transcript. There then follows a substantially complete collection of his contributions to railway magazines and journals and a list of his books.

Alan A. Jackson
H.W. Paar
Dorking and Chigwell,
June 1993

ABBREVIATIONS USED IN THIS BOOK

(A)	Article
BR	British Railways
Bradshaw	*Bradshaw's General Railway & Steam Navigation Guide for Great Britain and Ireland* (timetables)
BR (LMR)	British Railways (London Midland Region)
CSLR	City & South London Railway
District	Metropolitan District Railway
E&WID&BJ	East & West India Docks & Birmingham Junction Railway
EC, ECR	Eastern Counties Railway
EL, ELR	East London Railway
ER	Eastern Region of British Railways
GC, GCR	Great Central Railway
GE, GER	Great Eastern Railway
GN, GNR	Great Northern Railway
GW, GWR	Great Western Railway
	Hampstead Tube Charing Cross, Euston & Hampstead Railway
HJ, HJR	Hampstead Junction Railway
HL&D	Hertford, Luton & Dunstable Railway
JRCHS	*Journal of the Railway & Canal Historical Society*
(L)	Letter to the Editor
LB&SC, LBSC, LBSCR	London Brighton & South Coast Railway
LCC	London County Council
LC&D, LCDR	London, Chatham & Dover Railway
LM Region	London Midland Region of British Railways
LM&S, LMS, LMSR	London, Midland & Scottish Railway
L&NER, LNER	London & North Eastern Railway
L&NW, LNWR	London & North Western Railway
L&SW, LSWR	London & South Western Railway
LT	London Transport (London Passenger Transport Board/ London Transport Executive, London Transport Board)
LT&S, LTS, LTSR	London, Tilbury & Southend Railway
M&GN	Midland & Great Northern Railway
MD, MDR	Metropolitan District Railway
Met	Metropolitan Railway
Mid	Midland Railway
N&SWJ	North & South Western Junction Railway
NE	North Eastern Railway
NL, NLR	North London Railway
OS	Ordnance Survey
R&CHS	Railway & Canal Historical Society
RCH	Railway Clearing House
RCHME	Royal Commission on Historical Monuments England
RM	*The Railway Magazine*
RO	*The Railway Observer*
SECR	South Eastern & Chatham Railway
SE, SER	South Eastern Railway
T&HJ	Tottenham & Hampstead Junction Railway
U	*Underground*
UN	*Underground News*
wef	with effect from
WLE, WLER	West London Extension Railway
WLR	West London Railway
WR	Western Region of British Railways

PART ONE

An Interview with
H. V. BORLEY
on 19 November 1983

Present from the Railway & Canal Historical Society:
Graham Boyes (GB), John Norris (JEN), Harry Paar
(HWP)

HWP: Well, Mr Borley, we're very, very pleased that you've been good enough to come along today and talk to us about the North London Railway, because it's very difficult today after the years have changed the traffic patterns of Londoners and of railways in general to form any idea of what that line was like in its heyday. We see it today with the stations slighted and the traffic often minimal and it is difficult to form a picture of what it was like as a really high-powered going concern. The formal history of the line is fairly well covered, and the locomotive history is very well covered in the *Locomotive Magazine*, but it is much more difficult to build up, as it were, a social and a day to day history of the line, so we are mainly concerned today with talking to you about the things which were encompassed in your own experiences and particularly those perhaps prior to the Great War and maybe immediately afterwards.

HVB: When I became demobilised [1919] I was stationed at Headquarters and didn't have so much experience of stations. Of course, the traffic had begun to fall off when I first started work [in 1910]. The beginning of the falling off was the opening of the Central London Railway in 1900 and the electric trams and motor buses which occurred between about 1903 and 1914, and of course, that began; but you still had trains from the East End crowded with workmen, [paying] 2d a time, and you still had a considerable number of season ticket holders and people that couldn't advance the money to get a season and had to buy a third [class] return daily from places like Camden Town, Hampstead Heath, Finchley Road, Brondesbury, Willesden, and Acton.

JEN: You say [in the memorandum – see PART TWO] about a monthly, Mr Borley. Were there no weekly seasons in those days?

HVB: No, not in the time I'm talking about. Weekly seasons were very limited. They introduced some from Dalston to Broad Street fairly early but they then found that men worked six days a week and

somebody else used them on a Sunday and all that sort of thing. In fact somebody else often used them for an evening trip as well, so they didn't extend them. But, you see, originally they had a deposit on a season ticket. Well, a bit before my time, they only issued first and second class season tickets, for a period of three months and a substantial deposit. Well, that was quite beyond a large number of people. Before I went to Hampstead Heath, for instance, they issued 250 third returns in the morning. That was reduced to about 50 eventually because they'd just started some third class seasons, abolished deposits and for one month, which a few more people could manage.

HWP: Of course, their incentive to do this was just to cut the volume of daily ticket issuing work?

HVB: It was quite impossible for very many people to advance the money to start a second class three monthly season ticket with the deposit.

GB: What was the reason for the deposit?

HVB: It would probably have been beyond the resources of all four of us, I don't know, had we been sitting here in 1906, 7, 8, if you like.

GB: Why did they want the deposit?

HVB: To make sure they got the ticket back! That's why it's very, very difficult to find any specimens of old seasons. The season tickets were all sorts of shapes and sizes to help ticket collectors. As I think I put in the *Journal* of the Railway and Canal [Historical Society], the North London had all sorts of shapes and sizes: rectangles, octagons, circles, circular, various colours, two colours, and it was hardly necessary for a ticket collector that knew his job because they issued a circular about it. One of the circulars is in York [Museum] and of course that applied in many cases. Now, you see, you get a season ticket [and] the ticket collector that does his job properly, somehow he's got to see the stations, to see that you're not running past yourself. I mentioned there a rather interesting thing which I think the man concerned did manage to keep, that was a well known librarian of the Railway Club, named Bardsley; he had a season ticket which he kept, from Broad Street to Mansion House. Now that sounds a bit mad on the face of it, but the reason was he lived at Hampstead [and] worked at St James's Park. Well, if he were a little bit late, and got to Hampstead just as the train was going out, he'd got another train the other way five or six minutes later, so he could go that way. And of course, for mileage Broad Street to Mansion House both an ordinary ticket and a season ticket were ridiculously cheap. The third class fare round from Broad Street to Mansion House was 6d – that's *right round*, as you know, the Outer Circle, through Hampstead Heath, Willesden, Kensington and Victoria. A jolly good six pennyworth – brought you back nearly where you started!

JEN: So six pennyworth from Broad Street took you how far, as a minimum?

HVB: 6d from Broad Street? Well, I think Willesden was 5d – Broad Street to Willesden, 5d – and probably the next station was 6d. Anyway, Kensington Addison Road was 6d. So in a way you got the rest of the journey for nothing! I've no idea how many tickets to Mansion House they issued. From Hampstead Heath and places like that, we used to issue an occasional ticket to Victoria [for] people with luggage.

HWP: You started off in the booking office, Mr Borley, did you? Did you have any railway predecessors in the family at all?

HVB: No, but my father, grandfather and uncle took a certain amount of interest; my grandfather lived quite close to the station at Acton, Acton Central now. He retired there, to a country house it was. Very different now!

GB: Do you say that you started at Hampstead Heath station?

HVB: Well, I started at Gospel Oak, trained there. Then, being rather ambitious and that – well, many things went wrong; they got the date of my birth wrong, which was advantageous to me because I not only got more money but I got a job I should not, strictly speaking, be doing. And

anything that came along – they asked me about being a relief man, to which I agreed. Well, they wanted me to go, not exactly anywhere, but a bit more than I intended, but I pinned them down to Broad Street, Poplar and Kew Bridge. And then, you see, they wanted people to get a bit of outside knowledge, so I went as what they called a train register boy – that was what some companies called booking boys – in signal boxes.

Of course, the hours were pretty long everywhere and I used to go wandering about afterwards. My mother got a bit distressed; she thought I'd be making myself ill, not getting enough sleep, but it didn't kill me then, and it hasn't killed me now! I've managed to last eighty seven years! And, of course, [by] the date they got on the railway, I'd be about ninety, but the date of birth was wrong and it didn't come to light until I went into the army. But that went to my advantage. Also to my advantage [was] that I was nominated by a man who was a director of the railways and that sort of thing counted a bit in those days. And it wouldn't count so much today, perhaps wouldn't count at all. And so, of course, I had experience of many stations and in signal boxes. At the smaller stations, you see, they did things pretty simply then. If the station was open, shall we say, seventeen hours, well, they just split it between two men and alternate Sundays.

GB: To get on to the railway, you had to be nominated by somebody of influence? Was that common?

HVB: To be on the clerical staff, you had to be nominated by somebody.

GB: As an indication of good character, you mean?

HVB: Yes. You see, if your father was an inspector, or a guard even, or anything like that, or a driver, they'd join [you] as a clerk, but they wouldn't take on almost any Dick and Harry as a clerk, even if he had a reasonably good education. Of course, there were no such things as 'O' levels in those days – 'A' levels – and that. You either passed your examination and got a card at school or, if you were at the bottom, you stood a good chance of getting a ticking off, if not a cut with the cane!

That was the procedure. Well, you see, therefore I was enabled to work at various stations, including some signal boxes. Well, as I say, the most awkward time was the changing of shifts. As there were only two of you [in the booking office], you'd either got to work all day Sunday and have the other Sunday off, or work every blooming Sunday. Well, almost all stations chose to work all day Sunday and the shift was divided so that the morning shift was a bit shorter than the evening so that each person got his midday meal at home, something near one or two o'clock. Of course, there were no meal times allowed – you got no meal relief – you took other meals as best you could, even if dear old ladies reported you for talking to them with your mouth full! That did often happen. Well, of course, they knew that at Headquarters and they put the dear old lady off. But I saw one or two bits of correspondence of that when they were having a turn out in the war: 'Clerk Borley reported for speaking at passengers with his mouth full' – how you could avoid it, I don't know. [How] you can stand at a window without a bite of any kind! Of course, they provided everything for you – gas ring, stove to keep food warm, and also kettles. At Hampstead Heath, for instance, there were about three or four kettles for the various staff; including the signalman, I expect there were four.

The usual procedure was – well, I say usual – more or less half and half; take the late turn on Saturday and you got home about midnight on Saturday. You got yourself into bed; next thing you knew was the damned alarm clock ringing and you out of bed and off for Sunday, which was pretty well sixteen hours right off the reel, except for a bit of a break at church time [in] which the good people that look after religion thought you'd go to church, but I've never known a railwayman go to church in that, you see, he'd have to turn up in his working clothes – and it gave him a chance to have his one and only sit-down meal. Then you were on early turn on Monday. Well, of course, that gave you a weekend off the next week. The other way, of course, was to not have a weekend off, the early man taking the Sunday duty and the late duty following, you see; then he only got the clear Sunday off.

GB: How many turns did you work during the week? Was it five turns out of six?

HVB: You worked a full six-day week plus alternate Sundays. That meant the early shift was about nine hours – that's fifty four hours – and the late one sixty hours plus the full day Sunday. The church time was handy.

HWP: You mentioned you went into the signal box as a – what was the term you used, Mr Borley?

GB: Booking boy.

HVB: Train register boy – booking trains.

HWP: That was literally recording them in a register as they went by?

HVB: In the register, yes. At some of the stations, there was hardly time to breathe in the morning. You see, they had two boxes, two men in a box. At one time they had two separate signal boxes at busy places for the separate lines; but of course, when they had to economise, they concentrated in one box and two men there running backwards and forwards and it was no sooner banging 'Train out of section' when you got 'Is line clear?' for the next. And, of course, in foggy weather (and you got foggy weather round Dalston and Hackney like you never see today!) they had fogmen out almost everywhere, and round about Hackney and Bow in those foggy mornings, in the street you got a continual banging of fog signals both from the Great Eastern at Hackney Downs as well as the North London, and ditto at Bow. You see, the trains were so close behind one another between about seven and nine-thirty, that the distant was always on. God knows how many detonators they banged off! There was an instruction, if a driver found a distant on and didn't explode a detonator, he was supposed to report it. Well, if the fogman was here and the distant was there, he'd got another over there. Well, when his detonator [magazine] was exhausted, he'd got to take the best opportunity to get off to fill it up. So he couldn't always get the distant [detonator] on – all he could do was to hold up his red flag and say 'No.2 Up Line, Distant on' and hope the driver would see. Of course, the driver should have reported it but they didn't, not to my knowledge.

The North London had a little thing that

nobody else adopted, a 'calling on distant'. That is to say, at Dalston and other places, they could pull off the home and let the train [into section] and pull off this 'calling on distant'. Well, the detonator still had to be down and so all the fogman had to do then was to shout, 'The little 'un's off.' (I believe they sometimes said 'The little bugger's off'!)

GB: So all this time you were relieving, both in boxes and in booking offices, were you? You were doing both jobs?

HVB: I was fairly well experienced on both booking and accounts, and a certain amount of signal work.

GB: Very versatile!

JEN: But not goods booking, and not goods charging?

HVB: No. I didn't know much about goods, because I was never in the goods until I got to Headquarters. Then it was goods rates, not goods working. Despite the fact that the London & North Western took some sort of control over the North London line, the accounting system was a bit different, and was kept different, right up to the LMS days and later.

They had some of these signalling peculiarities. You see, on the North London, if you'd seen the tail lamp and if the starting signal was off, as soon as the train started you could bang off 'Train out of section' and accept the next one, which was not strictly in accordance with the RCH rules. RCH rules said, 'A quarter of a mile beyond the home signal, proceeding on its journey.' Well, that didn't work on the North London and it didn't work on parts of the Great Eastern, nor on the Met, nor on the District. God knows how they worked the District in steam days, but they did!

HWP: That was a quarter of a mile beyond the distant?

HVB: The RCH standard rule was 'A quarter of a mile beyond the home signal and proceeding on its journey.'

HWP: Were the fog signals placed mechanically, Mr Borley, in the time you're speaking of, with the machines, with the magazines?

HVB: Yes, if he put twenty or thirty in there, with trains following one behind the other and the distant almost always on, well, they'd get exhausted, and he's had to get across two running lines to get to the third line to put some in. He could attend to this one, just by there. They were supplied with refreshments after three hours and they were supposed to be on duty, I think it was, not more than thirteen hours.

GB: And how many days of fog would you get in a month during winter?

HVB: It varied considerably. Sometimes you got a week of it. Thirteen [hours duty] was the maximum. They tried to get relief, but it took a bit of finding! They got men out of the Carriage and Wagon Department and all sorts of people. They only paid overtime in very exceptional circumstances. The clerical staff didn't get overtime, nor Sunday pay. Even at Headquarters, you only got overtime pay if you were put on some job separate from your normal work. Talking about no meal times at stations, you got meal times at Headquarters – forty-five minutes – but there was no eating in between. If you were hungry, well, you had to wait until your authorised time. It wasn't until girls came in the office they started tea and coffee and all that sort of stuff. There were no facilities for making tea at Headquarters – you got your forty-five minutes – that was it!

JEN: When did girls start coming in the office? When did you start getting typewriters and things like that?

HVB: We had typewriters, if you're talking about the machine. Of course, in the early days, the girl was the typewriter just as the man that prints a book is a printer – the girl or man was the typewriter. My mother always referred to that like that – she'd say, 'Have you heard so and so's left school? She's a typewriter now.' My mother used that phrase to her dying day.

Yes, we had typewriters before I was at Headquarters, but not at stations. People, most of them, taught themselves. There was a variety of type-writers and, therefore, you couldn't really learn touch-typing. There was the normal keyboard you've got now, and there was a keyboard with no shift key, that's to say that the capitals and the figures were up there and the ordinary letters down here; and there was one with double shift keys, that's to say, you got the small letters, one shift key for the capitals and one for the figures, full stops and all like that. There was a variety of those; they were not standardised until about 1913 or '14 or so.

Yes, in addition to all my troubles and work [it] was the standard rule that clerks had to know shorthand and pass a test. Well, I hadn't touched shorthand but, just as I was leaving school, when my father fetched me out, he'd fallen on rather bad days financially and he thought it about time I earned some money. We had started learning French at school and I got rather interested in it, so in addition to my other duties I enrolled at what they always called a Night School in those days. (I believe they were officially Evening Classes.) It was a shilling for the term – some things were cheap in those days! Of course, I could only attend alternate weeks and, frankly, occasionally I was half asleep at the time, having been up since six (or before) that morning. I made sure I didn't attend an Evening Class on a Monday because, you see, [of my] having been at work all day Sunday and early morning Monday; it was generally Tuesday and Thursday, or something like that. Well, I managed somehow to pass the shorthand test [and] managed to get some sort of knowledge of French. I'd fail at any exam, but I can muddle round France, Belgium and Switzerland pretty accurately. I can read [it] – Faulkner gets some French magazines, which he brings here sometimes – [like] *La Vie du Rail* – which, as I'm interested in what they print, I can read it quite easily. But, as I say, I wouldn't pass an examination. So I didn't have much time for pleasure. For better or worse, I took no interest in football, cricket or anything like that. I went to a Music Hall occasionally, [the] Bedford, Camden Town. If I remember rightly, you could get in for about sixpence.

GB: What were you earning at that time? What was the pay you were getting?

HVB: The pay when I was training was £20 a year – a year, don't think it was £20 a week! – which was as good or better than most of my school friends. They all considered I was damn lucky getting on the railway. So I was, seeing I went on the railway transport [side] during the War instead of those poor devils that went in the Infantry and got blown to hell on the Somme and elsewhere. Then I should have gone to £25 or £30 but, as they thought I was older than I was, I went up to about £35 a year, and I think they gave me an extra £10 for when I was relief, because I had to go about and lodge anywhere where I could.

Of course, at some places, I used to lodge with railwaymen, and they were very pleased because, as I say in that [time], the Bow Works were partly closed owing to the combination with the London & North Western and some of the work was gone to Crewe and Wolverton. There I had another difficulty. My father said I should stand on my own feet and I suppose he was right. Well, they used to get me breakfast, perhaps bacon and sausages. Well, I soon realised that I was having bacon and sausages and they and two or three children were existing on bread and margarine. Well, of course, that was a bit too much for me and I said, 'Either we all have bacon and sausages, or we don't have any.' So we did the best we could, like that. Because with hungry kids around you with a bit of bread and margarine, it's a bit too much to stomach, bacon and sausages. Some people could do it, perhaps, but I'm damned if I could. There was considerable poverty round Homerton, Bow and that, and it was very distressing – I think of it now almost – to see a poorly clad kid, not properly clothed, begging a carrot or a turnip or a stale cake because they'd got an empty belly and no money. And, I mean I hadn't got the money; I did give them an odd penny, now and again, but I had to watch my pennies as well because [although] it was £35 or more, that didn't enable me to live in luxury.

HWP: Was this poverty attributable to the effect of the [works closure]?

HVB: It was made worse, but it was pretty bad enough [normally]. You used to have some of the amusing side of it. They used to run some excursions in the Summer – day returns – I forget

3. HVB was but three years old when this picture of Homerton NLR station was taken in July 1898 but it was to change very little in the ensuing 20 years and would be readily recognisable to him. Posters optimistically attempt to entice the somewhat underprivileged Homertonians to a special excursion to the Lakes of Killarney or into Corridor Trains for Edinburgh or Glasgow, whilst another draws attention to the improved train service to Llandrindod Wells, a matter of unlikely importance to a passer-by. Members of the local community are held back by an NLR porter under the bridge so as not to spoil the photo by smudging the very slow speed exposure but the two W. H. Smith & Son boys selling newspapers have managed to keep fairly still in a sitting position. The east end of the up platform may be glimpsed at the left side of the picture. *Official NLR photo: RCHS/Spence*

what it was – 2/6 or 3/6 or three bob or something like that. Some of the stations, [a] man would come up, with his family and ask for 'Two adults and three kids to Sahfend [Southend], please,' and plonk down a handful of small change; they'd saved that up week by week, sixpence and a shilling at a time, and it was always right! They were far more honest then than they appear to be now. I don't think I ever got diddled there, and they had certain opportunities, but it must have been hard to be honest with an empty belly. But there it was – well, enough of that!

GB: Had you, yourself, been brought up somewhere in North London?

HVB: I was born in Hampstead – lived in Hampstead, and both my parents. Well, when they were born, they were moderately well off. But, you see, if anything went wrong in those days, you suffered pretty badly. My mother was born in Kensington, near Addison Road station, quite a nice house, but the trouble was, her father got what they then called consumption, now called TB [pulmonary tuberculosis]. Well, if you got that you had to look after yourself as best you could; and the long and the short of it was, they had to leave that house at Kensington [and] go to live at Stratford, in a very small house. They fetched the eldest son out of school, at thirteen, which they could in those days; he managed to get a job as a messenger boy, at Stratford station. And my grandmother, she got a job as a cleaner there for a time – they had to get some money somehow; a cleaner in those days meant a bucket of water and a scrubbing brush, down on your hands and knees. The eldest daughter, she was taken out of school as soon as she could, to look after the house while mother went out to work. Meanwhile, of course, my grandfather, he lingered on and eventually died. They got some jobs for the boys; the eldest son became a Master Baker at Barnsbury and did fairly well until a lot of these other [German] bakers came along and more or less cut him out. You had good days and then you fell on evil times.

There were only two jobs for girls in those days – that was some sort of domestic service, or go in a factory. Well, there was an appalling factory at Stratford, making matches, and it was just a living death. Many girls had to go there. If they didn't leave soon to get married – well, they were as good as dead – [it] killed 'em off. It wouldn't be allowed for five minutes these days, but it was then. My mother got various jobs as a lady's maid, which was considered pretty good in those days. Eventually she got married. My father and uncle were in business. Then that was cut out. That was why, when it was time for me to leave school, I had to go into work. I didn't realise until I got there that such poverty did exist. Although I thought that my parents and I were poor, there were people a jolly sight poorer. Strange as I say, they seemed quite honest.

JEN: Can you remember the addresses where you lived in Hampstead? Do the houses still survive?

HVB: No. The house I was born in was destroyed in the Second World War, bombed to the ground (and all those round it).

4. Bow Junction and signal box in 1871, looking south towards Poplar, 4-4-0T no 1 is seen left, by the box, whilst 2-4-0T no.20 stands with an 8-ton wagon of 'Hirwain Coal & Iron Company Smokeless Coal' specifically labelled for the North London Railway Locomotive Department, which is being unloaded in baskets, each to be carried by two men.
Official NLR photo: RCHS/Spence

JEN: When you were working at Hampstead Heath, does the house where you lived then still stand?

HVB: I only lived in the one house at Hampstead, the one I was born in. I walked across the Heath to and from work – right across the Heath; it was safe to do it then. I doubt if it would be safe to come home at night, at midnight, right across Hampstead Heath now. All you met [then] was an occasional, what's politely called a 'Lady of the Town' or, in plain English, a prostitute, out for business, and I generally used to say, 'No time, no money, my dear; I'm tired!' I was [usually] a bit too late for the ladies of the town; they'd found their client or given up hope; it was only rarely I met one. But now, I mean, you'd probably get robbed there. You'd probably be all right in the early morning, going on duty for the early turn. But I'd have to come right round by the lighted streets. Same with Gospel Oak, West End Lane and that.

HWP: What about holidays, Mr Borley?

HVB: Two weeks holiday, and uniformed staff, one week. But, except the tip top people, you seldom got it right in the summer. I've had my holidays pretty well every month of the year! You usually, if you were lucky, got them in March, April or May, or September, October, November. Holidays, two weeks you got, either two consecutive weeks or one week. But you couldn't choose your time, often you didn't know only a few days beforehand, so you couldn't book up much or anything. And, on the first day, usually a Monday, you had to make sure that your relief was arrived. So you used to have to open up on Monday morning, which was part of your holiday, and wait 'til your relief turned up – unless you'd been able to arrange, the previous evening, with him which was very unusual. See, when I was on the relief, well, I couldn't usually get there until Monday morning and, of course, I used to have to get there as best you could. There was various ways. I had a bike at one time, but I was always a damn fool on a bike! That's why I've never had a motor car because I should never learn to drive it. I was hopeless [at] anything in the way like that, but I did have a bike – an ordinary bicycle, of course, not a motor bicycle. On a few occasions you [did]

what's called 'jumped a goods'. That was, of course, entirely unauthorised. You arranged, you see, if you knew a goods was 'bout time, if I was at say, Kensal Rise, I'd got to get to Kentish Town or something like that, I could get the signalman to forget to pull off his signals and when the train came along I'd shout to the driver where I wanted to get off and jump in the front van as he slowed down; by this time, his signals were off and [I was] hoping against hope that he didn't forget to slow down at Kentish Town and I'd drop out. I nearly went base over apex once or twice, but not quite! That was one of the ways we got to work.

JEN: You mention the 'front van'. Does this imply that goods trains normally had two vans, one at each end? Was that normal practice?

HVB: I don't know normal practice, but there was sometimes a van in front, yes, or perhaps it was the rear van with a guard. I mean, it's a long time ago, you know!

HWP: Holidays were paid, Mr Borley? Were they paid holidays?

HVB: Paid holidays? Oh, yes, yes! You got your salary, yes. You got your salary for a year. And they were reasonable with sickness, too.

GB: And privilege tickets?

HVB: Privilege tickets? Yes! Privilege tickets on all railways. A few of them wouldn't allow you on Bank Holidays and that sort of thing. Yes, you got privilege tickets and a pass for your holiday. You could usually get one on another railway, too. Clerical staff could. Yes, you got privilege tickets [at] quarter fare. That was a consideration! No limit on those. You'd get those at the station.

GB: And did you get some sick pay?

HVB: If you were sick, yes. But, of course, it was difficult reporting sick. You were sort of expected to carry on 'til they found some relief for you and that wasn't always easy.

GB: Were you actually employed by the London

& North Western Railway Company, or the North London Railway Company?

HVB: London & North Western. You see, because, at that time, they were cutting down a bit on the North London line, because the North London, you see, they were after dividends. For about twenty years the North London paid 7 [per cent], year after year, which was good! They had a huge passenger traffic, and all goods from the Great Eastern and east of England passed through the North London Railway; there was practically no other way. Some wanted a junction at Gospel Oak, but the North Western and the North London said no and there wasn't a junction at Gospel Oak, despite some people think there was, until the First World War. Incidentally, at Gospel Oak, the London & North Western did all the work, so I had experience of Great Eastern booking as well.

GB: You mentioned that you used to go down as far as Kew Bridge. Did they have their own booking office at Kew Bridge?

HVB: I could have gone to Kew Bridge, but never did. Kew Bridge was a curious station. There were two platforms there on the Hounslow line of the South Western and two there like that [on the N&SWJ]. Well, when it was opened the trains ran through there, stopped there, went on and went round the curve at Barnes and on to Richmond, and taken on by the South Western to Richmond and Kingston, the North London coaches were. Strange as it may seem, if you looked at it and were observant, you'd notice that the departure platform for Broad Street was an entirely different type – different lamps, different seats, different colour – than the other three platforms. There was a separate entrance belonging to the North & South Western Junction. The North London done

---

* This paragraph may be confusing to the reader since HVB was presumably drawing plans with his fingers on the table as he spoke. It should therefore be read in conjunction with the maps showing Kew Bridge in Part 3(iii) and HVB's notes on North & South Western Junction train services in Part 3(iv).

all the work on behalf of the North & South Western Junction – that was another problem with the South Western that I mentioned in there. This platform was [an] entirely different departure platform for Broad Street. There were North & South Western Junction porters on there, North & South Western Junction ticket examiner and booking clerks and tickets. When the train arrived at the other platform, South Western men attended to it; they were pretty conspicuous because South Western porters always had red ties in those days. A couple of those turned up and just looked through the train to make sure that nobody had left their umbrella or anything in there. Then the engine was detached, went forward on the South Western at New Kew Junction, ran back to Kew East Junction, and then backed on the train, shoved it forward again on the South Western, where the engine had been, and then drew into the North & South Western Junction platform, and eventually [got] right away for Broad Street. That was Kew Bridge.*

When the line from South Acton to Richmond was opened in 1869, which stopped the working of the through carriages to Kingston by the roundabout route, the North & South Western Junction put in a Bill, but they withdrew it, providing certain conditions were granted by the South Western. The result was there was a North London (or North & South Western Junction) booking office at Richmond. And the South Western would only have North London trains there, nobody else's trains; even when the North Western to some extent took over the North London, there were instructions issued that North Western carriages must not be sent to Richmond! Nor on the Great Northern services.

Then there was a trouble because the London North Western, so I was told, wanted to put some tourist and excursion bookings in from Richmond, which, it seems, they were quite entitled to do. But they sent along the tickets [headed] 'London & North Western Railway' and, of course, when the South Western saw that, that was like red rag to the bull! They weren't having that! They said only North & South Western Junction and, maybe, 'exercised by the North London' and nobody else. Off went these tickets, so stations in Scotland got tourist tickets headed North & South Western Junction Railway from Richmond. What they made

5. A North London line train from Broad Street to High Barnet bursts out of the tunnel into Highgate L&NER station headed by LM&SR 0-6-0T 7517, on 5 June 1937. *H. C. Casserley/RCHME*

of that, if there were initials, I don't quite know! But still, if it said Richmond to Inverness, that was all right for the ticket collector at Inverness! The South Western, you see, was very touchy about south of the river. D'you know Putney Bridge station? The boundary is not where you expect it to be, the south end of Putney Bridge. The bridge across the Thames was South Western (it's still British Railways Southern Region); the South Western insisted on that. They never run any bloomin' trains, except presumably, permanent way trains. Yes, the South Western was determined to have no other company south of the river! They didn't mind running powers [so] it's amazing the companies that ran to Richmond, even the Great Western! When I heard the Great Western trains were going to be withdrawn from Richmond, I nearly broke off my Christmas dinner to rush off to get a trip there before the end of the year. I managed it, I think, on the 29th December or something, the last Great Western to Richmond. The last Metropolitan had already gone about five years previously, so I missed

that, but I wasn't going to miss the last Great Western to Richmond! Yes, one time they had Met, Great Western, of course North London, and District, as well as South Western; of course, the South Western got there by that roundabout route – Waterloo, Clapham Junction, Chelsea & Fulham, Kensington Addison Road, curve round now, Shepherd's Bush, Hammersmith, Turnham Green, Richmond – all round, you'd cross the Thames about three times. That was the South Western's doing because they weren't having any other railway [company] making a railway to Richmond. Wouldn't mind your running powers, but ownership – no! And round they went! To this very day, the mileposts from Gunnersbury to Richmond are based on Clapham Junction, although there ain't no railway!

GB: I never realised that!

JEN: With all these through workings and running powers, what arrangements were made by the owning company that the other companies' men were conversant with their practices?

HVB: Well, they jolly well had to be!

JEN: Were they tested?

HVB: Well, the Great Northern, for instance – at one time a good third of the trains on the Great Northern suburban services were North London; they ran to High Barnet, New Barnet and Enfield (now Enfield Chase) and, at one time, to Hatfield, but, for many years, also to Potters Bar. Well, they had to be conversant; and they couldn't send a North London man that was in the habit of working between Poplar and Broad Street, they couldn't send him to New Barnet. They were provided with Great Northern Appendix and Great Northern Working Timetables, but they had to have some knowledge. You see, the Great Northern had 'Section Clear, Junction Blocked' which the North London didn't have. Well, they had to be conversant with that. The Great Northern was awkward, too. The Great Northern and the London & North Western had a great reluctance to put in facing points off a main line because they had one or two – or, rather, too many – cases where the signalman had changed the points under a train, You see, at one time, as soon as you had put your signal to danger, you could change your points. Well, if you smacked your signal to danger too smart and changed your points, you derailed your train. Well, in view of that, both at Gordon Hill (when opened) and Enfield and High Barnet, they wouldn't put in facing points. They made the train run into one station then back out. Well, if trains were close behind, you see, the man at High Barnet, for instance, to save time, he could accept it, 'Section Clear, Junction Blocked' from Totteridge, and the Totteridge chap would stick out a green flag and probably shout out, 'Section Clear, Junction Blocked.' Well, the North London man had to understand that.

The North London spent most of its career over other people's lines. It started a service – the first service from Willesden to Kew was North London. You see, the North & South Western Junction was sponsored by the North Western and the South Western. Having built it, then neither of them seemed keen to work any traffic over it – put forward excuses. The South Western started it by working some goods to Old Oak, which they continued to do right up to Nationalisation. The South Western worked there, but the North London eventually provided the [passenger] train service, which was very sparse originally because the only station was Acton – and Kew. But then, the Great Northern, which was very congested at King's Cross and Moorgate and something had to be done, and they made a curve, the Great Northern did, from Finsbury Park to Canonbury – one reason being to get their goods to Poplar, because previously the Great Northern goods to Poplar were exchanged at St Pancras Sidings; when I talk of St Pancras, I mean St Pancras Sidings on the North London, not the Midland affair! Then, of course, the Great Northern wanted to run to Broad Street. Well, that meant that some of the North London trains were [to go over] the North Western [as they] had a share into the Broad Street. You see, the North Western was a little bit artful. It always kept a bit of a hand over the North London; it bought a lot of the stocks and shares and appointed one or two Directors and all that sort of thing. And the North Western said, 'No, we're not having any other company into Broad Street.' And as the Richmond trains would had to have been shifted over to the North Western side, the poor Great Northern was unlucky. So the unusual system (rather unusual it was) [that] the North London trains took over from Broad Street right away eventually to Hatfield and Potters Bar. The Great Northern got a variety of trains at one time; they got some South Eastern from Woolwich and some London, Chatham & Dover from Victoria, and all those men had to be conversant with the Great Northern.

Another thing on the Great Northern: it's a very steep pull out of Finsbury Park to the High Barnet [line], and more than one train got stuck there. Well, it was always a North London thing to say, 'Well, plenty of trains get stuck there, but it's never a North London,' – and I believe they were right, because the North London had some damn good engines in their time. They looked a bit quaint, perhaps, when you saw them, but they were good engines in their time. And the next

6. High Barnet L&NER looking north, in the 1930s. North London train for Broad Street at right, King's Cross train in main platform. *Anon/Collection Nick Howell*

train, whatever it was, had to come along and give a shove. Well, on one occasion, what happened? A Great Northern failed, I'm told, and the next was a Chatham and they couldn't shift it; the third one was a North London. The North London come up behind [and] there were three trains struggling away. That was even too much for the North London so what the devil did they do? Well, the North London had to get a Wrong Line Order, I think, and come back and then, by that time, the Great Northern had got hold of a big engine and that was sent and shifted the two that were stuck. There was a big traffic to Alexandra Palace, too. You used to issue tickets to Alexandra Palace including admission.

GB: For special events there?

HVB: Mm! Crystal Palace included admission, too.

GB: What sort of things did they have on at Alexandra Palace in those days?

HVB: Well, various things happened from time to time but it was always a bit of a failure. It was a long time getting up to date. When I went there with my uncle – I suppose I was 12 or 13 or so, about 1908 – they were lighting everything with gas and that still, although there was electric light around. Lighting things with gas! [But] gas in many ways was much better. The Metropolitan had gas on the Inner Circle long after the railway was electrified, because it gave a better light. The electric light was liable to failure and gave a sort of yellowish brown light sometimes. The school I went to was built and opened by the London County Council in 1906 and that was entirely gas-lighted. Most of the streets were. As a kid I used [to] follow lamplighters round and was highly pleased when they let me shove the stick up and light a lamp. Yes, I believe in The Temple there may be still a few gas-lighted lamps. There were five years ago.

GB: I believe there are, yes.

HVB: And a few in the City of London. In those days, the men that lit them were supposed to come round 365 days, but I notice in the City of London, a few years back, over Christmas it was cheaper to leave 'em alight continuously over the three or four days of Christmas than it was to pay a man special duty to come round and put 'em out and light 'em again. But in the old days, the poor devil had to come round at four or five o'clock in the morning in the summer and put 'em out [and] light 'em again at eight or nine o'clock [in the evening].

GB: Was working for the railways in those days very disciplined?

HVB: Discipline was pretty strict, yes! But there was a man – who was the last Traffic Superintendent of the North London Railway and he went on to the North Western – his name was Ford, George Newton Ford. He was a most reasonable man. If any man got before him for discipline he'd patiently listen to him and then he'd probably say, 'Oh, dear! What a foolish thing to do!' And that sort of thing, you see. 'Why ever did you do that?' And he'd give him the least punishment he could, so to speak. Another thing, if a man was suspended from duty, which meant loss of pay – well, that was a very serious thing because most of those men, even signalmen, guards and that, more or less lived from hand to mouth, and it was the usual practice to club round a bit and help them out financially.

GB: What sort of things would they be suspended from duty for? Was this operating irregularities?

HVB: Yes, operating irregularities. But they didn't always; you usually got reprimanded [for] 'Late on duty.' But timekeeping was very good, really.

HWP: What was the loyalty of the staff under these quite hard conditions, long hours and short commons? Were the staff very loyal to the company?

HVB: Loyal, yes. I think 90% of them were. Yes, another thing, if a chap went sick suddenly, a porter or somebody'd come round, and if he found you in, he'd say, 'So and so's gone sick; you're wanted at the station.' Well, it was a sort of matter of honour to go round there, even if you'd done a morning

shift. I've done it more than once. And you got no pay for that; that was all part of the job! They used to say, 'Well, they're paying a man that's gone off sick; the railway's got to keep going.'

HWP: Was there much difference, Mr Borley, between the office staff and the running staff, the uniformed staff, in status?

HVB: Well, there was, but you worked one with the other. They hadn't thought of that, you know, 'One bloody man, one bloody job,' in those days. You worked with one another. There were occasions when you had to attend a call of nature. Well, you'd say to somebody, 'Have a look out; I'm going to nip downstairs.' Well, you used to do that best you could between two trains and it was nipping along and nipping back.

HWP: Was being in the office regarded as a cut above being on the line, as it were, would you say?

HVB: Well, in a way, yes. You were on a salary, and they were on a weekly wage, but you didn't get snooty or anything like that. You see, at Hampstead Heath there was an elderly porter there. Well, you were not supposed to smoke or drink on duty, but round about nine o'clock this porter would say to the ticket collector, 'Going for a pint.' Well, a train had just gone; that man would nip down to the pub – they knew he was coming – he had a pint of mild ale, two pence, drunk that, and he was back well in time for the next train. You could thoroughly rely on him. Always round about then, when he was on duty, 'Going for a pint.'

GB: What staff were there at these stations? Did you have a Stationmaster at every station on the North London?

HVB: No. They started, I believe, with Station-masters, but, except at Willesden Junction, there were no Stationmasters at all in my time. They had a Chief Booking Clerk and one or more under-clerks, according to the size of the station. And two Station Inspectors that worked shifts. Well, the Station Inspectors were skilled in all sorts of duties, including arranging single line working in the case of accidents and all that sort of thing, and signalling, and they usually had a smattering of booking office work. Officially the two [grades] were separate, but that didn't mean to say you held your head up in the air. The Chief Booking Clerk didn't think he was superior to the Station Inspector, although, of course, he was, and got a higher salary.

JEN: What was the chain of command then? The Chief Booking Clerk was responsible to whom?

HVB: The Traffic Superintendent at Headquarters at Euston, and the Inspectors were also responsible [to Euston]. But, you see, the Chief Booking Clerk couldn't order a porter to do anything; he could ask a porter to do something and the porter would do it. Of course, the porters, if there were no official office cleaners, the porters swept out and that sort of thing.

GB: How many porters typically would there be on a shift?

HVB: It varied. You see, at some stations, West End Lane, for instance, if I remember rightly, there were only three porters – [with] one permanently on the middle shift; that meant about twelve hours, with ten on Saturday. I was a little while at Willesden Parcel Office, the only time I was unhappy. Well, the hours at Willesden Parcel Office were 8.30 in the morning till 5.30 in the evening – in theory – but you went home when the last parcel was booked up. I was at a disadvantage there because I didn't know the district. I was sent there when a chap suddenly went sick. It was very awkward there; instead of going home at 5.30 you were lucky to leave at 6.30. You were not paid overtime for that. In fact, until the wages staff were paid for Sunday, it was just bare time there. You see, if an inspector got thirty bob a week, he got one sixth, in other words, five bob, for Sunday. ['Bob' is slang for shillings; one shilling became five new pence with decimalisation – Editor] They hadn't thought of time and a half and all that stuff then. And the signalmen worked three shifts round the clock, usually changed by working twelve hours on a weekend to give the other bloke time off. Three eights, twenty-four.

Nearly all the signal cabins were open perma-

nently until a bit later, when they shut some at night and Sundays. Train register boys worked about nine hours, I think, continuously. If a porter was on twelve hours right throughout the day, he did get a meal time, but they didn't like that. And some clerks at stations got a split turn. They didn't like that either! They wanted split turn to be at work when the busy time in the morning and ditto in the evening. They didn't want a chap coming on at eight o'clock and then hanging round there in the afternoon when there was little to do. So everything had to work out like that! You got your meals as best you could. Bank Holidays at Hampstead Heath – the August Bank Holiday was merry hell! Especially if it was a hot day.

GB: It was a popular place for people to go on the weekends, was it?

HVB: Hampstead Heath, yes! The North London always had a lot of spare rolling stock and engines; they were well provided with that. Even when they had to start running on the Great Northern, they'd got the rolling stock almost ready. They ran a lot of special trains; trains were one behind the other, people pouring out. Fortunately most of them had got return tickets if they hadn't lost it or left it in the pub! Another thing, there was practically no damage to trains or stations and very little graffiti as it's now called. If there was – what little there was – [it] was in gents' lavatories, and then more or less polite. You didn't see, like you often see, like at Mill Hill Broadway on the Midland when I was there, there was all sorts of filth written up in the waiting room and everything smashed that could be smashed. That was on a comparatively new line, the Bedford Electric. The Tilbury Company worked a train to Southend in the summer.

GB: From the North London?

HVB: Yes! From Chalk Farm, the London, Tilbury & Southend ran through. There were usually two on Sundays; one each weekday from June to September; and the people coming back, they were usually a bit merry but reasonably well behaved. Some chaps would come back, thumping their pockets, 'Lorst me bloomin' tickets.' So the ticket collector would look him up and down – it was usually the same ticket collector as was on in the morning – 'All right, mate! I remember you. Next time you go, take care o' your ticket!' What they used to do, they used to take their food with them to Southend and as '*bona fide* travellers' they could go in the pub all day long. Well, they went in the pub, to stop there till their money ran out, and then, when they got back, they'd got no tickets (sometimes) [or] usually had their tickets, but they'd got no money; they'd come back a bit merry. Yes, you know what was said about the '*bona fide* traveller' and the pubs? 'A *bona fide* traveller is a *bona fide* man that takes a *bona fide* walk to get a *bona fide* drink.' You got a lot of those at Hampstead. It was near a pub, and that pub was open from about ten o'clock in a morning till eleven o'clock at night, and at certain times they had a man on the door who used to question people where they'd slept the last night. There was a notice up saying, '*Bona fide* travellers'; you had to have slept three miles away. Well, they could say pretty well everything. Now and again a couple of policemen, usually a sergeant and a constable, came round and questioned everybody in there. Occasionally, when the sergeant and the constable came in, sometimes you'd see a chap nip out quick! But not always. That was the day at Southend. The kids used to make sand castles, mother used to sit there and watch them, and father would go to the pub if he'd got the money. But they used to take their own food. That was about the only outing they got. They'd saved up for about three months for that.

GB: Did people come from any distance on the excursions to Hampstead Heath?

HVB: The majority of the people were from Dalston, Haggerston, Shoreditch, Hackney, Bow, yes.

GB: What about Kew? Did you get them also going to Kew Gardens as well?

HVB: A fair number went to Kew. You see, a good many went to Kew and Richmond on Sunday. It was before the days of cinemas. Cinemas in London, but not outside London, were open on Sunday evening. After they'd been open for about ten years and more, it was found it was illegal to open on Sunday, but they managed to alter the law eventually and gave them permission. (I could tell you some funny tales about cinemas, too!) But Kew Gardens and Richmond – boating for people who'd got the money – and Richmond Park were open on Sundays.

Well, the fares were cheap; even the second class fares before the North London started third class were cheap. They only needed a few Parliamentary fares, Gladstone's 'Penny a Mile', because the seconds were below the penny, even from Dalston and that. Dalston to Hampstead Heath was – what? – 5d or 6d return and Kew Bridge from Dalston was about 9d. Kew Bridge to Richmond was about a bob. A good many of them could manage that on a Sunday. Yes, I was saying about cinemas; [at] Finsbury Park, just by the station there is, and was, on three boundaries, Islington, Hornsey – Stoke Newington, I think, was the other one. Islington and Stoke Newington were in the London County Council area; Hornsey was in Middlesex. And the bloomin' cinema was just in the corner of Hornsey, Middlesex. And, of course, Middlesex wouldn't allow cinemas to open [on Sundays]. London County Council bent the law and authorised them to open on Sunday. And that caused all the people who turned up there, 'Oo, it ain't open. Why's that?' Then somebody hanging round there, waiting for the pubs to open or something like that, would say, 'Well, you see, you're outside the London boundary now. You'd better get up to the *Nag's Head*.' (That was in the Holloway Road.) Yes, you got some interesting, funny things.

HWP: Did Hornsey actually prevent that opening, Mr Borley, in that case? Did they prevent that cinema from opening?

HVB: That cinema was never opened [on Sundays] because it was in Hornsey, Middlesex, and the licence said – gave the hours of opening, and that was weekdays, and that included Good Friday, and in some cases included Ash Wednesday. In Hertfordshire, I think it was, they wouldn't allow cinemas or any entertainment on Ash Wednesday. So they had what is still called Mardi Gras, which, in case your French is not all that, used to be Shrove Tuesday in English, what you might say 'Fat Tuesday', where, in Catholic countries, they generally have a feed up. But, of course, Ash Wednesday's not kept, not even in Catholic countries to the extent it was. Of course, London theatres were to a large extent closed throughout Lent in my young days. They used to say, if we opened very few people would go because Lent was supposed to be kept from Ash Wednesday to Easter Day. Good Friday was supposed to be a Holy Day, but it isn't everybody kept it holy.

GB: In the days you're talking of, you're saying that in the mornings during church services they didn't run trains on the North London?

HVB: They didn't run trains [i.e. passenger trains. Some railways, including the North London, continued to operate freight services in the Church Interval – Editor]. All railways were like that. It started with the London & Greenwich Railway. The London & Greenwich Railway had, I think it was every quarter of an hour or every half hour, something like that, from London Bridge to Greenwich; they had the same service weekday and Sundays, because at that time people lived near their work and they didn't start quite so early as subsequently. The first train on the London & Greenwich was about 7.30 morning and the last one about 10.30 or something like that. And the London & Greenwich started that. Well then, of course, the good people in the Church of England and in some Nonconformist churches thought these railwaymen should be able to go to church and they persuaded [the company] to have a break, usually about two hours, from eleven till one approximately between the services and [eventually] that applied to all railways that had a frequent service. At places like Baker Street and that, I just about remember them shouting out in a morning when we were hurrying to go somewhere, 'Hurry up! Last Richmond, last Richmond!' about 10.45 in the morning.

GB: And that continued till the war, did it?

HVB: That applied…That was pretty handy to have a sit-down meal of some kind. It was a bit of inconvenience because they'd got to find somewhere to put the trains. Well, with three or four trains finishing at Chalk Farm, where there's no room for them, they had to run a few of 'em into St Pancras Sidings. You had the extraordinary thing of a couple of trains standing in the platform at Dalston for about an hour and [a] half. In 1906 they curtailed the interval [to] about an hour and a half which today the union might have kicked up a row [about] because they lost a bit of lunchtime, you might say. It was also gradually – very gradually – abolished, was this Church Time. There was an article in *The Railway Magazine* about that many years ago [Vol.104, 686, pp.397, 420 (June 1958) – Editor]. The first one to do it was the South Western, I think you'll find, in 1901. Then when the District got in the hands of the American Yerkes, he said, 'Oh! Away with that!' and the District and the City & South London opened at Church Times, but the extraordinary thing was they nearly all did it at different times. The Great Eastern just about the time I started work abolished Church Time. But the Great Northern had about three hours of it. The Great Eastern was one of the first to abolish it. The Great Northern, the adjacent company, was one of the last. The same you got on the Southern: the Brighton was one of the last, the South Western was one of the first. In fact, the Brighton as such never abolished Church Time; it was the Southern that did it with electrification, although, on the South London line, the first bit that was electrified, they resolutely had this hour and [a] half or so Church Time there at first.

HWP: You mention the union, Mr Borley. Would that have been the ASRS at that time?

HVB: The union was, when I joined, the Amalgamated Society of Railway Servants. That was two or three amalgamated, and the drivers would not join and have not joined to this day. The locomotive men's union then, as now, was the Associated Society of Locomotive Engineers and Firemen. But some men did join. When it became the National Union of Railwaymen and one or two others, small unions, joined in, some men, some drivers and firemen and engine cleaners, transferred to that, to the National Union of Railwaymen. The Railway Clerks' Association was formed, I think, just after the First World War [HVB was incorrect here; the year was 1897 –Editor], and it was a very moderate affair and subsequently became the Transport Salaried Staff Association. But the clerks

7. 'North London trains were built to last for ever…' A posed photograph of NLR 4-4-0T no.31 and a standard train of twelve 4-wheelers at Devons Road (Bow) Carriage Depot looking north, 1898. This is the type of train that would have been very familiar to the young HVB. Notice luggage van/guard's compartment with 'birdcage' lookout at each end of the train. The Docklands Light Railway's Devons Road station now occupies the site of the signal box at the left.
Official NLR photo: RCHS/Spence

never joined in the National Union of Railwaymen.

HWP: Was it much of a force on the North London, the union, before the 1914–18 war, would you say, Mr Borley? Much of a power in the land?

HVB: Well, it varied. It was pretty strong round east London. It depends rather on the neighbourhood and the class of people that you lived amongst. The poor people were at the mercy of the Board of Guardians of the Poor, the Overseers of the Poor. The Board of Guardians were elected by the people, that was, at that time, men over 21, I think – not women. They were elected just as you elected the Borough Council; and they appointed a relieving

officer, but they didn't allow him much money and people often had to go almost on their hands and knees to get a few shillings. So that's how unions came to be formed. But, of course, it was a big effort to start a union and, of course, you'd got to pay your subscription; if it was only 6d a week, 6d was a lot of money to many people.

GB: What were unions actually able to do for their members in those days? Did they negotiate pay? Would the company take any notice of them?

HVB: They couldn't do very much because, at first, the railway companies wouldn't recognise them. And if they agreed to see anybody, they only saw

them as individuals. But, of course, it depends on that. With a man like Ford [George Newton Ford, last NLR Traffic Superintendent; see also PART 2 – Editor], they'd make some headway; because Ford realised, long ago, that the hours were too long and the pay too low. But, mind you, the pay was pretty fair compared with most other industries. And until all the poor devils were killed in the war, they all thought I was lucky to get where I was. And I was lucky, lucky for being nominated as I was, lucky for them thinking I was three years older than I was. Of course, there'd be a devil of trouble about that today! So as they wouldn't recognise the union; they didn't really recognise unions until after the First World War. That was when the eight-hour day was introduced. Incidentally, when I and a colleague were going in the army, they realised the hours were a bit too long and we trained three girls generally to two men. The girls were reasonably efficient but they didn't think they could stand the long hours. But there you are, the answer is that housewives generally work – often work seven days a week; they say they do at any rate! You're married; you probably know! And I think they're about right, sometimes.

HWP: What was the rolling stock, the condition of it, Mr Borley?

HVB: The North London trains were built to last

for ever, almost. The firsts were extremely comfortable, the smoking in leather and the other in blue cushions. The seconds had red cushions. They were lighted by gas. The thirds had wooden seats but [were] roomy and comfortable. The general percentage was about 40% smoking (the word 'Smoking' was on the quarter-lights), therefore 60% non-smoking. There was a notice inside of the North London (which was unusual) that smoking was prohibited. On the other railways they let it generally [be] understood that smoking was prohibited unless it was made [clear otherwise]. The thirds were five [compartments] to a carriage and the partition only went halfway up, so they had three lights to five compartments and these were gas lighted. They were turned very low. They were usually alight all day but turned very low, and turned up at Finchley Road on the up journey and turned down at Dalston, because of the tunnels, and very much the same on the other [direction], I think, controlled by the guard. The guards' vans were very big because at one time they had a lot of gas in there. Later that was done away with. They experimented with electric light about 1903, but things kept going wrong and so they did away with it. But the Mansion House Outer Circle trains, which were London [&] North Western always, they had electric light ever since I can remember, and they were a bit better rolling stock for comfort [but] not in build. The North London in its day had first class engines, with large destination boards in front.

And on Christmas Day specially, quite contrary to now, the Sunday service operated with some specials in the morning because there were a lot of people travelling to have dinner with friends, and I know I was retrieved as a child waiting on the platform at Hampstead Heath by my parents seeing the train coming in with a red disk, 'SPECIAL', on it. Then, of course, coming back at night at Acton, sometimes they'd run the Kew Bridge trains through. At Acton people had been trying to find seats and the porters or guard would shout out, 'Stand away! Stand away, please! 'Nother train following!' Of course, perfectly true the other train was following, [but] that had come from Richmond and was about as full as the other one!

But of course, the only lengthy holiday I had with my parents, my father had to stand nearly all the way to Kent – Sandwich – from Waterloo, Sunday morning; there were two trains. We went from Swiss Cottage to Baker Street and halfway round the Circle to Charing Cross. There, good people were trying to send us home, with placards saying we were going to Hell. Well, whether I'll finish up in Hell, I don't know, but I haven't got there yet! Whether my old parents are in Hell, I don't know. But, anyway, Father got some tickets and we got in the train at Charing Cross but, of course, it stopped in those days at Waterloo, Cannon Street, reversed, London Bridge; then it was damnably full at London Bridge. It stopped at one or two odd stations. We eventually got to Ashford and Minster; it was split at Minster, and part went to Margate and the other part round to Deal and Dover. That's how we got to Sandwich. There was a bit of comradeship. I know my Father with one or two other men took it in turns to sit down. They were non-corridor carriages. Like when I went with my aunt to Yarmouth, they were non-corridor. They stopped at Beccles. They shouted out, 'Stopping for five minutes' – see the people making for the conveniences, including me!

HWP: Was the stock kept pretty clean, Mr Borley?

HVB: The stock in my experience was *very* clean. People were much more tidy than now. Of course, in the smokers there was nowhere to put cigarette ends and matches; they did go on the floor. But there was, perhaps, not so much smoking as now – or perhaps not so much smoking as there was five or ten years ago; they say smoking's gone a bit out of fashion now. I don't know whether it has or not. I don't want to tread on anybody's toes; I see a gentleman there with a pipe! Although, of course, cigarettes, like everything else, were cheap – you'd get five Woodbines for a penny. It's even been said that you could get a couple of cigarettes for a halfpenny if you were short of money. Yes, you know, you could go in a pub with tuppence, get half a pint of mild ale or half a pint of porter for a penny, and a packet of Woodbines for another penny. There you got a drink and a smoke. And, of course, if you didn't like the cigarettes, you'd get a pinch of tobacco and a clay pipe for nixes [i.e. for nothing – Editor]. They kept clay pipes in pubs;

8. NLR composite First and Second Class five-compartment coach no.18, built at Bow Works in 1876 and gas lit. Photographed at Bow about 1898. *Official NLR photo: RCHS/Spence*

they'd give you a clay pipe if you bought a drop of beer. If you don't know what porter is, porter was an inferior kind of stout. It was rather famous at one time. You could also get in the saloon bar – those who could afford it – you'd get spiced ale or spiced wine. If you went in a pub for spiced ale now, they'd laugh at you, I should think, [though] I've never tried it. Yes, it used to be rather nice on a cold day, to have spiced ale.

GB: Going back to the carriage cleaning, was this done by – did they have women carriage cleaners or men carriage cleaners?

HVB: Mainly by men, but some companies, I think, had women.

HWP: It was all manual – there wasn't any automatic or semi-automatic?

HVB: It was manual. Pretty well everything was manual.

HWP: If the stock was clean, it was all the more creditable, really, wasn't it?

HVB: What they had out at Bow to do the cleaning of the carriages with cushions, I don't know. I should think they had some carpet beating and all that sort of thing. Of course, there were carpets in the firsts with NLR or L&NWR [woven in] to save you stealing 'em.

HWP: Did the North London employ many horses for shunting purposes, Mr Borley, as most companies did?

HVB: Not at any station where I was.

HWP: They didn't have station yards on those suburban-type stations, did you, normally?

HVB: Yes, well, they used to have an engine to do the shunting. The goods yards, except at first, were under the control of other companies, chiefly the

London [&] North Western, but the Great Northern had two or three and the Great Eastern one. You see, the Great Eastern goods at Hackney were very funny. Hackney Downs was up in the air; the North London was on the level. When the Great Eastern wanted a goods station they arranged with the North London to put it on the North London Railway – at Graham Road. So that meant another signal box there – the North London was good at signal boxes – and the Great Eastern worked through from Stratford via Victoria Park into this goods [station], and the Great Eastern passenger [station] at Hackney Downs was up in the air, so to speak. They had a connection between the two for passengers, officially called 'a covered footway and gallery'. There was an exchange booking office and ticket examiner there, a Great Eastern man. At Bow there was the same with a North London man. At Victoria Park everything was North London. At Gospel Oak, everything was London & North Western, including the Great Eastern [side], except the signalman, [who was] a Midland man attached to Highgate Road. So you had two Midland men working shifts under the control of the station-master at Highgate Road. The Midland signal box was at the Highgate Road end of the station; they were only less than half a mile apart. As I said, there was an exchange booking office there, but [with] Great Eastern tickets. Of course, they had different ways of dealing with children's tickets. The Great Eastern used to tear the singles in half and cut the returns diagonally, which seems to have been entirely abolished [on BR] now. But some companies used to cut a bit out of the bottom or have specially printed child tickets. Sometimes you cut the bit out the bottom and if you're busy you lost the bloomin' half, or nearly lost it. If you cut your bit out, if you couldn't produce the bit, you couldn't get credit for the half-ticket, you see.

GB: Did you deal with parcels at all, at suburban stations?

HVB: Parcels? Some stations there were parcels and cloakroom all together, but [at] others it was separate; it varied.

GB: Was it all 'to-be-called-for' parcels or was there delivery of parcels?

HVB: Usually delivery. But some stations it was 'till called for', yes.

JEN: And post was carried fairly short distances by train as well?

HVB: Yes, you had all sorts of things. At some of the stations you got an awkward thing; you got it so seldom that you were rather at sea when you charged for it. Dalston, especially, was a terrible place for tickets – more than Broad Street. You see, Broad Street booked, of course, for the North London and the Great Northern and the London & North Western. At Dalston you got all that packet, and Great Eastern as well. You see, if somebody living at Hackney wanted to go to Ilford, say, it was much better to go to Hackney (North London) and change at Victoria Park than to fiddle about from Hackney Downs to Bethnal Green. And so Dalston and Hackney got Great Eastern bookings, and Bow got Great Eastern bookings via Hackney to places like Chingford and Enfield. Yes, the number of sets of tickets at Dalston was colossal. There was almost always more than one clerk on duty at Dalston – and you needed it! We used to book up about ten o'clock at night. The London [&] North Western, all their accounts instructions were based on a place where there was just a few trains and you booked up after each train. They didn't have any proper instructions in the accounts instruction book for continuous working. And auditors used to come in, unexpected, of course.

Some auditors came in – I was at a station, alone – about 8.45 or nine o'clock or something like that. They came in [and] said they were the auditors. I said, 'Good morning, gentlemen.' Of course, I was attending to passengers, nineteen to the dozen there. They'd come from Northampton or some-where; they'd been transferred or promoted. They'd no experience of London stations. And I said, 'I can't book up or attend to you until after ten o'clock unless I shut down and send passengers without tickets, and that's not allowed.' So, of course, I was only a junior, but they eventually saw that it was impossible because they could see I was going nineteen to the dozen. So I think they went for a walk and came back and I did attend to them about ten o'clock. Later on, to economise, they had a Chief Booking Clerk between two or three stations – there used to be one at each station – and he wasn't there, and I was on my own. Well, I could manage a crowd , but I couldn't attend to auditors at the same time, and I had to tell them [in] pretty plain language. Oh, dear! Those were the days!

JEN: Could I just ask you one question, back on Kew Bridge?

HVB: Ask any question. Whether I can answer it is another matter!

JEN: You explained about the difference of the two platforms on the North London side or the North & South Western side; there is a house above the Broad Street departure platform. Do you know how old that would be? It is called Station House.

HVB: I don't know; I should think it's pretty old. There is another old house in the vicinity; it's now a certain number in Bollo Lane. It's against the level crossing on the Kew Bridge side. That's now entirely worked from the old [London &] South Western box. That house was erected in 1852 or 1853 because the Act of the North & South Western Junction provided for two level crossings and there was to be a gate house or lodge at each of those places. Well, the gate house or lodge still stands by the Bollo Lane crossing and it's now numbered a certain number in Bollo Lane. The one at Acton Lane – Acton Lane was a level crossing – between Acton and South Acton, that was just at the junction of the Hammersmith branch, originally. There was a gate house there and that stood until about ten years ago, I think. That was why that junction was often called Acton Gate House Junction, [though also] sometimes called Hammersmith Junction. The Hammersmith branch lost money from the day it was opened until the day it was demolished, and that's where they used to drop the carriage. You see, there were no continuous brakes at that time and a man with a shunting pole or a guard on the rear could snatch the coupling as the train slowed down. Like a goods train, you see, the couplings would be loose and the guard could snatch it and wave his hand and the train'd go on – slowed down and that was done. Both my grandfather and uncle swear to that and there was no reason to tell lies about it. It was probably

unofficial. I've never seen it in print but it was done. Then the whole service was altered when Broad Street was opened; they did away with the through carriages. They had through carriages to Stratford, too, which they dropped or separated at the junction at Victoria Park. But when Broad Street [was opened] they did away with these through carriages and people had to change.

But at Acton, you see, Acton Gate House, the bloomin' Hammersmith branch was arranged the wrong way round, so the local engine had to push the train to the junction points and then reverse and go on to Hammersmith. Well, when South Acton was opened, they extended the branch on to South Acton, and they ran on to South Acton, probably irregularly, because the [train] staff remained at the Gate House, the old junction, and they went on the single line without any token, but still, it was dead straight and nothing serious happened. But eventually, about 1909, just before my time, they decided to install the electric train staff and do away with the Hammersmith Junction, which they did. Then, of course, there was a complication because the North London engine shed was the other side of the Hammersmith branch, a place for six engines; whether there was ever six there, I don't know, probably usually four. Well, they could come out and cross the single line, right under the nose of the signalman, that was all right, [but] when they had the electric train staff, controlled from South Acton, that presented a bit of a problem. So they put a pillar in there, which the drivers could work; of course nowadays, they'd probably want extra pay for that – or go on strike! But there, in those days, they did as they were told. The driver could tap up the signalman at South Acton and he'd do something or other and release the staff, providing he was in a position to do so. And that was the way that was worked. That was all right then because you had a staff station at each end and an additional pillar at this engine shed. But, of course, you could only get one staff out at a time. So there was no danger of anything meeting.

GB: And the drivers used to get their own …?

HVB: The driver could get his staff out, you see, from his pillar, take it up to South Acton [and] hand it over to the signalman there, if he was going on to Kew Bridge to work a train. Then, of course, in the evening, when he was going back, he'd get a staff from the South Acton signalman, take it along and then put it in his pillar and clear it in the way that the electric train staff worked. Of course, when they abolished the passenger service, they did away with that. The passenger service finished in the First World War. They started three halts along there and a guard to issue tickets, and all that sort of thing, to economise. Then it was one engine in steam and it worked in a more simple way, more like the goods, a goods line – well, it was a goods line, of course, [and] the restrictions weren't so strict.

GB: I've not come across this, I don't think, any-where before, where you've got a section of single line with three token instruments.

HVB: You get that on some single lines in the country, where there's an intermediate siding. The train can get in that siding, put the staff in there and he's then locked in and they can deal with another train. You get that, I think, between Bedford and Sandy; you've got something like that. Then, when he wants to come out, he's got to get permission and the signalman will release him a staff if he's in a position to do so. You see, simple electric train staff is just from 'A' to 'B' and if you've got a' equal number of trains – well, it's all right, [it will] balance out, but if you've got an intermediate siding you've got to have some special arrange-ments, but it's quite safe if people abide by the regulations, and it's a job to break them because if you try to get a staff out and you haven't got authority, well, you'd need a sledge-hammer to break the blooming thing – and a strong man to wield the sledge-hammer!

GB: When you went into war service – into the Army – was that because you volunteered, and what were the arrangements with the railway company for the time you were in the war?

HVB: They hadn't introduced compulsory service then but it was in the air, so to speak. Many were going and I saw this chance of going in the railway transport service. You see, that was another thing that I must admit was rather unfair. I went to

Longmoor, and after about a fortnight there, learning mighty little about soldiering or anything else, I went off with certificates that I was proficient in all sorts of things, including railway bridge building, and I hardly knew anything about soldiering or engineer's work. Overseas I was to a large extent in the office but there, I mean, long hours on the railway, long hours there – well, you see, you got good times and bad times and there were times when you'd almost give anything to get a bit of sleep. And if the Germans bombed the rations – well, you probably had to go without. But then you thought of the poor devils in the front line; it wasn't particularly happy, you know, sending a train from the base loaded with 'reinforcements' as they called them, with officers in first class, the sergeants and sergeant-majors in the seconds and the troops in third class or trucks, going up there and you knew damn well that for many of 'em that was their last journey. It wasn't particularly happy and the carnage on the Somme for those four months …The most unfortunate people there were junior officers. Junior officers had got to give – a lieutenant and second lieutenant and to some extent captain – they'd got to give examples to their men, so to speak; they were perhaps the worst rank of all. But for everybody it was just murder and no other word for it.

HWP: Did you sense at the time, Mr Borley, how futile it really was or did you feel imbued with the fact that it was essential and had got to be done?

HVB: What do you mean?

HWP: Well, did your sense of duty overcome your sense of the fact that it was all a terrible waste?

HVB: To a large extent, yes. Another job I got after a few months in France – I'd got a knowledge of French and I used to talk to French railwaymen, and villagers for that matter – almost anybody sometimes – and they got in such a tangle because the French worked all the trains at first of all. Well, the French drivers, firemen and guards were being pretty well worked to death. There were collisions more often than should be, especially as they had a sort of semi-permissive block. That was, you see, they'd stop a train, and before they got 'Line clear' from the next one [box], they'd send the train forward with authority, telling him. Well, if the driver was half asleep, possibly there was a collision.

So they got some drivers from England and some that were in the Army, and some officer had seen me talking French and he had me in there and he said, 'You're a good French scholar, Borley.' 'No, sir, I have a slight knowledge of it'. 'Oh, well, you'll do,' he says. 'Look here, we're going to have some drivers that don't know French. You've got to go with some French drivers, learn a bit about it. We're getting some books out in English and French, explaining the signalling. You've got to do something with that. You've a couple of weeks to do it.' I said, 'It's a very short time, sir.' 'No matter, you've got to do the best you can.' So I went with these French drivers and studied this book, got a bit of a knowledge of it.

Then I was sent out with some English men, guiding them. Well, as I was a bit of a fool with a bike in my younger days, I was a bigger fool with a locomotive! So I didn't do much help there. Well, a fair number of good drivers and they'd got some British engines coming over then – as you know, they had to get some British because these French men, you see, in the French army, as in the British army, asleep on duty, on active service, means a court martial and could, in extreme cases, possibly mean a firing squad. But no French men got a firing squad but several of them were sent to join their regiment, the infantry. Well, of course, the more drivers they did that to, the less they'd got to run trains. So they got in a blooming predicament over that. So they tried to reduce the hours. Well, I don't deny that more than once, I've been asleep on a locomotive and, well, if you can keep awake on duty for 24, 28 or 30 hours on end, well, you're a superman! Fortunately, or unfortunately, some of those engines of the Northern Railway of France were extremely comfortable. It's all right for a driver working eight hours a day; he can squat on his arse and see everything ahead lovely. But if he's been there for about 24 hours and that, he's liable to doze off.

On occasions we were fetched out; at Rouen at one time, I was fetched out. You had [men] in squads, you see, and I was a sort of pilot. They knew damn well I couldn't drive. Fetched out about 3.30 one morning or something like that. Well, whatever the time, you appear before an officer; you got to be properly dressed, even at that time, on active service. So somebody came and fetched me. I said, 'Well, I'll get round as soon as I can.' So I got dressed, went round and they said, 'So and so train's got to go. Your lot got to take it.' I said, 'Begging your pardon, sir, but we haven't had a proper night's rest for more than two weeks. We only just got down to it, just before midnight. Now it's four o'clock; we won't be able to keep awake.' So the officer said, 'What the devil you mean, you can't keep awake? That bloody train's got to go and your lot's got to take it.' I said, 'Very good, sir. There's another thing, sir.' 'What now?' 'I see that's going to a place where I've never been. I don't know the road and the drivers won't know,' (because it was an English crew). He said, 'Well, get a pilotman at Longeau.' (Longeau was near Amiens.) Well, he knew there was about as much chance of getting a French pilotman at Longeau as there was meeting a polar bear in the Sahara Desert! So I said, 'Well, very good, sir, but I don't know how we're going to keep awake.' He said, 'That'll mean a court martial.' I said, 'Yes, sir, and a firing squad.' So I saluted and went off. There were three of us on the engine and I said, 'Well, you know the road this end, I'll get down and have a bit of a sleep.' Having been threatened with a court martial, the next thing I did was to go to sleep on duty on active service! But as you'll realise, it's the best thing to be done, because when I woke up, you see, and we were on a pretty level road the driver had a bit of a sleep, because otherwise we'd all have dropped off more or less the same time, and then the fireman. Then, of course, we got to Longeau [where] as I said – no pilotman. So I went in the signal box and had a look at the diagrams and all that. So I took a chance. We got to this place. We'd got a load of ammunition on, Germans were shelling it right and left, there was nobody about; we all three got down asleep in the brake van, there, with ammunition and Germans shelling. It was very near committing suicide, but the miracle was the Germans didn't hit the train nor explode anything near it, but there was nothing else we could do. I think the driver got out and nearly fell over in the darkness so he got back.

That was it, and so you went on, year after year. Later, there were a bit different arrangements and the drivers got to know things. They got hold of odd words and phrases to do with the railway. But for almost thirteen months, I never had a single day off. Then I came on leave. The manners and bad language of the people on the leave trains going home was mighty different from when they were coming back. Coming back, it was surprising what a lot of people were of illegitimate birth, if nothing worse.

HWP: Did you stick it out right to the end, Mr Borley – 1918?

HVB: Yes, I was demobilised about four, four or five months after that – demobilised at Crystal Palace. They gave us a week's pay. 'Course, the pay in the Engineers was considerably more than the Infantry. The Infantry pay in the first half of the war was a shilling a day. If you were married, they deducted sixpence for your wife; 'fighting for your King and your Country, all for a tanner a day.' Engineers, I think they made us – Sappers for a start, not Pioneers, Sappers. Three bob a day, I think, I got. I rose to the rank of corporal, about 4/6d a day.

GB: I think we ought to buy Mr Borley a drink now, don't you?

HWP: I think we owe him that, at least! I'd like to say, Mr Borley, that it's been a privilege, a real privilege and a pleasure talking to you, and I hope we have a further opportunity in the future.

PART TWO

Early Railway Journeys
and some remarks on
The North London Railway

Early Journeys

FROM AN EARLY AGE I took an interest in transport: trains, trams, omnibuses. I lived with my parents at Hampstead and we had relatives at Acton and Islington. We made rather frequent journeys on the North London Railway, nearly always on Sundays as my father worked six days a week. The guard's van had a raised 'look-out' and my father sometimes managed to arrange for me to travel with the guard, so I knew the road almost as well as he did. My grandfather knew the staff at Acton very well. On one occasion I was taken to the signal cabin and everything was explained to me, including the wheel which worked the level crossing gates. On another occasion I travelled on the engine of a local train from Acton to Kew Bridge and back.

I did not have many long-distance journeys. One was Liverpool Street to Yarmouth with my uncle and aunt, and another Kentish Town (Mid) to Southend, but I do not remember any details, except that the trains were non-corridor stock and

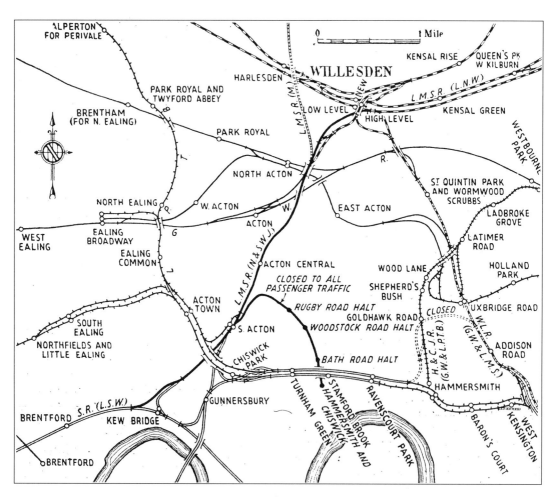

9. The North & South Western Junction Railway and adjacent lines as at 1923, showing the separate Broad Street platform at Kew Bridge. See also figs 21 and 23 of the North London Railway.
'The Railway Magazine'

always full. On a summer bank holiday I went with my parents to Crystal Palace from Hampstead Heath via Kensington and Clapham Junction. On return we got into the wrong crowd and eventually reached St Pauls (now Blackfriars). The railways had given up trying to control passengers from the Palace and tickets were accepted by any reasonable route, so we had no difficulty at St Pauls and then on the Outer Circle to Hampstead Heath.

At this time the Companies considered it most important that on the Inner Circle passengers used the shortest way and at most stations ticket examiners were at the foot of the stairs to see that this was adhered to. These men also shut the gate to prevent people joining a moving train.

I also went to Skegness with Mother, aunts and cousins. The GNR were helping to make this place popular by running very cheap day trips. It was the first time I had travelled in a really fast train.

I remember going to Sandwich for ten days in 1904. On a Sunday in summer, we left home about 8 o'clock, going by Metropolitan Railway from Swiss Cottage to Baker Street and then round the Inner Circle. Outside Charing Cross there were people with placards and bills telling us to go home as we were travelling to Hell. There were three classes and we booked second. The train was very long with a small engine, but the driver told us a large engine would come on the other end at Cannon Street. The train left Charing Cross at 10.02, and called at Waterloo Junction, Cannon Street and London Bridge, whence we left with two people standing in our non-corridor compartment. My father took it in turns to sit down. We stopped at a few suburban stations, then ran fast to Ashford, Canterbury and Minster, where the train divided, one part for Margate, the other for Deal. On the way the train stopped and was shunted on to the up line as the down was being relaid. This greatly interested me. At Sandwich the signal cabin was by the level crossing; my father soon made friends with the signalmen, and I frequently went into the cabin.

On a fine Sunday in January we went by omnibus to Pimlico but the weather suddenly changed and snow began to fall. We left earlier than intended and my mother secured a seat inside but father and I had to go on top; the driver looked like a snowman. At Chalk Farm, the man with the 'cock-horse' attached this horse to the front. Snowing had stopped but

froze and soon the conductor said, 'Will the genulmen get out, please; the 'orses can't make it.' My father, in silk top hat and frock coat, took charge of one horse (he had had some experience with horses) and we eventually reached Hampstead Town Hall. Here the driver said, 'We can't go no furver. You'll have to walk.' So the horses were taken to the stables in the High Street and the vehicle was parked for the night. We all walked, including the ladies in their long skirts.

In 1910 I entered the service of the London & North Western Railway. I had been nominated by a man who was a director of that Company and the North London Railway. This was of considerable help to me. Also my date of birth came to be recorded as three years earlier than the correct date, with the result I not only received a higher salary but occupied positions which I should not have done.

After a month's training at a few stations at a salary of £20 per annum and having passed a test, I was appointed as a booking clerk at a salary of, I believe, £35 and was soon placed on the relief staff for stations between Broad Street, Poplar and Kew Bridge, and paid a further £10 a year.

The North London Railway and associated lines

I GIVE DETAILS of the lines concerned. The original *North London Railway* as opened in 1850–51 ran from Bow (junction with London & Blackwall Railway) to Camden (Chalk Farm) (junction with L&NW); the train service weekdays and Sundays was every quarter-hour from and to Fenchurch Street.

The *Hampstead Junction Railway* extended from Kentish Town Junction (Camden Road) to Old Oak Junction via Hampstead Heath, opened in 1860 and was extended to Acton Wells Jn in 1885. The first trains were NL and the line was worked and managed as part of the NL from 1862. The Hampstead Junction Company was dissolved in 1867, being amalgamated with the L&NW, but the NL remained in control until 30 June 1872 after which the NL continued to control bookstalls, advertising and season tickets.

The *North & South Western Junction Railway* ran from a junction with the L&NW main line at

Willesden to Old Kew Junction (L&sw). There were two main road level crossings – Acton Lane and Bollo Lane; also a 'track' (now Churchfield Road) crossed on the level. Acton Lane crossing was abolished in 1874, the road being taken under the railway. The original intention appears to have been to provide a through service from Euston to Brentford and Hounslow. A small station was built at Acton with neither footbridge nor subway; it was rebuilt on the same site by the NL in 1876. Gate-houses or lodges were provided at Acton Lane and Bollo Lane; the latter still stands as a residence. The passenger service began in 1853 with four NL trains to Kew, where a platform was constructed. A station was built a year or two later. There was a branch (opened for goods in 1857 and for passengers in 1858) to Hammersmith from Hammersmith Junction (or Acton Gate House Jn). Here the train stopped and detached a carriage, but later the vehicle was 'dropped' by the guard snatching the coupling as the train slowed or the gate-keeper detached it with a shunting pole. My grandfather and uncle saw this at the crossing. The vehicle was then worked forward to Hammersmith.

Through carriages were also worked by the NL to Stratford and Stratford Bridge (later called Stratford Market). The train stopped at Hackney Wick Jn (later Victoria Park) and detached one or two carriages. When traffic was heavy, Stratford carriages worked through specially from and to Chalk Farm (now Primrose Hill). Upon the opening of Broad Street in 1865 services were entirely altered and in each case through vehicles ceased. The Hammersmith carriage was propelled from Acton station to the junction. Upon the opening of South Acton in 1880 the single line was extended thereto but the physical connections remained at the Gate House. When the original HJ line was abandoned in 1892 a two-way junction was made at Old Oak Jn between the substituted HJ line of 1885 and the N&SWJ lines. This enabled the NL goods trains to go forward and then reverse into Old Oak Sidings.

Working Timetables

As the NL was based on Fenchurch Street, the line remained 'up' to Fenchurch Street and Poplar. In the working timetables Fenchurch Street was at the head, with Broad Street a third of the way down the page. When the NL ceased to use Fenchurch Street, Mint Street (GN Goods) and Haydon Square were at the top and this remained until the formation of the LMS.

The Staff and Hours

All NL stations were under the control of a Chief Booking Clerk and two Station Inspectors. Later one Chief Clerk had charge of two or three stations. Most staff worked early and late shifts, six days a week. The change-over time was usually 1.30pm so that both could have their mid-day meal at a reasonable time. The shifts were changed on Sunday, the late-turn man taking the Sunday duty (about 16 hours) and early turn Monday. This gave the other man a clear weekend off. At some stations, however, the early-turn man took the Sunday duty and late turn Monday. At the more important stations, there were additional staff, usually working a split turn so as to be on duty at busy times. At these stations, staff usually worked about eight hours on Sunday. Clerks usually booked up at about 10pm; money taken after this being left for the following day. Signal cabins were open continuously, three men each working eight hours a day. At busy cabins there were one or two additional men. All except clerks were paid a day's pay at ordinary rates for Sunday duty. From 1912, clerks were also paid for Sunday duty. Servants' (i.e. employees') trains were provided before the first and after the last public train. That between Devons Road and Broad Street consisted of a third class brake carriage; that between Devons Road and Chalk Farm was ordinary passenger stock. There was also a Servants' train at night, from Hampstead Heath to Willesden.

From 1914, to relieve staff of Sunday duty, men from Goods stations and Parcels offices worked a turn on Sunday at Passenger stations.

Clerks and inspectors were granted two weeks' annual leave, lower grades one week, usually in early spring or autumn. One had to wait the first day for the relief man to arrive. No time was allowed for meals at stations, but facilities including kettles were provided for heating food and water.

10. Bow station NLR, looking south to Poplar about 1905, Broad Street train entering.
Commercial postcard by Charles Martin

At headquarters 45 minutes were allowed for lunch but food was not allowed to be consumed at any other time.

There were two guards on Kew Bridge and Richmond trains until 1909 and on trains to and from the GN until 1915.

Discipline was strict; if a man was suspended with loss of pay, others, irrespective of grade, clubbed together to help him financially.

The L&NWR takes over the NLR

IN CONSEQUENCE of the opening of the Central London Railway, tramway electrification and motor buses, the NL lost much traffic. In 1908 agreement was reached with the L&NW and the senior officers of the NL retired at the end of that year. Control was taken by L&NW officers, who were responsible to the NL Board of Directors. The NL remained an independent Company. The Traffic Superintendent, George Newton Ford,

went to Euston and in 1911 was appointed also District Officer of the Southern Division of the L&NW – it was said jocularly that the NL had taken over the main line to Stafford. The NL Permanent Way and Maintenance Officer, stationed at Camden Town, whose area included the N&SWJ, also took control of the HJ.

The agreement with the L&NW led to the partial closing of the Locomotive and Carriage & Wagon works at Bow. Some men were given the opportunity to go to Crewe or Wolverton (moving expenses paid), others were given two weeks pay in lieu of notice. There was already much poverty in East London. People bought groceries in very small quantities; some brought a cup or bowl for some loose pickles or treacle. They seemed mainly to live on bread and margarine, then usually pronounced correctly with the 'g' as in 'garden'; it looked more like lard. It was very distressing to see, as I did, hungry poorly-clad children begging stale cakes, biscuits, carrots or apples from shops. The unemployed were at the mercy of the Guardians of

11. The impressive Bow Road frontage of Bow station NLR, incorporating the 'Bow & Bromley Institute', about 1903, looking north east. *Commercial postcard by Charles Martin*

the Poor, who appointed Relieving Officers who could not give much assistance. I found the poor people generally honest. The fares for a day trip for the family to Southend were paid sometimes in a variety of coins, which had been saved week by week over several months. Ford was a very popular officer; he paid frequent visits to stations and was always welcomed. He too was very distressed at the poverty but could not help much. I became very well acquainted with him as we were both interested in the history of the NLR.

The Stations

THE STATIONS were in most cases substantial buildings, half or more of the length of the platforms being covered. There were usually first and second class waiting rooms and toilets on each platform and plenty of seats for third class passengers and smokers on the platforms.

The Trains

TRAINS ON THE NL consisted of close-coupled carriages, second class in front on the up journey. Third class had wooden seats; from 1907 these were changed to leather, although the work proceeded very slowly. About 40% of the compartments were labelled 'Smoking' on the quarter lights; 60% were non-smoking, with notices inside reading, 'Smoking prohibited.' The vehicles were gas-lighted but the thirds had only three lights to five compartments.

Train Services and Church Interval

MOST SERVICES were every 15 minutes daily, with an interval on Sunday at morning Church Time; this enabled staff to have lunch. For many years, the interval on the NL was two hours, reduced to one and a half in 1906 and abolished in

12. Bow Junction signal box in the 1930s, looking north into Bow station. *RCHME*

1921. During the interval trains stood at various places, including St Pancras sidings.

For many years, the last two trains from Poplar before the Sunday morning interval terminated at Dalston, the working being as follows:

The train arrived at the eastern platform at Dalston as usual; the engine was detached, and reversed on to the other line and proceeded to Eastern Junction. Meanwhile, the guard having reported that the train was complete, the light engine was accepted from Eastern Junction by a block telegraph special code and was attached to the rear of the train, which it pushed forward and then back on to the other line where it stood until the train service was resumed.

The second train then arrived, but stood at the platform until the first train had resumed the service to Poplar. The procedure then was the same as in the case of the first train. (The 'up line' was from Dalston Junction station to Eastern Junction.)

One or two Chalk Farm trains were sent empty to St Pancras sidings as necessary to relieve congestion at Chalk Farm.

(On the District and Metropolitan Railways in the Church Interval certain trains terminated at various stations with sidings, remaining there, on the running line in some cases, until the train service resumed.)

Sunday services operated on Christmas Day and Good Friday but morning and evening traffic was heavy and special trains were run. The engines carried red discs with 'Special' in white letters. Engines carried large destination boards; these included 'Dalston' and 'Camden Town', only used on Sunday, and 'Bow NL' for the Plaistow train. One of each obsolete board was kept at Bow; these were Fenchurch Street, Hatfield, Southend. Side destination boards were carried on brake-vans.

After the agreement with the L&NW, work continued much as before. Instructions were issued that L&NW carriages were not to be sent to Richmond nor to GN or LT&S stations, and the NL continued to work cross-London goods transfers. The Outer Circle was always worked by the L&NW

but never ran from Broad Street on Sundays. In 1912 these trains were diverted to Kew Bridge. On summer bank holidays, the NL ran many additional trains to and from Hampstead Heath, Kew and Richmond. The LT&S ran a train daily in summer (usually two on Sundays) from Chalk Farm to Southend and back from 1907 till 1914.

Fares and Tickets

NORTH LONDON FARES were always on a low basis, the second class usually at or below 1d per mile. Before 1869 NL tickets were issued from Fenchurch Street and Stepney, and also from Blackwall when NL trains ran there. Between adjacent stations in many cases the fare was 1d second class. Third class was introduced generally in 1875, at still lower fares, but the second class penny fares were increased to 1½d. Return tickets available for return the following day were usually fare and a half, issued for all trains. Through fares were in operation to GN suburban stations via Canonbury and Finsbury Park, to GE suburban stations via Hackney or via Victoria Park or Bow, to the LT&S via Bow, to the L&NW via Willesden and to the L&SW via Kew Bridge or Richmond. At Hackney an exchange clerk and ticket examiner was provided by the GE, and at Bow by the NL. After the footways and galleries were closed, through bookings continued, passengers crossing the public streets. Down-line tickets were white, red and green respectively for first, second and third class; up line tickets were respectively yellow, blue and buff. Many Poplar line tickets were two colours, or bore stripes. The tickets bore large numbers indicating destination: Broad Street No.1 to Chalk Farm No.9; Hackney No.10 to Blackwall No.16; Kentish Town No.17 to Richmond No.29. Local tickets were cut in half for children (returns diagonally) but through tickets had a piece cut out at the base. In some cases, specially printed tickets were supplied. The GE cut the tickets in half. The GN cut only singles in half; returns had a piece cut out. The GN had bookings from Broad Street, Dalston Junction, Hackney, Bow and Poplar to all GN stations, and GN tickets to stations north of New Barnet. The L&NW had bookings from Broad Street, Dalston Junction and Camden Town, and

tickets to stations north of Willesden. The GE provided tickets from Victoria Park, but all staff were NL.

Workmen's tickets were issued between Broad Street, Poplar and Chalk Farm at a charge of 2d. Formerly there were six sets of tickets, one for each day of the week; later there was only one set. Tickets were issued from Broad Street to Mansion House; the original fare was (I understand) 9d third single, reduced gradually to 6d. Season tickets could be obtained. A member of the Railway Club, Harry Walker Bardsley, obtained perhaps the only one. He lived at Hampstead and worked at St James's Park, so if he missed his usual train, there was one a few minutes later to Broad Street; he joined that, thence travelling on the Inner Circle to St James's Park.

The N&SWJ had its own booking office at Richmond (closed 1917) and N&SWJ tickets (same type as NL) were issued from Gunnersbury, Kew Gardens and Richmond. This practice was continued by the LMS until nationalization (1948). When the L&NW introduced some tourist and excursion bookings from Richmond they supplied tickets headed 'L&NWR' but the South Western said this was contrary to the agreement and insisted on 'N&SWJ' tickets, and this was done.

Season tickets were issued from the Season Ticket Office, Broad Street, including those for the HJ and the N&SWJ. Third class seasons were introduced in 1902, but deposits were not abolished until 1909. Many people could not pay the deposit and so took third returns daily. In 1903, Hampstead Heath issued about 250 third returns to Broad Street each weekday, but the number gradually dropped. In 1911 only about 50 were issued.

The NL published large timetables, giving also other Companies' connecting train services and lists of fares and season ticket rates from each station. In 1911 these were replaced by small 'pocket size' books which gave much less information.

Signalling

I WAS GIVEN an opportunity of working as a 'Train Register Boy' in signal cabins for a few months. The NL had special block instruments, supplied by Pryce & Ferreira. Installation was complete by 1895

13. A 1930s view of Canonbury Junction; former NLR lines to left and former GNR tracks curving round to the southern entrance to Canonbury tunnel and Finsbury Park at centre. *RCHME*

and extended to Gospel Oak, including Finsbury Park No.1 (GN) and Channelsea (GE), and also Old Oak Jn to Acton (GW) and New Kew Jn (L&SW). Kew East Jn to Old Kew Jn was controlled by L&SW permissive block, and South Acton to Bollo Lane Jn by Preece's and thence to Richmond by L&SW lock and block. Broad Street, passenger and goods, was controlled by four cabins and a rather complicated system was installed, I believe, about 1892. Very good in its day but out-dated in LMS days, it remained in use until about 1960 and is now in the Museum at York with other NL instruments.

The Hammersmith branch was controlled at first by train staff and ticket from Acton Gate House. Upon the opening of South Acton station in 1880, the single line was extended thereto but the only physical connection remained at Acton Gate House, which controlled staff and ticket working. In 1909 it was decided to abolish Acton Gate House Jn (or Hammersmith Jn) signal cabin, remove the points and install electric train staff

working, with a new connection at South Acton. This work was completed and operated from 1 September 1910. A pillar was provided at the engine shed [near the former junction] to enable drivers to obtain a staff with the permission of the signalman at South Acton.

At one time there were 43 NL cabins (not including HJ and N&SWJ) and for many years separate cabins were provided for the No.1 and No.2 lines at many places, but these were gradually phased out between 1907 and 1909 and concentrated in one cabin.

Exceptions to normal regulations were authorised at many places and an unusual feature was the calling-on distants. These had very short arms, were notched and showed no light when 'on'; a small green light showed when 'off', indicating 'home off, starting signal on'. Apparently these signals were first installed at Dalston in 1893, and later at a few other places. The NL was subject to much fog and a considerable number of men were stationed at distant and other signals. The detonator was not taken up if only the calling-on distant was off, but the fogman shouted, 'The little 'uns off.' Refreshments were brought out to fogmen after three hours duty. Where trains passed near signal cabins in foggy weather, the 'Register Boy' had to shout to the driver, 'No.2 up advance starter on,' or 'No.2 up, right away to …', as the case may be.

At one time the NL code differed considerably from that of many other companies, and this resulted in a serious collision in tunnel at Canonbury in December 1881. As the NL man at the junction could not accept an up train, he correctly gave seven bell beats to Finsbury Park No.1, described in the NL code as: 'obstruction, permissive block,' meaning 'line temporarily blocked with permission.' But 'permissive block' in the code used by the GN meant 'stop and caution' and did not apply to passenger trains. The GN man, looking hurriedly in the NL code, misunderstood the meaning and exhibited a green flag, pulling off the signal, and a collision resulted. The NL drivers did not understand the significance of the green flag. The derailed vehicles probably tightened the wire, causing the distant to 'droop'. The wording of the code was subsequently altered to 'temporary obstruction.' From 5 October 1884 the NL adopted a new code, only slightly different from the standard RCH code.

Signalling at Kew Bridge was under L&SW control and L&SW staff attended to NL trains on arrival. The N&SWJ had its own entrance, booking office, clerks and porters under the control of the N&SWJ Station Master, including the goods station. The departure platform was obviously in N&SWJ style and was maintained by the NL on behalf of the N&SWJ. In 1918 the L&SW took full control of passenger arrangements.

The NL instruments remained until replaced in 1957–1961 by British Railways instruments. The Hammersmith branch reverted to 'one engine in steam' when the passenger service was withdrawn in 1917. The connection at Old Oak Jn (installed in 1892) was taken out of use with effect from 6 November 1977 and removed, and the cabin closed.

Later developments

No.1 UP LINE south of Dalston Junction station to Broad Street was taken out of use on 2 January 1966. No.1 down line was taken out of use on 5 November 1969. No.1 lines (down and up) went out of use on 8 November 1976 from south of Dalston Junction station to Western Junction. Between Camden Road Jn and Canonbury Jn, the No.1 lines (up and down) went out of use on 5 October 1981.

South Acton Jn and Bollo Lane Crossing were concentrated at Bollo Lane Jn cabin on 23 August 1970. Canonbury Jn was controlled by Western Jn, Dalston, from 12 May 1974.

A note on the
Great Eastern Railway
at Gospel Oak

14. Gospel Oak station looking east in the 1920s, North London platforms to the right, disused L&NER platform at left. *RCHME*

THE Tottenham & Hampstead Junction Railway was authorised in 1862 to construct a railway from a junction with the GE at Tottenham Hale to a junction with the Hampstead Junction Railway at Gospel Oak. Construction began at the Tottenham end but, by the time the work reached Highgate Road, the coffers were empty and no more capital could be raised, nor would the GE, the L&NW or the NL advance any money. The line was sponsored by the GE, who at first provided a fairly good service, weekdays and Sundays, from Fenchurch Street to Highgate Road from 21 July 1868. The trains reversed at Tottenham Hale. However, the resident population was very small and passengers very few, although the fares were low having regard to distance. The service was gradually reduced to one or two trains a day and was withdrawn in January 1870.

The T&HJ Railway was distinct from the Hampstead Junction, which was sponsored by the L&NW and NL.

Although the line could not be completed west of Highgate Road, a brick bridge over Gordon House Lane (now Gordon House Road) had been built, and so had some circular brickwork for a turn-table at Gospel Oak. Matters remained thus until the Midland constructed a short line from Kentish Town to Highgate Road (High Level) and began a goods and passenger service in 1870.

In 1888 the GE and Midland decided to complete the line to Gospel Oak, but the L&NW and NL refused to agree to a physical junction. The Midland did the work, including a substantial one-platform station with waiting rooms and an interchange booking office. The GE then began a service from Chingford to Highgate Road on 1 August 1885, and from 4 June 1888 this was extended to Gospel Oak. In summer months from 1891 to 1909 the GE ran a through train (or through carriages) to Southend, usually on Sunday but in some years on weekdays also. The GE provided tickets, those to T&HJ stations being GE type but headed 'Tottenham & Hampstead Junction Rly,' later 'Tottenham & Hampstead Joint Rly.' Bookings were restricted to Chingford, North Woolwich and intermediate stations, and also single, day and week-end excursions to Southend. Passengers to North Woolwich were practically 'nil' as the Victoria Park route was quicker. There were no Midland trains, nor Midland bookings.

There is no evidence that a turn-table was ever installed at Gospel Oak and when I saw the place in 1910 the brickwork was visible but the pit was full of earth and overgrown with grass and weeds, and even trees. Some OS maps marked the place 'turn-table', but evidently the surveyor anticipated matters incorrectly.

The L&NW staff attended to the day-to-day work at Gospel Oak station and the permanent way and station maintenance was performed by the Midland. A signal cabin at the east end of the station was manned by Midland men, under the control of the Stationmaster at Highgate Road.

A physical junction between the Tottenham and Hampstead Junction lines was made during World War I and an L&NW junction signal cabin was installed. It was brought into use on 30 January 1916, but taken out of use in 1922. The cabin remained unused and empty until the junction was reinstated on 11 March 1940, again for wartime contingencies.

No regular passenger services have ever worked through the Gospel Oak connection. Regular goods services virtually ceased in 1920 but recommenced in 1940.

The last passenger service from the Tottenham platform was on August Bank Holiday 1939. Later the platform and booking office built by the Midland were demolished.

A new terminal platform was brought into use on 5 January 1981 and a service between Gospel Oak and Barking commenced on that day.

15. L&NER Chingford to Gospel Oak train of ex-GER coaches leaving Chingford
(Stanley Road–Beresford Road footbridge in background) on 1 June 1925, hauled by GER J69 0-6-0T 7363.
F. Agar/North Woolwich Museum Collection

PART THREE

Contributions
to
Periodicals

(i) On General Matters

Use of Non-Imperial Units

IN 1965 the Government decided with the full support of the British Standards Institution and the Confederation of British Industry to adopt the Metric System and the target date for completion in 1975. The railways then arranged to begin making a change and among other things some kilometric posts were erected. Later the Metrication Board was formed to facilitate the change and is doing the work the Government appointed it to do. Many members and former members of the British Commonwealth followed the lead of Britain but some of them seem to be moving much faster than we are doing.

Because of the removal of some connecting lines and junctions the railways need remeasuring in some instances, and in any case existing mile posts will not last for ever. The new London Transport cars have been constructed to metric dimensions. Many County and Town Councils now stipulate for tenders in metric quantities and it is, I submit, far better for the railways to make the change rather than being left in splendid isolation in 1975. Of course the change will cost money, and it will not become any cheaper or easier by postponing it, but there is good reason to think it will be most beneficial in the long run.

(L) *RM* 117, p.101 (2/1971)

Metric Measures

I WAS VERY INTERESTED in the article about kilometre posts, in which the writer says it is doubtful if there is much enthusiasm for metric. I have always been in favour since I first used metric in the science lab 76 years ago. We all thought how lucky French and German children were after we had spent three years trying to master rods, poles, perches and square ditto, also furlongs, pecks, bushels, stones, scruples, drachms and many more. Metric was legalised in Britain by an Act of 1897 and most countries of the British Commonwealth are now 'all metric'.

(L) *UN* 256, p.86 (4/1983)

Kilometre Posts

WITH REFERENCE TO *UN* 255, March 1983, I found this article most interesting. I think it is the first time that railway distances have been calculated by way of an exchange point such as Mile End, where there is no physical junction.

When British Rail acquired the line from Moorgate to Finsbury Park the line was measured in km from Moorgate. At the same time, in connexion with electrification, kilometre posts were erected from King's Cross to Royston, the zero point being the buffer stops at King's Cross. Posts coloured blue were erected at each km and midway between each was a slightly smaller post bearing the figure 5 in a square; this represented 5 hectometres. The posts were not very substantial and many have disappeared.

When the pylons were erected these were marked in km. Under the number of kilometres is another figure indicating the first, second, third, etc. pylon in the kilometre zone. Therefore, the figure 10 represents 10km from King's Cross and, if the figure 4 appears underneath it, this indicates the fourth pylon from the km point. Upon reaching km 11 the lower figures start again at 1. The first pylon bearing km 10 is not necessarily exactly 10km from King's Cross, but perhaps a few metres beyond. Numbers 4 upwards are well on the way to km 11.

The pylons from Drayton Park to just south of Finsbury Park are, of course, based on Moorgate.

(L) *UN* 257, p.97 (5/1983)

24-hour clock

I THINK it very undesirable to mix the 12hr method with the 24hr method. Certainly one can say, 'fourteen o'clock.' The railways of India adopted 24-hour time very many years ago, and officers and men who had been in the Army in India and whom I met during the First World War frequently spoke of fourteen o'clock, fifteen o'clock etc.

In German one says, 'Vierzein Uhr,' which is fourteen o'clock. 'Uhr' is clock; the German for hour is 'Stunde'. In the Scandinavian languages one finds; kl. 14, kl. 14.25 etc; 'kl. 14' = klockan fjorton = clock fourteen. The word 'hundred' sometimes used in England and which the Astronomer Royal has described as 'illogical and absurd' does not occur in other languages.

(L) *U* 12, 4, p.56 (4/1973)

Crime on the Underground

T HERE HAVE ALWAYS BEEN and probably always will be prostitutes hanging around tube stations in the West End. Recently I was talking to a solicitor who attends Courts in the West End, and whom I know very well. He stated that the Act which came into operation a few years ago, relating to soliciting by prostitutes, has altered the 'profession' in some respects for the worse.

Formerly these women were 'honest' in as much as having agreed a price for their favours they carried out their part of the bargain and would not think of picking their client's pockets or robbing him in any other way. Since the Act, these women seem only too ready to get money by false promises, 'mugging' or any other form of robbery and giving little or nothing in return.

(L) *U* 11, 11, p.168 (11/1972)

Chronology of London Railways *

M ENTION MUST BE MADE of V. Badman, who arranged the details ready for typing and printing, and A. M. Jervis, who did the typing so carefully that enabled the work to be photolithoed, thereby greatly reducing the cost.

As regards the area covered, this comprises the whole of Greater London, usually to the first station outside the boundary. In addition, as there was a through service from Mansion House to Windsor via Ealing (with GW engines from that place) from 1 March 1883 until withdrawn 1 October 1885, stations to Windsor were included; for the same reason Southend and Shoeburyness (LMS engines from Barking) were included.

I regret it is impracticable to give a general date to which the contents are correct. Although the Jubilee Line is given, this does not mean the information is complete up to 1979. As stated in the Introduction, much of the work was completed five or more years ago. A publication of this nature can never be complete. I have tried to have it accurate and reliable; in this respect I regret I or the typist failed in a few cases, those relating to London Transport being:

Page 15, Note 6/9 – Add: Passenger trains continued to East Finchley; withdrawn 3 March 1941.

Page 16 – Deptford Road Jn – New Cross: LB&SC date to read 1 Jan 1886.

Page 30, Item 6 to read: Kilburn Park.

Page 33, Note 14/29 – Goods consisted mainly of material and stores for MD Trains worked by L&NW and Mid.

Page 39, Item 4: King William Street closed 25 Feb 1900 (as page 66).

Page 50 – Chesham year to read: 1889 (as page 36).

Page 54 – Eastcote: 'All' to read 'Pass.'; add Goods, 1913.

Page 55, Note E7: Year of fire was 1875.

Page 61, Note H14: Date of rebuilding to read: 1906-08.

Page 78 – Rayners Lane: 'All' to read 'Pass.'; add Goods, 1929.

(L) *UN* 250, p.224 (9/1982)

*Borley, H. V., *Chronology of London Railways*, Railway & Canal Historical Society, 1982.

Ceremonial Openings of Railways and Stations

I T WAS FORMERLY the general practice for a ceremonial opening (if held) to take place a day or a few days before a line or station was opened for public traffic, but within the last 30 years or so the ceremony has often taken place some days, or in some cases some considerable time, after the building has been in general use by the public. This causes confusion to historians and leads to incorrect dates being quoted.

The opening ceremony of the present station at Letchworth was performed on 16 May 1913, and the new building was opened to the public on Sunday morning, 18 May 1913. On the other hand, the new Kingsferry Bridge connecting Sheppey with the mainland was opened for road traffic on 29 February 1960 and for rail traffic on 10 April 1960. Then on 20 April the Duchess of Kent visited the bridge and performed what was described as the opening ceremony.

Among railway stations, Elm Park and the new stations at Welwyn Garden City, Leigh-on-Sea and Carpenders Park all had ceremonial 'openings' after they had been in general use. It is difficult to see how these visits by notable people can be correctly described as the opening of the building, especially in the case of Leigh-on-Sea, where the Mayor of Southend, who performed the ceremony, only spent some ten minutes at the station. For the guidance of future historians, I set out below the actual dates of opening to the public and the dates of the ceremonial visit in some of the cases which are often wrongly quoted:

Station	Opened to public	Ceremonial visit
Welwyn Garden City (2nd sta.)	20 Sept. 1926	5 Oct. 1926
Leigh-on-Sea (2nd sta.)	1 Jan. 19344	Jan. 1934
Elm Park	13 May 1935	18 May 1935
Carpenders Park (2nd sta.)	17 Nov. 1952	27 Sept. 1954

(L) *JRCHS* 7, 3, pp.58–59 (5/1961)

Station Names

LONDON TRANSPORT apparently sometimes quietly drop part of the name of a station. Chancery Lane (Gray's Inn) lost its suffix some time ago, and Holborn (Kingsway) seems to have been dealt with in a similar way.

LT ceased to use the second portion of the names of Amersham and Chorley Wood stations about 1950 but apparently never officially advised BR and so the LM Region continued to use the full title. At the same time LT reduced the name of Chalfont & Latimer and had some plates made reading 'Chalfont'. However, LT quickly had second thoughts and scrapped the new plates and reinstated the old ones.

I have known Gospel Oak station for about 70 years. The name boards always read Gospel Oak, so did the tickets. For some reason the words '(for Highgate)' were included in the entry in some time tables. It was rather confusing as Gospel Oak is a full mile from Highgate, which is of course at the top of the hill.

The LMS added '(for Northwick Park)' to the name of Kenton when the Metropolitan station opened, but seemed to have dropped it some years ago.

LT do not appear to be able to decide on the name of Totteridge & Whetstone but agreed with me in a letter a year or so ago that the correct name is Totteridge & Whetstone. This is logical as the station is on the Middlesex side of the brook which forms the boundary and is therefore in Whetstone. This station would probably have been called Whetstone but for the fact that this name was proposed for another station opened about the same time which it was eventually decided to call Oakleigh Park.

(L) *U* 13, 3, pp.40–41 (3/1974)

Sunday etc. Closures

WHEN THE Metropolitan Railway first opened, most of the operating staff worked every Sunday, a short turn in the morning, the next Sunday a long turn. This was soon changed to a full turn on alternate Sundays, often for 15 or 16 hours. The intention of the church interval was to enable railwaymen to attend church, but I have not known any so doing. They would have been conspicuous in uniform or working clothes. The interval did, however, enable men to have one uninterrupted meal on Sunday, as no meal time relief was granted. When the church interval was abolished the staff on Sunday was increased by men from the Goods department and in some cases from Headquarters. The pay was one day at the ordinary basic rate.

The church interval on the Ongar branch and the Fairlop loop and on other GE lines was abolished in 1910, the first Sunday with continuous operation being 1 May 1910. On the High Barnet line, including Mill Hill East, the first Sunday with continuous working was 6 May 1923.

It should be borne in mind, especially in the case of smaller railways, that *Bradshaw* was sometimes a month behind in making alterations to the services. Great Eastern stations were closed as follows:

Hainault, entirely with effect from 1.10.1908, last
  train 30.9.1908; reopened by L&NE on 3.3.1930.
Barkingside, wef 22.5.1916, last train 21.5.1916;
  reopened 1.7.1919.
Chigwell Lane (later Debden), wef 22.5.1916,
  last train 21.5.1916; reopened 3.2.1919.

Central Line Reconstruction – It is definite that the L&NE trains between Ilford and Woodford were withdrawn after traffic on Saturday 29.11.1947, but my notes indicate that a bus or coach service ran on 30.11.1947. The bus service was gradually curtailed as the sections opened. There was no connecting bus after traffic on Saturday 13.12.1947 between Ilford and Newbury Park.

Brill Branch – Sunday service began on 5.4.1903, one train each way in the morning chiefly for milk and farm produce. The up train had a connexion for London at Quainton Road, the down train no connexion. From 1.5.1904 one train ran on Sunday afternoons also. From Sunday 5.6.1904 the morning train worked forward to Aylesbury, not advertised, and returned after the arrival of the first train from Baker Street, thereby giving a service to Waddesdon Manor, Quainton Road and Brill for the first occasion. Sunday services on the Brill branch were withdrawn wef 2.5.1920, last Sunday train 25.4.1920.

Verney Junction – The Aylesbury & Buckingham Railway did not run any trains on Sundays. With the opening of Waddesdon Manor on 1.1.1897, the Metropolitan provided an improved service, including two trains each way on Sundays between Aylesbury and Grandborough Road, but the morning down train left too early to connect with a train from London. Commencing in October or November 1900, these trains ran to and from Verney Junction. The first service on Sunday morning from Baker Street was provided by the Brill train from 5.6.1904 as far as Quainton Road, thence to Brill. The Sunday service to Verney Junction was withdrawn wef 2.5.1920, reinstated 2.7.1922 and finally withdrawn 3.5.1931, last train

26.4.1931. Great Central trains served Quainton Road every day from 1906.

Waddesdon Manor (Waddesdon from 1.10.1922) – The very last trains to call were the up and down L&NE main line trains on Sunday 5.7.1936, the station being permanently closed on and from 6.7.1936.

Quainton Road – remained open on Sundays for L&NE main line trains until morning trains withdrawn 21.9.1958, last 14.9.1958; down evening train withdrawn 23.11.1958, last 16.11.1958; up evening train withdrawn 10.5.1959, last 3.5.1959. Closed entirely for BR passenger trains 4.3.1963, last trains on Saturday 2.3.1963. Metropolitan trains previously withdrawn after traffic on Saturday 4.7.1936, resumed in 1943 (not advertised, advertised from 7.1.1946 on weekdays only). Last Metropolitan train ran on Saturday 29.5.1948.

Mill Hill East – It is not possible to say whether trains actually ran on Sunday 10.9.1939 (my records say they did) or whether the substitute bus service operated but, in any case, one had to obtain tickets at the station ticket office and this remained open every day, even when trains were not running; so can one really say that the station was closed? It may be mentioned that the Dollis viaduct was originally built in 1867 for double track.

Highbury & Islington – From Sunday 7.4.1968, LT took over the reconstructed entrance and ticket office of the North London Railway and henceforth dealt with all booking facilities. Escalators were provided.

Park Royal – From its opening, open every day but from about 08.00 to 20.00. From 1908 opened at 06.42 on weekdays, other times unaltered. From 1912 opened normally.

(L) *UN* 260, p.150 (8/1983)

Sunday Church Interval

THE Church Interval still operated when I started work on a railway now part of BR. I never heard of any railwayman going to church in the interval – uniformed staff would be obliged to attend in uniform. Very many had to work all day, often 16 hours, and the interval was the only opportunity for a proper sit-down meal.

When the interval was finally abolished, the District with effect from 26 July 1903 and the Met gradually wef 7 April 1907 and entirely wef 3 October 1909, some of the staff from Goods depots, and in a few cases from Headquarters, were rostered to do a Sunday turn at passenger stations, thereby enabling regular staff to work shorter turns on Sundays.

(L) *UN* 306, p.105 (6/1987)

Train Services on Christmas Day – 1

THE TRAIN SERVICES on Christmas Day in recent years have been drastically curtailed and it may therefore be interesting to place on record the general position in the first half of the present century. It should be borne in mind that in the nineteenth century trains on Sundays were very few and even long-distance trains stopped in many cases at all or nearly all stations. On the other hand, a considerable number of branch lines had a train each way morning and evening. The services were gradually improved in the present century, but many branch line services were withdrawn about 1917 and not resumed. It should also be noted that 26 December, commonly called Boxing Day, was not a public holiday until the passing of the Bank Holidays Act 1871.

For about 100 years most railway timetables included a note: 'On Christmas Day and Good Friday trains will run as on Sundays,' and this was generally the position, but in many cases traffic was heavier than on an ordinary Sunday and additional trains were run.

The final section of the London & Greenwich Railway was opened on 24 December 1838, and it is recorded that a large number of the inhabitants of Greenwich and neighbouring places travelled on the railway on Christmas Day. Similarly, the first section of the District Railway was opened on 24 December 1868 and the line was very well patronized on that day and on Christmas Day.

As far back as any record can be traced the Great Eastern Railway provided one or two trains each way on the morning of Christmas Day on all or nearly all of its branches which did not normally have a Sunday service, and this practice was continued in a modified form by the London & North Eastern Railway. On the Great Northern, the down main line stopping train, originally the 'Parliamentary', was followed to Hitchin by the through carriages for Cambridge, which on Sundays were on the rear of the main train. Both trains were made up to full strength and there were few, if any, vacant seats.

Prior to electrification London suburban railways observed a 'church time' interval of about two hours on Christmas Day and Good Friday, as well as on Sundays; this resulted in passengers thronging the stations before and after the interval. On the Richmond line of the North London Railway special trains were run on Christmas Day immediately prior to the last train before church, and prior to the first ordinary train after the church interval. The engines of these trains carried red disks bearing the word 'Special' in white letters in place of the normal white disks.

London Transport at one time ran full Sunday services on Christmas Day, all stations being open, but on that day in 1963, including BR stations served by LT trains, 87 stations were closed and another 20 stations part of the day.

Finally, a word about the staff. On the main lines comparatively few enginemen and guards were needed, but in the London suburban area a considerable number were required for duty. The station staff generally took their normal early or late turn, but if Christmas Day fell on a Sunday the usual Sunday arrangements applied, which meant a few hours at a country station but often sixteen or even seventeen hours at a suburban station. It was not until comparatively recent times that payment was made for duty on Christmas Day, for that purpose it was just a day in the ordinary week's work. From about 1890 most railways gave the wages staff a day's pay (one-sixth of the weekly wage) for Sunday but many companies did not pay the clerical staff for Sunday duty until about 1913.

(A) *JRCHS* 10, 2, p.25 (3/1964)

Train Services on Christmas Day – 2

UNTIL ABOUT 1946 the full Sunday service had been run on that day [on the Underground] and the only stations closed were the two or three normally closed on Sunday at that time.

The main railway companies also ran full Sunday services, frequently with some additional trains in the morning.

(L) *UN* 160, p.44 (4/1975)

[As a footnote to the above, HVB recalled to me in 1988 that on Christmas Day 1910 he was on duty as a booking clerk at Hampstead Heath station from just before the first train at 07.45 until just after the last at around 23.00. A Sunday service was being worked, with a slightly reduced Church Interval of just under one hour. Extra trains were required as many people were travelling to visit relatives and friends; business was brisk in the ticket office until around 11.00. His mother brought him his Christmas dinner and he opened the booking office door to take it in. Meat and vegetables, and a large piece of Christmas pudding – 'good stuff made with rum and wine' – as well as mince pies, were shared with the other staff on duty, a ticket collector, two porters and a station inspector, the feast taking place during the Church Interval. After he returned home that evening, he had a quick supper and went to bed at midnight. The next day, Boxing Day, he did an early turn in the ticket office from 07.00 to 14.00 – Editor]

Railway Letter Service

TERMINATION OF the Railway Letter Service in June 1984 appears to have passed almost unnoticed. This service was introduced in 1891 and letters or documents fully addressed with correct postage could be handed in at the parcels or booking office at virtually any station for conveyance by the next train to the nearest station to the firm or person to whom it was addressed. The items had to be endorsed either to be called for by the addressee or posted from the station.

The extra charge was originally two pence and for some years the service was fairly well patronised. However, as charges were increased less use was made of the facility. By 1965 the charge was one shilling. By subsequent inflation the charge reached one pound in addition to the postage and, as the use had virtually reached zero, the service was quietly discontinued in June 1984.

The foregoing only relates to the agreement of 1891 with the various railway companies. The present agreements with certain members of the Association of Minor Railways are not affected. Also, in December 1984, British Railways entered into a new agreement with the Post Office whereby the Railway Letter service could be resumed for special occasions, such as the Great Western 150 celebrations at Swindon.

(L) *RM* 131, p.285 (6/1985)

(ii) On the London & Blackwall Railway

Some Lesser Known Features of the London & Blackwall Railway

FOLLOWING a private opening on Saturday 4 July 1840, the London & Blackwall Railway was opened for public passenger traffic on 6 July 1840. As is well known, rope traction was used, but on the opening day only one line was ready, the trains running every thirty minutes between Minories and Blackwall, the intermediate stations being Limehouse, West India Docks and Poplar. Apparently Stepney station was not quite ready and the actual date of opening cannot be traced. The second line was brought into use on 3 August 1840 and Stepney station was then open, the service being every 15 minutes. The timetables for 1841 show the service commencing at 8.30am, and terminating at 8.45pm in winter and 9.45pm in summer; the Sunday service was the same as on weekdays except that trains ceased running from 10.30am until 1pm. For many years the trains started earlier and continued running later in summer than they did in winter.

Fenchurch Street station was opened on 2 August 1841, on weekdays only as the Act authorizing the extension to this station prohibited the running of trains on Sundays. This was repealed by Act of 31 May 1842, and the Sunday trains commenced to run from and to Fenchurch Street on 5 June 1842. The ropes extended from Minories station to just short of Blackwall station. The trains left Fenchurch Street by gravity and were attached to the ropes at Minories. The stationary engines were underneath Minories station and the ropes extended thereto. The vehicles which had been detached from the rope on arrival at Minories were re-attached and, after travelling a short distance, were again slipped from the rope, having gained sufficient momentum to travel the quarter-mile to Fenchurch Street.

Shadwell was opened on 1 October 1840, and Cannon Street Road on 21 August 1842. With rope traction it was not possible to travel locally between certain intermediate stations, and the facilities provided varied slightly from time to time, but during all or most of the period of rope operation carriages were provided to convey passengers from Cannon Street Road, from Shadwell and from Stepney to Blackwall and return. Uniform fares were charged originally, 6d first class, 3d second

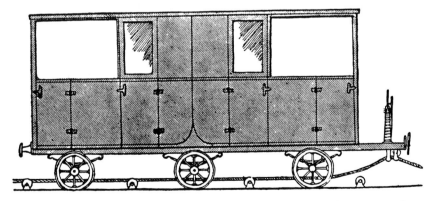

16. A London & Blackwall Railway composite coach. The apparatus for gripping and releasing the endless rope may be seen at the right hand end. *Anon*

class. The latter was soon increased to 4d, and subsequently return tickets at 10d first class and 7d second class were introduced. The fares fluctuated from time to time.

When the railway was first opened Poplar station was not conveniently situated and the buildings were of a temporary nature. This station, often referred to as Brunswick Street, was rebuilt with direct road access from Poplar High Street, the work being completed in 1845.

The gauge of the railway was originally 5 feet (some records give 5ft 1in) and when powers had been obtained to construct a branch to Bow and a junction with the Eastern Counties Railway it was necessary to alter the gauge to 4ft 8½in, which gauge the Eastern Counties had recently decided to adopt. It was also decided to work the railway by locomotives. To enable the work to be carried out the trains had to be worked on one line and, from October 1848, the service was reduced to intervals of 30 minutes. The last day of working the railway by ropes (on the south line) was 14 February 1849 and the following day the trains were hauled by locomotives (on the north line), the service interval being 40 minutes. The conversion of the south line was then proceeded with, and from 2 April 1849 normal up and down line working was instituted, the trains running every 20 minutes. The branch to Bow was opened on the same date with a 20-minute service. From 11 August 1849 the trains ran every 15 minutes, on both the main line and the branch. During the reconstruction of the railway Cannon Street Road station was closed, probably in November 1848, and not reopened. Minories was closed on and from 15 February 1849, the day steam traction started. This station was reopened on 9 September 1849 and finally closed on and from 24 October 1853. It is not clear whether up trains called at Minories when hauled by locomotives.

The joint station with the Eastern Counties was referred to by various names: Bow, Bow & Bromley, Victoria Park & Bow, Victoria Park & Eastern Counties Junction, and Old Ford. The Eastern Counties would not, however, permit a physical junction to be made. From the opening of the branch the Bow trains were combined with the Blackwall trains but, after a collision at Stepney when the carriages from Bow were being attached to the main train, it was decided, commencing 11 August

1849, to work the branch trains from and to Stepney. This led to complaints and from 9 November 1849 the Bow service was made half-hourly, the trains running through to and from Fenchurch Street. From 18 March 1850 the Bow trains ran every quarter-hour independently of the Blackwall trains.

The trains of the East & West India Docks & Birmingham Junction Railway (later renamed the North London) commenced to run to and from Fenchurch Street (using the south side of the station) on 26 September 1850, and the London & Blackwall trains to and from Bow were withdrawn from this date. The North London service was every 15 minutes and, although in the public timetables both trains were shown as leaving Fenchurch Street at the same time, actually the North London train preceded the Blackwall train as the former ran non-stop to Stepney.

In 1854 the Blackwall Company agreed to the Eastern Counties running trains to and from Fenchurch Street and the Eastern Counties then connected the lines at Bow, which enabled the London, Tilbury & Southend trains to run from Fenchurch Street from 13 April 1854. The service between Fenchurch Street and North Woolwich via Stratford Bridge commenced on 1 June 1854 but, owing to complaints of late running from the Blackwall Company, the trains were withdrawn on and from 16 October 1854. The North Woolwich trains were reinstated on 1 May 1855, and commencing 1 June 1858 some were diverted to run via Bromley but did not at first call at that station. Meanwhile, on 22 August 1856, the branch of the Eastern Counties to Loughton was opened and that company worked a service from Fenchurch Street to stations on that branch.

Under an agreement made in August 1840, the London & Blackwall operated through bookings to Woolwich, and in 1841 to Gravesend, in conjunction with various shipping companies using Brunswick Pier, Blackwall. Later, similar bookings were instituted to Greenwich and Erith. Vessels sailing to and from certain coastal resorts also used Brunswick Pier. From 22 June 1849 express trains were run between Fenchurch Street and Blackwall in connexion with the Gravesend boats, the rail journey taking five minutes. These expresses were withdrawn on and from 6 November 1854; there were only a few each way daily. The boat services from Brunswick

17. Stepney Junction, looking east, in 1936; the former GER lines and platforms are at the left and the by then disused former London & Blackwall Railway platforms at the right, occupying the site of the present day Limehouse station of the Docklands Light Railway. *RCHS/Spence*

Pier gradually declined and through bookings were withdrawn on and from 1 October 1866. A small amount of goods traffic was conveyed locally from January 1842, but other railways requested accommodation for goods on the London & Blackwall. The branch to Haydon Square was constructed by the Blackwall Company but used exclusively by the London & North Western from opening on 12 March 1853 after a brief temporary opening in February 1853. Haydon Square station, as well as the branch leading thereto, became the absolute property of the London & North Western on 15 April 1864. Commencing in May 1858, the goods trains to and from Haydon Square were operated by the North London Railway.

The Eastern Counties and the London, Tilbury & Southend had accommodation for goods at Minories, at first on the south side of the line and, from 1861, on the north side – later known as Goodman's Yard. Both the Great Northern and the Midland had accommodation on the south side at Minories. These goods stations were known as Royal Mint Street, the Great Northern's being opened on 8 December 1858 and becoming their property from 1 February 1861. The Midland station was opened on 1 October 1862. For a few months the North London worked the Great Northern traffic, but subsequently the Great Northern worked their own trains, at first via St Pancras Junction (NLR), later via Canonbury Junction. The Midland's goods traffic was originally worked via Hitchin (GNR) and St Pancras Junction (NLR), the North London working the trains over their line to Royal Mint Street. When the Tottenham & Hampstead Junction was connected with the Midland, that company worked their own traffic via the Tottenham & Hampstead line and Stratford. Both stations at Royal Mint Street, as well as Goodman's Yard, were severely damaged by enemy action and have been closed. Great Northern goods trains started to run to East India Docks on 23 December 1859. Midland goods ran to Poplar via Limehouse curve from 1882. A branch for goods traffic to and from London Dock (East Smithfield) was opened on 17 June 1864.

Soon after steam operation commenced it was found necessary to widen the line between

18. The exterior of the Blackwall terminus of the London & Blackwall Railway, looking east at Brunswick Quay, 1936. This handsome building, designed by Sir William Tite, was demolished in the late 1940s for the construction of the Blackwall Electric Power Station. *RCHS/Spence*

Fenchurch Street and Stepney, and a portion at the London end, together with additional accommodation at Fenchurch Street station, was completed in 1854. The third line (for up trains) was operated from Stepney from March 1856. An additional down line to Stepney was completed in 1895.

In accordance with the Act of 1844, Parliamentary fares were put into operation where the second class fare was more than one penny per mile and when, in 1849, it was possible to travel between any pair of stations, additional Parliamentary fares had to be introduced. No special carriages were provided for passengers with Parliamentary tickets, which at first were issued by one train and subsequently by two trains a day. First, second and third class carriages and fares were provided by all trains from 1 June 1869, the single fares to Blackwall being 6d first class, 5d second, 4d third; return fares, 9d first class, 8d second, 6d third. The fares prior to this date were 6d first, 4d second single, with return fares 10d first, 6d second.

In 1864, the Great Eastern offered to purchase the London & Blackwall, but the Board of the latter Company would not agree. It was, however, arranged for the Great Eastern to lease and work the line from 1 January 1866. The Great Eastern made a further attempt to absorb the Blackwall Railway in 1896, but again without success.

When Broad Street station was opened on 1 November 1865, the North London trains ran between Fenchurch Street and Broad Street, but from 1 August 1866 the North London service was between Fenchurch Street and Bow. These trains commenced to call at Shadwell on 1 October 1866. (The timetables are not very clear but this information has been verified from other sources.) The last North London trains from and to Fenchurch Street ran on 31 December 1868, but in lieu thereof the Great Eastern worked a local service between the same points every 15 minutes. From 1 March 1877 this service was half-hourly and it ceased on and from 4 April 1892, on which date a covered footway and gallery connecting Bow (NL) with Bow Road (GE) was opened. This footway was closed in 1917 and later removed. The North London had their own tickets from Fenchurch

Street, and probably from Stepney also, until 1868, but it was not then the practice to print the name of the railway on the tickets.

When the Poplar line of the North London was under construction in 1851 the North London sought permission for a junction at Poplar, but the Blackwall Company would not agree. In 1852 this consent was given and a single-line junction made, facing towards Blackwall, with the London & Blackwall down line only. The North London then requested permission for their trains to run to Blackwall but this was refused. The Blackwall Company did, however, construct an overbridge and improve facilities for the exchange of passengers at Stepney (previously passengers crossed on the level). From 1 September 1870 North London passenger trains ran to and from Blackwall, the junction having been rearranged for through working. North London tickets were issued from Blackwall and at first there was a North London staff at that place. The North London trains passed through but did not stop at the London & Blackwall Company's station at Poplar. Through bookings from North London stations to Woolwich and Greenwich by boat from Blackwall were arranged, but these were withdrawn on and from 1 October 1886 owing to curtailments in the boat services. In consequence, the number of passengers to Blackwall declined and the North London ceased to run through to that place

on and from 1 July 1890. The junction was removed by the Great Eastern in August 1890. (Some accounts give the date as 1900, but both North London and London & Blackwall records give August 1890 and there is no record of the junction being reinstated and subsequently removed.)

An additional station, Millwall Junction, was opened on 18 December 1871 at the same time as a service of trains, chiefly for dock workers, commenced to run on the Millwall Extension Railway between Millwall Junction and Millwall Docks (Glengall Road). The service was improved and extended to North Greenwich on 29 July 1872. A portion of this line was opened by the Dock Companies and, as the bridges were not strong enough for locomotives, horse traction was used for part of the journey. The carriages were provided by the Great Eastern. Subsequently the bridges were strengthened and from 23 August 1880 the trains were hauled by Dock Companies' locomotives. A service on Sundays commenced on 29 August 1880.

In connexion with the opening of the Millwall Extension, additional sidings were provided by both the Great Eastern and the North London Railways for the exchange of merchandise traffic between the two systems at Millwall Junction (Harrow Lane) as well as for the transfer of trucks to the Docks lines.

19. The interior of the London & Blackwall Railway terminus at Blackwall, looking east, 1936. Brunswick Quay and the river Thames lie behind the wall at the right and the ship seen at the left is in the East India Export Dock. This site was used for the construction of an electric power station in the late 1940s. *RCHS/Spence*

In 1874 the Great Eastern and London & Blackwall acquired Potters Ferry which ran between North Greenwich and Greenwich Town. The ferry service was discontinued on and from 1 November 1902 owing to the opening of a tunnel by the London County Council. The Council paid £8,000 compensation to the railways, who thereby surrendered all rights to the LCC, including the landing places.

Burdett Road station was opened in 1871, Bow Road on 1 October 1876, and Leman Street in 1877. The construction of the latter was started in 1872 but the work was left in abeyance. The Midland Company's branch to Poplar Dock was opened in 1882.

In 1874 it was necessary to reconstruct the bridge over Commercial Road, Stepney, and the work was commenced in 1875. Stepney station was closed (except for trains to and from Blackwall); down trains normally calling at Stepney called instead at Burdett Road, and up trains at Burdett Road or Shadwell. The work was completed and normal service resumed on 17 July 1876.

An interesting, but short-lived, service started on 1 January 1880 between Palace Gates and Fenchurch Street. The Limehouse curve was opened on 5 April 1880 and, from 1 September 1880, the Palace Gates service was diverted to and from Blackwall. This service was withdrawn on and from 1 March 1881. There were also some through trains between Blackwall and Southend and Southminster on Sundays in the summer months in 1890 and 1891. Midland Railway goods trains also used the Limehouse curve.

(A) *JRCHS* 3, 6, pp.105–107 (11/1957) and *JRCHS* 4, 1, pp.12–14 (1/1958)

The Eastern Counties and Blackwall Railways at Bow

THE Old Ford branch of the London & Blackwall Railway was opened on 2 April 1849 and was worked by locomotives. Contemporary maps show a station in Bow Road and another where the branch joined the Eastern Counties line. Whether a physical connexion was made is doubtful as relations between the two companies were not harmonious. *Bradshaw* for most months says there were trains every fifteen minutes to Bow and the Eastern Counties Junction; no other time-tables are available. The Minute books of the Blackwall Railway refer to their station as Bow & Bromley. The name of the exchange platforms is given in EC Railway records as Victoria Park & Bow. I have not been able to obtain definite information but it would appear that the Blackwall Company's trains only went forward to the exchange platforms when necessary to make a connexion. The number of EC trains calling at the exchange platforms was comparatively few.

The North London Railway was opened from Bow Common to Islington on 26 September 1850 and provided a regular quarter-hourly service from Fenchurch Street to Islington. The Blackwall Company's service to Bow & Bromley was withdrawn from the same date and the station closed. EC trains still called at the exchange platforms but these were finally closed with effect from 6 January 1851. The connecting line was not used for regular traffic until the London Tilbury & Southend Railway was opened from Forest Gate Junction to Tilbury on 13 April 1854.

The junction with the NL Railway was later known as Gas Factory Junction and was under NL control and maintained by them for many years after that company ceased to use Fenchurch Street. The GE and LT&S Companies contributed to the cost.

When opened, the NLR was known as The East & West India Docks & Birmingham Junction Railway. The Company had few carriages and no engines and hired rolling stock from the Blackwall Company together with some of that Company's enginemen and guards. The NL also obtained some L&NW engines but perhaps not until a temporary junction with that Company at Camden was made on 15 February 1851.

Bradshaw shows the trains to Blackwall and the NL trains leaving Fenchurch Street at the even quarter hour although there was only a double track at that time. It would appear, however, that the NL train left first and ran non-stop to Stepney. NL passenger trains ceased to use Fenchurch Street with effect from 1 January 1869 but the GE worked a service from that station to Bow (NL) until 1892.

(L) *JRCHS* 20, 2, p.50 (7/1974)

(iii) On the North London Railway

20. The armorial device of the NLR. Inside the garter is a quartered shield emblazoned with the arms of the cities of London and Birmingham (the latter unofficial and not precisely those eventually granted in 1878) and those of the East and West India dock companies. *RCHS/Spence*

The North London Line

O N THE OPENING of what was called the North London City Extension, to Broad Street, *The Railway News* commented: 'The history of the North London line is in some respects a curious one, and if a railway be a sensitive thing it must feel as much astonished in being brought into Broad Street as Christopher Sly, the tinker, felt when he found himself metamorphosed into a duke. Its projectors had as much idea of its ever turning out to be an important passenger line as they had of running it to Grand Cairo.' As originally contemplated, the North London was to be little more than a long siding of the London & Birmingham Railway, linking Camden goods station with the West India

Docks, and its initial importance was that it provided the last link in a chain of railways connecting the Mersey with the Thames.

While the scheme was still before Parliament, the London & Birmingham was amalgamated on July 16, 1846, with the Grand Junction Railway and the Manchester & Birmingham Railway to form the London & North Western Railway. Nevertheless, the North London scheme retained the word 'Birmingham' in its original title, and emerged as the East & West India Docks & Birmingham Junction Railway, incorporated by Act of August 26, 1846, to build an eight-mile line from the LNWR at Camden to Poplar. A further Act was obtained in 1850 for a short line at Bow connecting with the London & Blackwall Railway, and this changed the

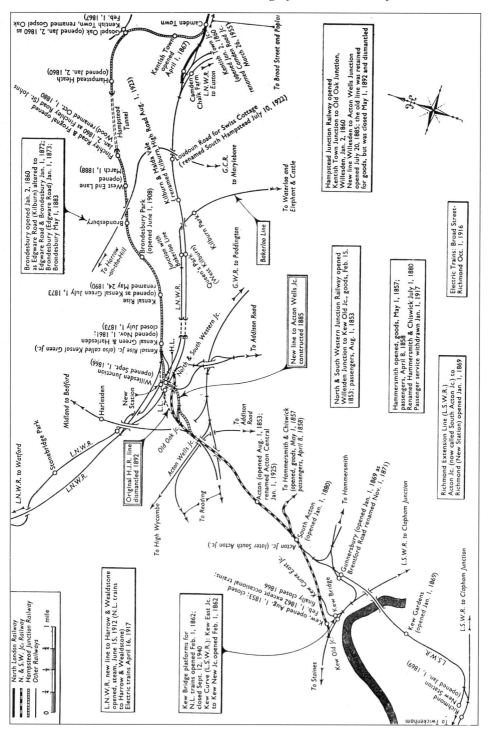

21. The western portion of the North London Railway and its associated lines, showing the pre-1923 ownerships. The chronological details were compiled by HVB. '*The Railway Magazine*'

22. The Broad Street terminus of the L&NWR and NLR, as opened in November 1865.
The structure remained substantially unaltered (apart from some additions in the forecourt) until demolished for the
Broadgate Offices Development in 1985. *From 'The Illustrated London News', 3 February 1866.*

complexion of the undertaking, as it gave access to Fenchurch Street, the first railway terminus in the City of London. The route made a great detour, as the engineer had carried it beyond the limit of the bills of mortality to avoid a heavy outlay in construction costs. Even so, it was felt that the railway had great potentialities as a passenger line, as travellers might be expected to prefer, even with the longer mileage, 'the easy and rapid conveyance by rail to the lumbering roll of an omnibus.'

The line from Islington to a junction with the Blackwall Extension Railway at Bow was opened on September 26, 1850, with a 15-min service to Fenchurch Street, and intermediate stations at Stepney, Bow, and Hackney. Kingsland Station was opened November 9, 1850. The service was extended to Camden Town on December 7, 1850, and to Hampstead Road on June 9, 1851. Coal traffic began to be conveyed in December, 1851, and goods traffic from January 1, 1852. Because of its cumbersome legal title, the line was called

popularly the 'Camden Town Railway' in its early years, but the legal name was changed to the North London Railway by an Act of 1853. With the rapid growth of the northern suburbs in the 1850s, the circuitous route failed to attract sufficient of the new traffic and the North London City Extension from Dalston to Broad Street was built under an Act of July 22, 1861, at a cost of upwards of £1m for some two miles of railway. It shortened the journey to the City by about four miles for all stations west of Kingsland. This important branch was opened for public passenger traffic on November 1, 1865. At the formal opening, the Rector of Bishopsgate said that the railway had given liberal treatment to persons displaced by the building of the line. Broad Street Station is today substantially as constructed, but the lines and platforms have been altered, and the booking offices were originally at street level.

Of the original stations from Bow to Hampstead Road, all that remains is the entrance to Kingsland, which is now houses. This station was

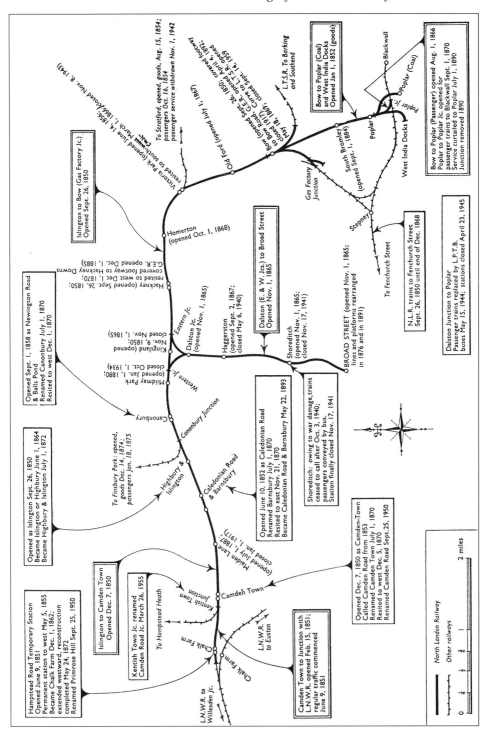

23. The North London Railway and connecting lines.
The chronological information was compiled by HVB.
'The Railway Magazine'

24. Shoreditch NLR frontage, at the corner of Old Street (left) and Kingsland Road in the 1900s.
A summer scene, with services and fares to Southend-on-Sea well advertised. *London Borough of Hackney. P.1739*

closed on the opening of Dalston Junction in 1865. Poplar passenger station was opened on August 1, 1866, and was almost entirely destroyed during the second world war. The next stations were South Bromley and Bow. The NLR works were situated at the latter. The present station was completed in 1870, and the Poplar and Fenchurch Street lines meet here. There is also a branch to the London, Tilbury & Southend Railway. The next stations were Old Ford and Victoria Park; at the latter point there is a junction, with the Great Eastern Railway. The first Victoria Park Station, in Wick Road, opened in 1856, was used as houses until 1957; the second station, resited, was opened in 1866. The next stations were Homerton and Hackney.

At Eastern Junction, Dalston, the line to Broad Street diverges. The original line proceeds past Kingsland, Western Junction, Mildmay Park (closed), Canonbury (junction with the Great Northern Railway), Highbury & Islington, Caledonian Road & Barnsbury, Maiden Lane (closed for passengers, but an important goods station for Caledonian Market), St Pancras goods junction with the GNR and Midland, Camden Road (formerly Camden Town), and Primrose Hill (formerly Chalk Farm). The stations between Dalston and Camden Road were entirely remodelled when the line was quadrupled, a task completed in 1871. The whole line suffered severely during the last war and stations between Dalston and Poplar were closed to passenger trains in 1944.

The Hampstead Junction Railway, an associate of the LNWR, was incorporated on August 20, 1853, to link the NLR with Willesden and the NSWJR. The line, which was opened on January 2, 1860, leaves the NLR at Camden Road Junction (formerly Kentish Town Junction). It was worked by the NLR from opening. The original stations were Gospel Oak (at first named Kentish Town), Hampstead Heath, Finchley Road and Edgware Road (later Brondesbury). Kensal Green & Harlesden Station was opened in 1861 and closed in 1873. Its buildings and portions of the low staggered platforms, the only ones on the system, are still there. Near here the original HJR line to Kew diverged, and part of the embankment remains. Originally the HJR crossed the LNWR by an overbridge; there was no station at Willesden until 1866. A goods curve, now known as the City Goods line, connected the two systems.

The North & South Western Junction Railway was incorporated on July 24, 1851, to provide a connexion between the LNWR at Willesden and the LSWR Windsor loop at Kew. A limited amount of goods traffic was begun on February 15, 1853, but no passengers were conveyed until August 1, 1853, when a service was provided by the NLR. The connexion with the HJR at Old Oak Junction was opened in 1860. The Hammersmith branch (single line) was opened from Acton Gate House for goods in 1857 and to passengers in 1858. The LSWR from Kew Curve East Junction to Kew Bridge Station and Kew New Junction was opened in 1862, and the South Acton to Richmond line seven years later, in 1869.

Throughout its career, the policy of the North London was always to run its trains at 'even times.' It has been already noted that the original 1850 service was at 15-min intervals. When the line from Broad Street to Dalston Junction was opened on November 1, 1865, regular 15-min services were instituted between Broad Street and Chalk Farm and between Broad Street and Fenchurch Street. A half-hourly service was operated between Broad Street and Kew Bridge. In 1866 the Fenchurch Street service was diverted to Poplar, a local service of North London trains running between Bow and Fenchurch Street until the end of December, 1868, when the North London ceased to use Fenchurch Street. Beginning on January 1, 1869, alternate Kew Bridge trains were diverted to Richmond over the newly-opened line from South Acton. A local service was provided between Acton and Kew Bridge in connexion with the Richmond trains. The service on the Hammersmith branch was at first hourly from Acton, and later half-hourly from South Acton. Early in the present century the service to Richmond was made half-hourly, passengers for Kew Bridge – with a few exceptions – changing at Acton.

In 1911 a scheme was sanctioned by the directors for the electrification of the lines from Broad Street to Chalk Farm, Kew Bridge and Gunnersbury; thence to Richmond had already been converted by

25. Shoreditch, looking to Broad Street, in the 1930s. A Poplar train headed by LM&SR 3F 'Jinty' 0-6-0T no.7351 is entering but will not produce much work for the solitary porter in attendance. Platforms were provided here for all four roads. *RCHME*

26. A Poplar–Broad Street train pauses at Hackney in the murky weather of January 1927, in charge of an NLR 'No.1 Class' 4-4-0T. *H.C. Casserley*

the LSWR. The Kew Bridge and Richmond service was brought into operation on October 1, 1916, but under wartime conditions little improvement could be made in the train service, although the journey time was reduced. The electric services to Chalk Farm and on to Watford commenced on July 10, 1922, although a few through trains to the latter place had been run via Hampstead Heath since 1917. After the end of the first world war, services were gradually improved and remained so until the outbreak of the second world war in 1939 when some reductions were made, though the latter were not as drastic as in the first war. Soon after the end of the second world war services broadly on the lines of those worked in 1939 were operated, and remained with little alteration until 1962.

27. A fogman's hut is prominent in this 1930s view of Haggerston, looking south to Broad Street from the end of the platforms. The electrified Richmond lines are to the right. *RCHME*

When the policy of basing fares more strictly on distance travelled, rather than on those of a competitive shorter route, was adopted on September 1, 1952, the North London was one of the lines on which travellers were affected adversely. By reason of its circuitous route, many of its fares were well below the strict mileage scale, and these were brought up more nearly to the distance charge, making journeys on the North London less attractive than those on other services between similar points. During the next decade some traffics had reached a disappointing level, and from September 10, 1962, the Monday to Friday frequency of the Broad Street –Richmond service was reduced, and withdrawn after mid-evening. At the same time the Broad Street –Watford Saturday evening service was also discontinued. On September 27 the Hampstead Borough Council agreed to support a campaign against the possible closure of the line to passenger service, but British Railways announced that the changes were aimed only at reducing the loss on the service and not its withdrawal.

A revised timetable for the Broad Street – Richmond line came into operation on January 7, 1963. The running time was reduced by five minutes, and a regular 20-min service instituted throughout the day on Mondays to Saturdays. On Sundays there was a 30-min interval and the service was limited to the period from about 11am to 10pm until April, 1963, when a 20-min service was operated on Sundays throughout the day until September. The Sunday service has now reverted to that operating in January, 1963.

With the publication on March 27, 1963, of the report on *The Reshaping of British Railways* (the so-called Beeching Report), however, the Broad Street–Richmond line was scheduled among those on which all passenger services would be withdrawn. Later, the end of 1963 was suggested for the withdrawal, but a six-month reprieve was given. The Hampstead Borough Council, which throughout had taken an active part in opposing the closure, recently passed the following resolution: 'This Council recognising that the facilities and standards of service available to the travelling public on the Broad Street–Richmond railway would be much improved by its integration into the London Transport system, urges the Minster of Transport to transfer the control and administration from the London Midland Region of the British Railways Board to the London Transport Board. It further invites other local authorities concerned to support the proposal and urges them to seek the backing of Members of Parliament for such a plan and resolves that this resolution be sent to the Minister of Transport and the Member of Parliament for the Borough of Hampstead.'

Throughout the line of route, similar steps are being taken by respective local authorities and campaign committees. Representatives of the various committees have decided to set up a joint co-ordinating committee with the objects of co-ordinating and publicising the fight against closure. This is to be called the Broad Street – Richmond Line Joint Committee, and, at the time that these notes were being written it was intended to hold the first meeting on January 23, to elect officers and agree the future plan of campaign. The foregoing notes, which are but an outline of some of the principal features in the history of the North London Railway and associated lines, have been compiled in the hope that they will prove of interest to many who are actively interested in the future of this pioneer London suburban railway.

(A) *RM* 110, pp.204–210 (2/1964), (with C. E. Lee)

North London Railway Express Trains from Fenchurch Street

COMMENCING on October 21, 1857, the North London Railway ran two express trains from Fenchurch Street to Camden Town; these expresses were at first described as 'Through Trains' and the method of working was as follows: additional carriages were attached at Bow to the rear of two up trains which formed the 4.15pm and the 5.15pm from Fenchurch Street. The additional carriages were therefore on the front of two trains from Fenchurch Street which stopped at Stepney in the usual way. The additional carriages were detached at Bow bank, and ran forward express, arriving at Hampstead Road a few minutes after the previous train. The remaining carriages went forward from Bow bank by gravity to Bow station, where an engine was attached, and the trains worked forward to Hampstead Road in the ordinary way. The carriages

28. Dalston Junction station as the young Borley knew it. This view of about 1905 looks north and shows four of the six platforms – the west side – with a Broad Street train entering. The then spacious street level buildings are seen on the right, with a portion of the covered footbridge above the train. There was a second footbridge to all platforms at the Broad Street end of the station, behind the photographer.
Commercial postcard by Charles Martin/RCHME

of the express portion of the 5.15pm train continued to Kew. Presumably the reason why the trains were divided on Bow bank and not in Bow station was to enable the express to make a good start on the falling gradient. Subsequently the expresses are shown as calling at Camden Road station.

The Hampstead Junction Railway was opened on January 2, 1860. The two expresses ran as before, but passengers for Kew changed at Camden Road by either train. In the up direction, express trains commenced running February 1, 1860. An additional train left Hampstead Road at 9.18am, and the carriages of the 8.20am from Twickenham were attached at Camden Road; the train then ran through to Fenchurch Street calling at Hackney and Stepney. On March 1, 1860, another up express started to run, which left Hampstead Road at 8.18am, the carriages of the 7.50 from Kew being attached at Camden Road, the train then running on to Fenchurch Street calling at Islington and Stepney. Commencing on the same date, the 9.50am from Edgeware Road (Kilburn) had

through carriages to Fenchurch Street, but these were attached to an ordinary train at Camden Road. The 8.18am from Hampstead Road was discontinued from November 1, 1860, but the other trains ran until the end of September, 1861, when it was announced that from October 1 express train running between Camden Town and Fenchurch Street would be discontinued for the winter months. The 8.10am from Twickenham continued, however, to have through carriages which were attached to an ordinary train at Camden Road, and worked through to Fenchurch Street.

The express service recommenced on May 1, 1862, when additional carriages were attached to the 5.0pm from Fenchurch Street, which were detached on Bow bank and ran express thence to Camden Road and Hampstead Road, passengers for the Hampstead Junction line, Kew and Twickenham changing at Camden Road.

The up expresses recommenced December 1, 1862, with the 8.10am from Twickenham which ran from Camden Road to Stepney without

29. Poplar. A picture which well portrays a North London winter scene totally familiar to HVB. Although taken in the LM&SR era (16 January 1927), the train remains composed wholly of NLR four-wheeled stock, but the loco is an ex North Staffordshire Railway 2-4-0T numbered 1451 by the LMS. *H.C. Casserley*

30. A L&NWR Birmingham (New Street)–Broad Street 'City to City' Express, passing a NL train just west of Mildmay Park Station about 1912. The loco is no.1913 'Canopus'. *Anon, RCHS/Spence*

stopping intermediately. The 9.45am from Kew also had through carriages to Fenchurch Street, but these were attached to an ordinary train at Camden Road. From the same date, the express carriages off the 5.0pm from Fenchurch Street worked through to the Hampstead Junction line and Twickenham.

From January, 1863, there were two up and two down expresses and also one up ordinary stopping train with through carriages from or to the Hampstead Junction line and beyond. From this date until the end of October, 1865, the service continued, with certain alterations and additions. The maximum number of expresses in any month was three in the up direction and four in the down. Some of these worked from and to Twickenham and, from July 1, 1863, Kingston.

The details given above relate to weekdays, and until the end of August, 1864, the service on Saturdays was identical with that on other week-

days; subsequently, the Saturday service only differed very slightly.

When the through service between Hampstead Road and Twickenham commenced on May 20, 1858, about half the trains were formed of London & South Western carriages. It is not clear whether any of this company's vehicles actually worked through to and from Fenchurch Street. Probably the London & Blackwall company would have objected to this. However, there is some evidence that, in the latter part of the period under review, all the trains were formed of North London carriages.

At Fenchurch Street, the trains carrying an express portion were indicated by notice boards: 'The express train for the Hampstead and Kew line is at the end of the platform.'

Broad Street station was opened on November 1, 1865, and from that date the North London trains to Kew and Kingston ran through from

31. Exterior of Broad Street station (left) in 1905, looking east and showing its position relative to Liverpool Street GER (centre) and Liverpool Street Metropolitan Railway (centre right). The forecourt accretions. with staircases from platform level were subsequently to be 'modernised' by the LMSR. *Commercial postcard by LL*

Broad Street calling, generally, only at Shoreditch, Dalston Junction and Camden Road on the North London Railway. On Sundays they called at all stations. From February 1, 1868, they called at Islington instead of at Shoreditch.

(A) *JRCHS* 2, 3, p.37 (5/1956)

WITH REFERENCE TO the article headed 'North London Railway Express Trains from Fenchurch Street' in the *Journal* for May 1956, some members have expressed doubt as to whether the trains were actually divided on Bow bank, as there would be some risk that the brakes would not hold the rear portion on the falling gradient. No further information can be obtained, but it is possible that, during part of the time these trains were operated, the dividing took place in Bow Station, the express carriages being beyond the platform.

(L) *JRCHS* 4, 1, p.14 (1/1958)

The Victoria Park Branch of the Eastern Counties Railway and North London Trains to Stratford Bridge

THE Victoria Park Branch of the Eastern Counties Railway was opened on 15 August 1854, but very little use was made of the line until the North London Railway began running a passenger train service on 16 October 1854. Regular goods trains started on 1 January 1855; these were worked by the North London, and consisted of merchandise transferred from places on the Eastern Counties Railway to places on the Great Northern, London & North Western and London & South Western systems. It will be observed that early in its active life the North London began working trains over other railways, and also transferring goods across London, these operations continuing throughout its career.

The branch of the Eastern Counties joined the North London at a point then known as Hackney Wick or Victoria Park Junction, but in later years usually called Victoria Park Junction. When the passenger service was started in 1854, additional carriages, usually two, were attached to certain trains from Hampstead Road, which was nearly on the site of the present Primrose Hill Station, formerly named Chalk Farm. These carriages were dropped – that is, detached at the junction – and worked forward to Stratford Bridge by a North London engine, calling at the Low Level platforms at Stratford, which in consequence were often referred to as the North London station. At that time, only North London trains used the Low Level platforms at Stratford.

There was no station at Victoria Park at that time, and those trains which had a connexion to or from Stratford Bridge had to stop at the junction to drop or pick up the branch carriages. The train left Hampstead Road for Fenchurch Street with the Stratford Bridge carriages at the rear, but on the return journey various methods were tried; at one period it was the practice to attach the additional carriages at the rear, at another time they were attached in the front, the Stratford Bridge engine then working through to Hampstead Road, the other engine remaining at the junction to work the next train forward to Stratford Bridge. No method seemed to be entirely satisfactory, but the arrangement continued in various forms after the opening of the original station at Victoria Park. There were a few minor collisions and near-collisions, and it was eventually decided that the through carriages would not be worked after the end of December 1859. On and from 1 January 1860, passengers had to change at Victoria Park, except on occasions as described later.

The original station at Victoria Park was opened specially on 29 May 1856, in connexion with the Peace celebrations held in Victoria Park that day marking the termination of the Crimean War. This station was shown in the timetables as 'Victoria Park, Hackney Wick' until the end of 1859; it was sited before the junction, and consisted of two short platforms, and was at first without shelter of any kind. The entrance in Wick Lane was a substantial one. It was converted into a pair of dwelling houses now known as 339 and 339A Wick Road, and is still standing. This station was opened for regular passenger traffic on and from 14 June 1856, and subsequently the platforms were partially covered and waiting rooms provided. The original station was closed when the new one, situated immediately beyond [i.e. south of] the junction, was opened on

32. The main building of the 1866 Victoria Park station, NLR, in Cadogan Terrace, about 1905.
'BDV', a cheap tobacco, is well advertised, but the more affluent might prefer Freeman's Darvel Bay 'Segars'
available from the shop at the right. Other needs were met by the *Railway Tavern* (left).
Commercial postcard by Charles Martin

1 March 1866; this station originally consisted of four platforms, but the one on the line to Stratford was used only by the through trains from Chalk Farm (the locals starting from the platform adjacent to the North London up platform) and was reached by crossing the line on the level, no subway or bridge being provided. This platform was not in general use after 1866, and was later removed, the work being completed 15 August 1895. A footbridge in the centre of the station, connecting the three platforms, was brought into use on 24 February 1891. An additional entrance from Riseholme Street (near Wick Road) with No.2 Booking Office was opened on 1 February 1899. Local people had asked for an entrance from Gainsborough Square, but as it was considered that it would be too costly to comply with this request the new entrance was made from Riseholme Street, and was known as the Hackney Wick entrance.

Victoria Park was a very popular place, especially on Sundays in the summer, and the two carriages usually allocated to the Stratford Bridge service, worked in conjunction with the Fenchurch Street and Hampstead Road trains, proved insufficient. From 1855, the Stratford Bridge trains worked from and to Hampstead Road on Sundays in the summer months – usually May to October, inclusive; this practice continued until 1866. In August 1864, the trains worked through on weekdays and Sundays, but this was not repeated in subsequent years. Hampstead Road station was renamed Chalk Farm 1 December 1862.

There were two through trains each way daily between Hampstead Road and Tilbury via Victoria Park Junction and Forest Gate Junction in July, August and September 1855, but the service was not repeated. The trains consisted of North London carriages but possibly the Eastern Counties Railway worked the trains forward from Stratford main line station. From 1 September 1866, the North London ceased to work trains to Stratford Bridge, but instead ran a through service from Chalk Farm to Barking, worked by North London engines throughout; passengers for the North Woolwich line were conveyed via Stepney. This service lasted only two months. From 1 November 1866, all through working ceased, and the Great Eastern Railway started to work a local service between Victoria Park and Stratford Bridge. From 1 November 1867, the North London again took over the service, which remained a local one, and the Great Eastern and North London continued this arrangement in alternate years until 1874. The last North London passenger train to and from Stratford Bridge ran on 31 October 1874.

From the opening of the new station at Victoria Park on 1 March 1866, the local trains started back from the platform at which they had arrived. From 1 October 1895, the locals ran between Victoria Park and Canning Town, generally using a terminal

platform at the latter place, the rails serving which have now been removed. At various periods since this date some of the trains have worked through to North Woolwich.

The Great Eastern service, which had been half-hourly since 1870, was reduced to hourly service from 1 January 1917. In 1921, the weekday service was much curtailed, and the Sunday service was withdrawn entirely on and from 7 October 1923. What remained of the weekday service was withdrawn on and from 1 November 1942.

Stratford Bridge station was situated approximately on the site of the present Stratford Market station, but the entrance was in Bridge Road. The present building dates from 1880, and the name Stratford Market was adopted on and from 1 November 1880. In the Great Eastern timetables, the station was usually styled Stratford Market (West Ham).

The Hackney Wick, or No.2, entrance to Victoria Park station was open only during certain hours from 11 July 1920, and was presumably closed

33. Victoria Park Junction and signal box, looking north west from the London end of the Stratford platform, Bow train entering, about 1905. *Commercial postcard by Charles Martin/London Borough of Hackney*

34. Southend–Chalk Farm LTSR train stopping at Bow, NLR, on 25 June 1912; the loco is LTSR 4-4-2T no.31, 'St Pancras', built in 1892. Seen across the photo is the long footbridge connecting all four NLR platforms with Bow Road station, GER. *Anon/London Borough of Tower Hamlets*

from 29 January 1940, when the LMS service to and from Poplar was curtailed. The station was closed entirely from 8 November 1943; it had been closed on Sundays from 31 March 1940, from which date the Poplar service ran only on weekdays; this service ceased to run on and from 15 May 1944. The station buildings at the No.1 entrance still stand, as do the platforms and some of the buildings at platform level. The Hackney Wick entrance has, however, been removed entirely.

(A) *JRCHS* 3, 2, pp.28–31 (3/1957)

North London Railway Trains to Southend-on-Sea

THE CONNEXION between the North London and the London, Tilbury & Southend Railways was originally at Stepney, and from 16 October 1854 at Stratford also.

Commencing 1 July 1855, the North London ran two through trains Sundays and weekdays between Hampstead Road and Tilbury via Victoria Park Junction and Forest Gate Junction. These ran up to and including 30 September 1855 and were most probably hauled by Eastern Counties locomotives between Stratford and Tilbury.

There was no further through working until 1 September 1866, when a through service was started between Chalk Farm and Barking by the same route. This service ran only during September and October 1866, engines and carriages being provided by the North London throughout. Hampstead Road station had been renamed Chalk Farm on 1 December 1862.

The North London obtained powers to construct a curve from Bow to Bromley forming a junction with the London, Tilbury & Southend line which had been opened in 1858. This curve was opened for normal passenger traffic on 18 May 1869, a service of through trains between Chalk Farm and Plaistow being operated from that date. The previous day was Whit Monday, and on that day the North London worked two through excursion trains from Chalk Farm to Southend and back, calling at all stations to Bow, then at Tilbury, for Gravesend.

During the summer months, June to September, from 1869 to 1886, the North London ran a through train on Sundays and Mondays to Southend and back, calling at all intermediate North London stations, also at Plaistow and Tilbury, North London engines working throughout. During certain years up to 1886, through North London carriages ran daily in the summer between Chalk Farm and Thames Haven or Chalk Farm and Tilbury in connexion with boats to Margate. These carriages were attached to and detached from London, Tilbury & Southend trains at Plaistow. If the traffic was heavy, the Great Eastern (and subsequently the London, Tilbury & Southend) worked the North London carriages forward specially.

When the railways adopted continuous brakes, that used by the North London differed from that used by the London, Tilbury & Southend. It therefore became impracticable to combine the trains of the two companies, and the Tilbury objected to the North London trains, as serious difficulties might have arisen in the event of a locomotive failure. Consequently, there was no through working after 1886 until 1907.

Meanwhile the Chalk Farm and Plaistow service which, as stated, started running on 18 May 1869, ceased on 30 September 1871. From 1 October 1871 the trains worked locally between Bow and Plaistow, but from 1 June 1877 until the end of January 1878 the Plaistow train again ran through from and to Chalk Farm. After this the service was a local one until it finally ceased on and from 1 January 1916. In later years, to avoid confusion, special destination boards reading 'Bow (NL)' had been provided, and when the London, Tilbury & Southend withdrew second class on 1 April 1893, the North London did likewise on its Plaistow train which consequently was the first North London train on which second class was not provided.

During the summer months, June to September, from 1907 until 1914, the Tilbury ran a through train daily from Chalk Farm to Southend on Sea, returning in the evening. This train called at all stations to Bow, at Plaistow or Barking, and at Leigh-on-Sea and Westcliff-on-Sea. In 1909 there was an additional train on Thursday afternoons, returning in the evening, and from 1910 there were two trains each way on Sundays. The through trains did not run on Bank Holidays as the Tilbury was too busy with its own local traffic. When necessary, the North London ran a relief train from Caledonian Road & Barnsbury to Southend, returning to Chalk Farm. The London, Tilbury & Southend provided a pilotman from and to Plaistow, the North London engine running on light to Shoeburyness shed. The last day these trains actually ran is not recorded. On Friday 31 July 1914 both the North London and Tilbury trains ran to schedule. War was then imminent, and on both the following days the North London relief train reached Plaistow, but a pilotman was not available, and the passengers were transferred to London, Tilbury & Southend trains. The through London, Tilbury & Southend trains do not appear to have been run on these days nor subsequently.

There have been no more regular booked trains of the category detailed above, but on various days in the summer months subsequent to the termination of the first World War, through excursions have been run from Willesden or from Watford to Southend by this route.

From 1 January 1923 there were a few through trains, weekdays only, between Broad Street and Shoeburyness via Upminster, and from 1 October 1923 via Tilbury also. These trains did not call at any intermediate stations on the North London, and the last train ran on 27 April 1935.

Through tickets between North London and Tilbury stations continued to be issued, available via Bow (NL) and Bow Road (W&B) until 1945, when bookings to stations between Dalston and Poplar were also withdrawn after the train service had been discontinued.

(A) *JRCHS* 3, 5, pp.87–88 (9/1957)

IT MAY BE ADDED that during the years 1907 to 1914 the trains ran via Upminster. As it was the standard practice for all North London trains to carry an indication of their destination, a supply of 'Southend' boards was kept for these trains. The London, Tilbury & Southend Railway also had 'Chalk Farm' boards.

(L) *JRCHS* 4, 1, p.15 (1/1958)

Calling-on or Station Distant Signals: North London Railway

In 1876 the North London Railway had some home and distant (or auxiliary) signals. The home signal was placed close to the signal cabin and if the station platform was beyond the cabin a starting signal was also provided for that line. Drivers were instructed to be prepared to stop at the distant signal when at danger, whistle, and if they saw the way clear, to proceed cautiously to the home signal. The home signal was locked with the starting signal and the former could not be lowered until the starting signal had been taken off. When the section ahead was blocked and it was necessary for a train to draw forward to the starting signal the signalman authorized the driver to do so by means of a green flag or lamp.

In 1889 revised regulations came into operation. The home signal was free from the starting signal and Station signal cabins generally had starting, home and distant signals, the distant being locked with both home and starting signals, except at Dalston Junction (No.1 line and Poplar line) and at Tilbury Junction (Bromley branch) where the distant was locked only with the home signal. At these cabins, however, the signalman had instructions not to take off the distant unless and until both home and starting signals had been lowered, except in the case of passenger trains booked to stop at the station, in which case it was the practice to take off the home and distant only.

This arrangement was found to be unsatisfactory and it was decided in 1893 to provide a supplementary distant signal at certain places. These signals were similar to calling-on arms, which had been introduced on the North London Railway in 1889, but the arm was notched. They were placed underneath the ordinary or through distant and showed a small green light when off, but no light when on. When off, these signals indicated that the home signal was off but that the starting signal was at danger. They were named station or calling-on distant signals and the first was installed at Dalston Junction No.1 up line and brought into use on 6 November 1893, followed by Tilbury Junction in 1894; Dalston Junction (other lines), Poplar and Victoria Park in 1895. These signals were particularly useful in foggy or misty weather and at Dalston where the signals in the tunnels could not be readily seen owing to curves. Fogmen left detonators on the rail whilst the through distant was on but told the driver if the calling-on distant was off. Calling-on distants remained after the NL became LMS, the last being removed in 1940. These signals do not appear to have been adopted by any other railway.

(A) *JRCHS* 5, 4, pp.73–74 (7/1959)

The Blackwall and North London Railways at Poplar

The Act of 26 August 1846 incorporating the East & West India Docks and Birmingham Junction Railway authorized that Company to construct a railway from a point at or near the Camden Town Station of the London & Birmingham Railway in the Parish of St Pancras to Poplar. Actually the railway started at a point (later known as NL limit) in Hampstead parish, on land the property of the London & North Western Company.

The line authorized was to cross the London & Blackwall Railway at two places: at Harrow Lane, Poplar, and near Prestons Road, Poplar, the two branches diverging just north of Poplar High Street. As the railway had to pass under the High Street and almost immediately cross the Blackwall Railway the Act authorized the crossing either by an overbridge or on the level, such crossing to be constructed by agreement with the Blackwall Company and if on the level to be under the absolute control of that company and the Blackwall line protected by strong and effective barriers. The E&WID&BJ Company's trains were to stop five yards before reaching the Blackwall Railway. The other crossing, near Prestons Road, was to be by means of a bridge and as the distance from Poplar High Street in this case was considerably further than in the case of the crossing by Harrow Lane the gradient would not be abnormal.

As the Blackwall Railway Company were running a 15-minute service of passenger trains they definitely refused to agree to a level crossing so the E&WID&BJ Company (whose title was changed to North London Railway Company as from 1 January 1853) was obliged to build a bridge at

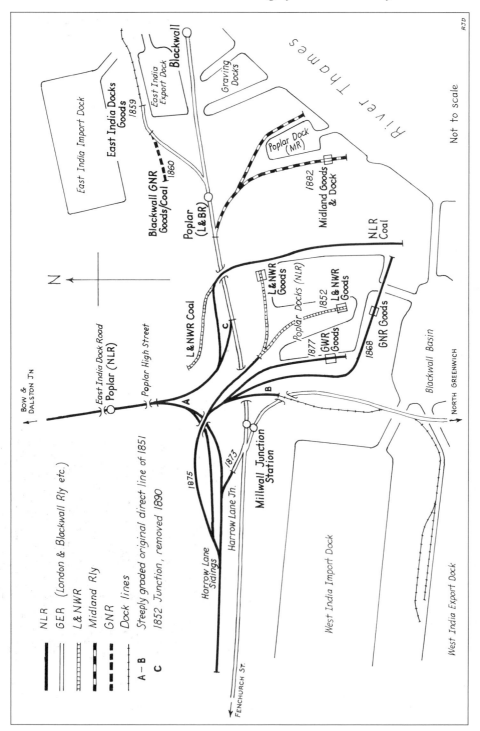

35. Simplified sketch plan of the railways in the Poplar Docks / Blackwall area about 1914.

Harrow Lane with steep gradients each side, that from the High Street to the north side of the bridge being 1 in 34 for about five chains, and that on the south side 1 in 29. Both bridges were completed in 1851 and brought into operation for normal goods and mineral traffic on 1 January 1852. In 1852 a junction was constructed joining the North London and the Blackwall railways near Prestons Road by means of a short spur from the NLR eastwards. This was known as Poplar Junction. The layout was rearranged in 1870 to facilitate through running of North London passenger trains to and from Blackwall: the junction was taken out in 1890 when the service was withdrawn.

When the railway to Poplar was completed the North London wished to run a service of passenger trains to and from Blackwall but the Blackwall Company declined to agree. The North London

Company then constructed a passenger station in East India Dock Road, Poplar, and worked a service between that station and Broad Street from 1 August 1866. This service was extended to and from Blackwall from 1 September 1870.

As the goods traffic was increasing rapidly further accommodation was necessary and land was acquired on the west side of Harrow Lane, part of this thoroughfare being closed and replaced by a footbridge under the new railway connexion to sidings on the recently acquired land. These sidings, known as Harrow Lane Sidings, were brought into use in 1866.

The steep gradient already mentioned led to considerable difficulties in handling traffic to and from Poplar Docks and both the railway companies who had goods stations on the NLR at Poplar pressed for better facilities. These companies were

36. Demolition of Poplar station, London & Blackwall Railway, in 1936 looking east towards the Blackwall terminus. The masts of a vessel in the East India Export Dock are visible above the signal box in the background. The single line to the left in front of the box leads to Blackwall Goods Depot (GER/L&NER) and East India Docks Goods (GNR/LNER). *RCHS/Spence*

the London & North Western from 1852 and the Great Northern from 1868. The North London therefore decided to abolish the direct line from High Street to the Docks, and construct an additional bridge over the Blackwall Railway on the east side of and adjoining the existing bridge, thereby providing additional running roads to the goods stations. The company also arranged to increase the siding accommodation at Harrow Lane and to construct a loop line from the sidings to the overbridges. Thenceforth vehicles for the Docks (except those by the Prestons Road route) would go into Harrow Lane Sidings and subsequently be taken over the loop line to the Docks. It was also arranged to put in a junction, known as Harrow Lane Junction, connecting the North London with the Blackwall Railway just west of Millwall Junction passenger station, but the actual date of the opening of this junction cannot be traced; it was, however, in use by 1873. The Loop line was

brought into use in 1875, the whole of the work being completed in October of that year. In 1877 the Great Western Company opened a goods station at Poplar, the trains being worked by the North London from and to Acton GWR.

At one time there were five NL signal cabins at Poplar, viz, East India Dock Road, High Street, Harrow Lane, Loop Line Junction and Blackwall Bridge, but from 9 September 1888 the first two were concentrated into one new cabin, named Poplar Central, and in March 1909 Harrow Lane cabin was closed, the points and signals on both the High Level and Low Level lines being worked from Blackwall Bridge; at the same time the number of running roads across the two adjoining bridges was reduced, the remaining roads being signalled for traffic in either direction. In addition there is a signal hut at Prestons Road.

(A) *JRCHS* 5, 6, pp.101–103 (11/1959)

37. Poplar NLR station looking north from Poplar High Street bridge in the the 1900s;
at the right, a train from Broad Street has just terminated. This site is now the Docklands Light Railway
Poplar All Saints' station. *Anon/London Borough of Tower Hamlets*

38. Poplar NLR station frontage to East India Dock Road, looking east, about 1907. The Docklands Light Railway
Poplar All Saints' station now occupies this site. *Commercial postcard, publisher unknown*

The Merchandise Train Services of the North London Railway

THE North London Railway began to carry merchandise on 1 January 1852, but a few tons had been carried during the last few days of 1851.

Land had been obtained from the East & West India Dock Company at Poplar, part of which had been purchased, the remainder leased. Extensive sidings had been laid down, and warehouses and appliances constructed. A timber pond had been converted into a dock. The warehouses etc. were let to the London & North Western Company, for use as a waterside goods depot, and brought into use on 1 January 1852.

Coal depots were constructed at certain places on the NLR, and coal trains were worked from Poplar and Blackwall to these depots by the Northumberland & Durham Coal Company's own engines. This arrangement terminated in 1859 when the NLR bought out the rights and the engines of the Coal Company. In 1870 it was arranged that the L&NW Railway should take over these coal depots, some of which were enlarged to deal also with general merchandise.

Meanwhile, on 12 March 1853, the London & North Western had opened a goods station at Haydon Square on the Blackwall Railway.

Additional sidings, warehouses and appliances were constructed at Poplar for the use of the Great Northern from 1868 and the Great Western from 1877. The Great Northern usually worked their own traffic to Poplar, at first over the North London from St Pancras, but from 14 December 1874 from Finsbury Park via Canonbury. The Great Western traffic was always worked by the North London from Acton GWR.

The main work of the North London Railway so far as goods traffic was concerned consisted of hauling trains across London from one company's exchange sidings to those of another company, and from the opening of the various junctions merchandise trains were regularly worked by the North London Railway as set out hereunder:

(1) From Acton (GW) to St Pancras for GN, and to Stratford (later to Temple Mills) for GE.

39. A cattle train hauled by an ex-NLR 0-6-0T, coming off the LT&SR curve from Bromley, at Bow station, LM&SR, looking south east, about 1925. *Anon/RCHME*

(2) London & South Western traffic from Old Oak Sidings, Willesden, to the places named above.

(3) London & North Western traffic from Willesden or Camden to the places named above; also to St Pancras for Midland Railway.

(4) Great Northern traffic until 1874 from St Pancras to Stratford; commencing 14 December 1874 from Finsbury Park, East Goods Yard or Clarence Yard via Canonbury to Stratford (later to Temple Mills).

(5) Until 1870, Midland Company's traffic St Pancras to Stratford and to Royal Mint Street; and until 1882 to East and West India Docks.

The North London also worked exchange traffic to and from Plaistow, LT&S Railway, and all L&NW goods traffic to and from Haydon Square, L&NW, and Upton Park, L&NW. To other L&NW depots that company usually worked its own traffic.

The Great Northern worked their own traffic, originally from St Pancras, later from Finsbury Park, to their Hackney Wick goods station, opened 1 March 1878, Poplar, Royal Mint Street and Victoria Docks. In early years the North London took a share in working the Royal Mint Street traffic.

On 7 May 1894 the Great Eastern opened a goods station called Hackney Downs on the North London at Graham Road. The Great Eastern worked their own trains to this station over the North London from Victoria Park.

The arrangements detailed above apply equally in the reverse direction, and continued after the formation of the LM&S Railway.

NOTE: St Pancras refers to the sidings of that name on the North London, and not to St Pancras goods station, Midland Railway.

(A) *JRCHS* 6, 2, pp.21–22 (3/1960)

Red for Danger

IT IS TO BE REGRETTED that Mr Rolt* did not correct a small error in his account of the accident at Kentish Town in 1861. Had the staffing and working arrangements been as Mr Rolt sets out there would have been a target on the previous train and the collision would probably have been avoided, but the staff at the stations and those with the ballast train were L&NW men. All the passenger trains were North London, and that company did not provide targets to indicate a special train following. At that time there was no telegraph communication of any kind between Kew and Willesden, and the station-

84

40. A NLR 0-6-0T on a loaded loose-coupled westbound coal train from Poplar Docks passing Homerton, looking east, about 1925. Note the running number hung on the loco bunker to assist signalmen to identify the working. *Anon. RCHME*

master at Kew sent forward the special train when ready. In an effort to avoid a recurrence the North London took entire charge of the Hampstead Junction line for about twelve years and telegraphic communication was provided between Kew and Camden Road and intermediate stations, together with improved signalling and interlocking.

(L) *JRCHS* 13, 2 p.34 (4/1967)

[* The reference is to Rolt, L. T. C., *Red for Danger*, David & Charles, 1966.]

The North London Railway †

SOME MORE DETAILS have come to light since the latest edition of *The North London Railway* went to press, and the additional information on pp.28 and 29 should be amplified as follows:

– The construction of the Tottenham & Hampstead Junction Railway between Gospel Oak and Highgate Road (p.13) had been started in 1868 and the bridge over Gordon House Road practically completed, but funds had then run out and no more capital could be raised.

– The junction with the District Railway at South Acton (p.15), although closed for regular working in 1915, was not removed until 1930.

– The junction at Poplar (p.16, line 9) used by NL trains to and from Blackwall was taken out in August 1890 (not 1900) and the connecting line used as a run-round siding.

– Acton Gate House (p.14) was situated where Acton Lane crossed the railway, until 1874 a level crossing. The place was subsequently named Hammersmith Junction and remained the physical junction with the branch even after South Acton station had been opened in 1880, and the branch extended thereto. The section between this junction and the terminus at Hammersmith continued to be worked by train staff and ticket, but the short extension to South Acton was worked 'one engine in steam'. For many years there does not appear to have been any train staff or mechanical device to ensure this, but it was decided in December 1891 to counterlock the signal at the Hammersmith Junction cabin with that at South Acton. This was one of the first cases on a single line where the signal at one end was interlocked with the signal at the other end. These arrangements applied until 1909, when the electric train staff was adopted between South Acton and Hammersmith station, Hammersmith Junction cabin being closed at the same time. The physical connexion was resited at the north end of South Acton station. As the engine shed was actually on the branch, an instrument was provided there to enable the driver or fireman to obtain a staff after having obtained permission of the signalmen. In 1917, after the passenger service had been withdrawn, the branch was worked with train staff, one engine in steam.

– A joint station with London Transport at Highbury & Islington was brought into use 7 April 1968. New entrances to Hampstead Heath station and to Caledonian Road & Barnsbury station (from Caledonian Road) are practically completed and will probably be in use when this appears in print. The original entrances will then be closed.

(L) *JRCHS* 14, 4, p.71 (10/1968)

[† Robbins, Michael, *The North London Railway*, Oakwood Press, 1967]

The Directorate of the North London Railway

T HE MAXIMUM NUMBER of directors stipulated in the Act of Incorporation was eighteen, and it was agreed by the promoters that not more than ten should be representatives of the L&NWR and three of the East & West India Dock Company, leaving five to be appointed by the other shareholders. Actually the total number did not exceed fourteen but at least half of these were also on the board of the L&NWR.

(L) *JRCHS* 9, 1, p.18 (1/1963)

North London Railway Station Entrances

M EMBERS may like to note that the new entrance to Hampstead Heath station was opened on 22 July 1968. A new entrance to Kensal Rise, almost on the site of the original entrance which was closed about 1890, was opened on 15 December 1968. The new access to Caledonian Road & Barnsbury was brought into use on 16

December 1968; it is on the south side of the railway, the previous entrance from Caledonian Road (closed 1920) was on the north side.

(L) *JRCHS* 15, 2, p.37 (4/1969)

The North London Railway At Poplar

[see fig 35]

T O REACH the docks at Poplar the East & West India Docks and Birmingham Junction Railway (later renamed North London Railway) had to cross the Blackwall Railway, and that Company was asked to agree to a level crossing, but naturally the Blackwall Company declined. The NLR therefore constructed a bridge.

The date when the line from Poplar Docks to Bow was opened is a little obscure. Sidings for coal had been constructed at Hackney, Kingsland and Islington in 1851 and these were taken over by the Northumberland & Durham Coal Company on 20 October 1851. The Coal Company worked coal trains with their own engines and men from Poplar Docks to these depots from that date or very soon afterwards. A little later sidings were made at other places and where the railway was above public streets 'coal drops' were provided. The NLR took over the working of the coal trains on 20 January 1858, purchased the Coal Company's engines and wagons and paid compensation to that Company.

From 1 January 1852 the London & North Western Railway worked a service of trains carrying general goods over the NLR to and from Poplar Docks. In 1852 a curve connecting the NLR with the Blackwall Railway, facing towards Blackwall, was brought into use.

About 1865 an additional line was constructed by the NLR; this crossed the Blackwall Railway to the east of the direct line. About the same time Harrow Lane Sidings, to the west of the original line, were brought into use. A physical connexion with the Blackwall at Harrow Lane Junction, Millwall Docks, was brought into use in 1873.

Meanwhile a passenger service between Broad Street and Poplar Station, in the East India Dock Road, began on 1 August 1866. The curve of 1852 was reconstructed for through running and the passenger service extended to Blackwall on 1 September 1870.

Through bookings from NL stations to Woolwich and Gravesend were put into operation, available by steamer from Brunswick Pier, Blackwall. The Blackwall service was, however, curtailed at Poplar on and from 1 July 1890 and the junction with the Blackwall Railway severed in August 1890.

The original direct line to the Docks entailed a severe gradient each side of the bridge over the Blackwall line. This bridge was replaced in 1875 with a curve, suitably graded, and a new bridge over the Blackwall Railway. This bridge was widened from time to time. There were therefore still two separate bridges over the Blackwall line.

From about 1853 the NL had worked Great Northern goods traffic from Holloway via St Pancras Sidings to Poplar, and some ten years later the GN worked their own traffic to and from Poplar. Commencing in December 1874 the trains were routed via Canonbury. For many years the service was from Ferme Park or East Goods, Finsbury Park, to Poplar; in the reverse direction the trains usually ran to Clarence Yard.

Beginning in 1877 the North London worked Great Western goods traffic from Acton GW to a depot at Poplar rented from the North London.

The grouping of the railways made practically no difference. The Poplar passenger service was withdrawn wef 15 May 1944. The final closing of the Blackwall Railway east of Millwall Junction Station and removal of the tracks enabled access to Poplar Docks to be simplified. Work on a new direct line to the West Quay was begun in January 1968 and brought into use in May 1968. This resulted in the old high level line becoming redundant and removal was completed about a year later, July 1969. The eastern line, constructed about 1865, also remains in use.

(L) *JRCHS* 20, 3, pp.70, 71 (11/1974)

[Editorial note: HVB subsequently informed me as follows. The 'additional line' mentioned in paragraph 4 of this letter was in fact a widening of the 1851 bridge referred to in paragraph 1 and the date in the last line of the letter should therefore read 'in 1851', not 'about 1865'.]

North London Railway Engine Boards

THE North London Railway retained at Bow engine boards for Fenchurch Street, Hatfield, Southend long after their trains and engines ran [had ceased to run] to those places.

(L) *UN* 292, p.53 (4/1986)

41. A watercolour impression of the interior of the Broad Street terminus about July 1876, showing a Blackwall train in charge of NLR loco 67 and (right) a NLR 12-coach train for Alexandra Palace, GNR, with NLR loco 47. *Painted by J. F. Vickery, 1943*

(iv) On the North & South Western Junction Railway

The Early Train Services of the North & South Western Junction Railway

[see figs 9 and 22]

THE North & South Western Junction Railway was incorporated by Act of 24 July 1851 to construct a railway from a point in the parish of Hammersmith near West London Junction on the London & North Western Railway to a junction with the London & South Western Railway at Brentford. This junction, formerly known as Kew Junction, is now known as Old Kew Junction. The length of the railway was 4 miles 8 chains* and at first only a single line was laid although provision had been made for a double line of railway. The Company entered into an agreement with the L&NW and L&SW Railways under which these two Companies were to work the line and as the North & South Western Junction Company expected both goods and passenger trains to run through between the L&NW and L&SW lines the Junction

---

* This distance included a short curve at Kew facing towards Barnes, which was not constructed by the N&SWJ, and the powers lapsed. A curve, following approximately the same course, from Kew East Junction to New Kew Junction, was later constructed by the L&SWR and opened for goods traffic in 1861, and for passengers the following year. The entrance at Kew Bridge station for passengers for North London trains was on the east side of Lionel Road, where a staircase led down to the booking office which was on platform level. This entrance was bricked up, the staircase removed by the booking office closed in 1918. [This sentence is printed as originally published. It should read: 'This entrance was bricked up and the staircase was removed after the booking office closed in 1918.' At Richmond the separate booking office for NL trains was closed in 1917 – Editor]

Company did not at first consider it necessary to provide stations.

On 15 February 1853 the London and South Western Company commenced working goods trains to and from the L&NW Railway at a point then usually referred to as Kensal Green but now known as Old Oak Sidings. As neither the L&SW nor the L&NW Company was willing to work a passenger service the North & South Western Junction Company decided to construct a passenger station at Acton and to ask the North London if they would work some trains from their terminus at Hampstead Road to Brentford. The North London agreed to work the trains and sanction was obtained from the L&NW for such trains to pass over their line but the L&SW Company declined to have the North London trains at Brentford or at any other place on their system. The Junction Company thereupon hurriedly erected a temporary platform at Kew and the passenger service commenced on 1 August 1853. The North London Company's station called Hampstead Road was on a site partly covered by the present Primrose Hill Station, the entrance being from the road now named Regent's Park Road, just by the Adelaide Tavern. The service consisted of four trains on weekdays only between Hampstead Road and Kew, calling at Acton, a distance of 8 miles, the journey time being 20 minutes. (Some accounts say that there was no intermediate stop, but contemporary records state that Acton Station was opened from the commencement of the passenger service; it was a small building with neither subway nor footbridge. The present station on the same site was built by the NLR and completed in 1876.) The railway was made double track just before the opening for passenger traffic. These trains, except the first down, had connexions from or to Fenchurch Street. A service on Sundays consisting of four trains each way commenced on 2 April 1854, with connexions from and to Fenchurch Street.

As a result of negotiations with the London & South Western that Company agreed to haul some of the North London trains through to Windsor from 1 June 1854. At the same time the service over the N&SWJ was improved. From this date there were seven trains each way, of which three went through to and from Windsor hauled by L&SW locomotives on that railway. The Windsor service was not very satisfactory seeing the first down train did not arrive in Windsor until 12 noon and the first up train did not leave until 12.15, NL coaches not being stabled overnight at Windsor. The Sunday service consisted of three trains to and from Windsor and one more each way as far as Kew.

The working on Sunday was rather unusual. The first down train from Hampstead Road ran to Windsor but as carriages were not stabled at Kew this train consisted of a double set of vehicles some of which were taken forward from Kew to Windsor by an L&SW engine, the NL engine bringing back the other carriages as the first up train. The journey time from Fenchurch Street to Windsor was two hours. The Windsor service ran for the last time on 31 October 1854.

After the withdrawal of through running to the L&SW Railway the service to and from Kew fluctuated between four and eight trains on weekdays and four or five on Sundays. The trains had connexions from and to Fenchurch Street except the first down on weekdays which latterly had a connexion from Bow. These arrangements applied generally until 1858.

From June 1855 until October 1866 inclusive a market train conveying passengers and cattle ran from Windsor to the Metropolitan Cattle Market [There was no rail access into the Market. Caledonian Road was the nearest NLR station – Editor], usually on Monday, but sometimes also on Friday. It was worked by the L&SW calling at Datchet, Staines, Feltham, Hounslow, Brentford, Kew, Acton, Kilburn and Hampstead Road, the NL Company working forward from Kew. The train returned from the Market in the afternoon.

From May 1855 through bookings were re-established with Windsor line stations, passengers making their own way between the two stations at Kew.

On 1 June 1855 some of the Kew trains commenced to call at Kilburn LNWR.

Commencing 21 October 1857 the 5.15pm train from Fenchurch Street had special carriages; these were detached from the main train near Bow and ran non-stop thence to Hampstead Road where passengers joined the train for Kew.

In 1858 the N&SWJ, NL and L&SW agreed to through trains to and from Twickenham, both the NL and L&SW supplying carriages, the L&SW working all the trains and supplying guards between Kew Junction and Twickenham. The trains, which did not call at Chiswick or Mortlake, had to reverse at Kew Junction and in Barnes station. The service started on 20 May 1858 and there were eight trains each way on weekdays all of which went through to Twickenham; on Sundays there were seven to Twickenham and one more as far as Kew. The journey time from Hampstead Road to Kew was 20 minutes. The time from Fenchurch Street was 40 minutes more. Commencing in August, all the Sunday trains ran through to Twickenham. Through covered carriages were attached to three trains from Fenchurch Street on weekdays, returning from Twickenham in the evening. A special day return fare of one shilling was charged. This arrangement applied during the summer months of 1858 to 1861 inclusive. The service on Sundays was reduced during the winter months.

The Twickenham service was at first shown in the L&SW Company's ordinary public time books but was omitted after a few months. The service was not very popular with L&SW officials who feared loss of traffic from their own route to Waterloo. The working time tables of the L&SWR show these trains calling at both stations at Kew and passengers were booked from the L&SW station at Barnes and beyond on these trains. The NL Company issued sheet time tables headed North London, Blackwall, Hampstead Junction, North & South Western Junction and South Western Railways.

The Hampstead Junction Railway was opened on 2 January 1860 and this resulted in considerable improvement in services. This railway left the North London Railway just to the west of Camden Road station and joined the N&SWJ Railway on the west side at a point just north of Old Oak Common Lane bridge in Acton parish. The original stations were Kentish Town (renamed Gospel Oak 1 February 1867), Hampstead Heath, Finchley Road and Edgeware Road [so spelled – Editor]. The initial service was Camden Road to Twickenham five trains plus three as far as Kew and thirteen to Edgeware Road. In the up direction there were four from Twickenham plus four from Kew and thirteen from Edgeware Road. Two trains from Fenchurch Street on weekdays ran express to Camden Road in connexion with trains to Twickenham. On Sundays there were four trains to and from Twickenham plus two between Camden Road and Kew. Commencing 1 February 1860 the 8.20am from Twickenham, which consisted of L&SW coaches, ran through to Fenchurch Street calling at stations to Camden Road, then at Hackney and Stepney. The L&SW coaches usually returned from Fenchurch Street attached to an ordinary NL train. All trains were diverted to run via the Hampstead Junction line from the date of opening and this added about fifteen minutes to the journey time. The express trains between Fenchurch Street and Camden Road, however, saved fifteen minutes. The market train from and to Windsor ran non-stop from Acton to Camden Road.

Beginning in March 1860 additional up trains ran through to Fenchurch Street and in the summer months the service to Kew and Twickenham was substantially increased, especially on Sundays.

In May 1861 the service settled down to six trains weekdays and Sundays to or from Twickenham, and an additional eight on weekdays and four on Sundays to and from Kew. This applied until the end of December 1862. From 1 December 1862 the 5.0pm train from Fenchurch Street had through coaches for Twickenham, which were detached at Bow and ran express thence to Camden Road. Additional through workings were put into operation from time to time.

The reversing of the trains at Kew and Barnes wasted time, and was liable to cause delay to other trains. The N&SWJ gave serious consideration to applying for powers to construct a line of its own to Richmond. The L&SW opposed this but agreed to apply for powers to make curves at Kew and at Barnes. These curves were constructed in 1861 but a difference of opinion arose as to payments for the new station at Kew Bridge, and, further, the NL trains carried a considerable number of passengers to and from Barnes; the new curve avoided that station. It was eventually agreed that the NL (on behalf of the N&SWJ Co.) would be responsible for

maintenance of their own booking office and the platform used by NL trains to London and the L&SW Co. for the other platform at the new station at Kew Bridge. The former platform therefore always had NL characteristics but was entirely surrounded by platforms, etc., obviously L&SW. These arrangements operated from 1 February 1862 from which date the trains ceased to use Barnes station, but commenced to call at Chiswick and Mortlake. The running time between Kew and Twickenham was reduced by about eight minutes.

From 1 January 1863 the weekdays service was much improved; there were eighteen trains each way between Camden Road and Kew, of which seven continued to and from Twickenham. The Sunday service remained at six to and from Twickenham plus four as far as Kew. All Twickenham trains were extended to Kingston using the terminal (or low level) station from 1 July 1863. There was little change in the weekday service until the end of October 1865 except that the number of through trains to Kingston was increased to nine in some months and ten in others. On Sundays, however, there was a new development; in the summer months of 1864 and 1865 a regular half hourly service of through trains in the afternoon and evening ran between Bow and Kew. The Kingston service was eight trains in the summer and five in the winter on Sundays.

The whole service was revised on 1 November 1865 by the opening of the NL line between Broad Street and Dalston Junction. On weekdays a regular half-hourly service operated between Broad Street and Kew, the journey time being 50 minutes. Nine of these trains were worked forward to and from Kingston. There were two trains on Sunday morning and an hourly service in the afternoon and evening. Five of the Sunday trains ran to and from Kingston.

Commencing in May 1865 for the summer season, there were three down trains on Sunday mornings and a half-hourly service in the afternoon and evening to Kew, eight of these going forward to and from Kingston. The service to Kew continued until the end of 1868, but from October 1866 the Kingston service was reduced to six trains on weekdays (not four as stated in another account) and five on Sundays, and was not subsequently altered. About the same time (the actual date cannot be traced) the L&SW Co. ceased to provide any coaches for the Kingston and Broad Street service but continued to work the NL trains as between Kingston and Kew.

Meanwhile the N&SWJ Company had revived their scheme for a direct line to Richmond and submitted a Bill to Parliament; this alarmed the L&SW Co. who thereupon submitted a Bill which included a line of railway covering much of the ground included in the Junction Company's Bill. Parliament passed the L&SW Bill subject to certain concessions in favour of the Junction Company and in consequence rejected the N&SWJ Company's own Bill. The concessions permitted the Junction Company to have their own booking office and clerks at Richmond and supply their own tickets to stations on the N&SWJ Railway and beyond. In addition, the NL Co. (on behalf of the Junction Co.) were to run their own trains to and from the new terminal station, alongside the old station, at Richmond. These arrangements operated from the opening of the line on 1 January 1869. On this date the N&SWJ Co. sent two inspectors and two points-men to Richmond to look after their interests. The L&SW Co. objected to this and after some cor-respondence the inspectors and pointsmen were withdrawn.

From 1 January 1869 alternate trains on weekdays ran to Richmond leaving the old line at Acton Junction (later known as South Acton Junction). In addition two express trains were added to the service, in the morning in the up direction and down in the evening. At first these ran non stop from Camden Road to Brentford Road (renamed Gunnersbury 1 November 1871) but a little later called at Willesden and Acton. Commencing February 1869, on Saturdays the evening down expresses were altered to leave during the afternoon. The diversion of certain trains to Richmond reduced the service to Kew Bridge by approximately half. This resulted in complaints and in mid-January a service of local trains was added, operating between Acton and Kew Bridge in connexion with the Richmond trains. On Sundays all trains served both Kew Bridge and Rich-mond. There were two trains in the morning, and in the evening an hourly service operated. This latter was worked at first in a rather unusual way. The down train from Broad Street ran through to Richmond (a local train connecting from Acton to Kew Bridge); the train then returned from

Richmond to Acton (connecting with a train from Kew Bridge to Broad Street). The train under notice then worked from Acton to Kew Bridge and finally Kew Bridge to Broad Street. Thus on the down journey passengers for Kew Bridge changed at Acton and on the up journey passengers from Richmond changed at Acton; in either case the waiting time was only a few minutes. The local trains were referred to in the timetables as 'short' trains and a siding with facing connexion was laid down at Acton to accommodate them.

This Sunday service only operated for three months, as from April 1869 another train was added in the morning serving Kew Bridge, and in the afternoon and evening an additional hourly service operated to and from Kew Bridge, the other train working through to and from Richmond. There was, therefore, a train each hour for Richmond and each half-hour for Kew Bridge.

The service started in 1869 remained basically in operation until 1906 on Sundays and 1909 on weekdays, the only substantial alterations being the provision of later trains, commencing 1 July 1875, and experiments with earlier trains at various times which, being poorly patronized, were with one exception soon withdrawn. An additional express train began to run in 1873. The express trains started to call at Hampstead Heath 1 June 1871 and subsequently at certain other stations on the Hampstead Junction line.

Additional stations were opened: South Acton on the N&SWJ line 1 January 1880; and on the Hampstead Junction line, Kensal Green & Harles-den 1 November 1861, replaced by Kensal Rise (at first named Kensal Green) 1 July 1873, Willesden Junction 1 September 1866, Kentish Town (in Prince of Wales Road) 1 April 1867, West End Lane 1 March 1888, Brondesbury Park 1 June 1908.

Commencing May 1906 an additional down train was provided on Saturday afternoon; this ran non-stop to Gospel Oak calling at most inter-mediate stations thence to Richmond. On Sundays the service was entirely revised, through trains to and from Richmond running every half-hour throughout the day, except for a short interval during the forenoon. There was also a service of local trains between Acton and Kew Bridge.

From 1 May 1909 through trains ran to and from Richmond every half-hour on weekdays and the express trains were altered to run non-stop from Broad Street to Hampstead Heath, except Saturdays when the first stop was Gospel Oak. In the up direction the trains ran non-stop from Gospel Oak to Broad Street. There was a half-hourly service locally between Acton and Kew Bridge.

Starting July 1909 some additional local trips to and from Kew Bridge on Sunday morning were worked, and on Sunday afternoon and evening additional through trains from Broad Street and Kew Bridge ran every half-hour, giving a quarter-hourly service as far as South Acton.

In 1910 additional services to and from Kew Bridge on weekdays were instituted; these were worked by a [steam] Rail Motor Car loaned by the L&NW Railway. As from 1 October 1911 it was arranged that the L&NW Co. provide a service between Willesden and Kew Bridge in lieu of the NL local train between Acton and Kew Bridge. Commencing 22 April 1912 these were replaced by a through service of L&NW trains on weekdays between Broad Street and Kew Bridge. (These L&NW trains had previously worked between Broad Street and Earl's Court.)

The war of 1914–1918 caused a reduction in the services, but starting 1 October 1916 a service of electric trains ran between Broad Street and Richmond and Kew Bridge. At first the electric trains merely replaced the steam service but the running time was quicker. The service was considerably improved commencing 1 May 1919. From 9 May 1920 there was a quarter-hourly service to and from Richmond on Sundays, and from 10 July 1922 on weekdays also.

This account does not include services on the Hammersmith branch nor the Midland Company's trains. These will be dealt with later.

As previously stated the Hampstead Junction line originally joined the North & South Western Junction line on the west side, and as the North London goods trains for Old Oak sidings always travelled by the Hampstead Junction line this necessitated the trains drawing forward towards Acton Wells and reversing into Old Oak sidings. In 1885 the London & North Western Railway constructed a new line from Willesden High Level to Acton Wells Junction, with facing connexion with the original North & South Western Junction

42. The original terminal platforms at Richmond – the so-called Richmond New Station – looking west about 1870, with L&SWR train for Ludgate Hill via Kensington and, at right, a NLR train via the North & South Western Junction Railway. Subsequently a fourth platform face was added on the north side (i.e. behind the NLR train). *Anon/Richmond Local Studies Library*

line at Old Oak Junction. This enabled the North London goods trains to run clear of the passenger lines before reversing into the sidings. Henceforth the original lines between Willesden High Level and Acton Wells Junction were not used for passenger trains. The old HJR lines between Willesden High Level and Old Oak were closed on and from 1 May 1892 and removed, but certain earthworks are visible today.

The buildings of the old station at Kew, near Old Kew Junction, remained as a dwelling house until 1956; portions of platforms can still be seen. Another building which remained until 1957 was the 'gate-house' at the corner of Acton Lane and Bollo Bridge Road. Here, originally, was a level crossing but in 1874 Acton Lane was diverted under the railway, and the crossing closed on and from 20 August 1874. At this place the Hammersmith branch single line joined the main line.

The Hammersmith branch was opened for coal and certain classes of merchandise traffic on 1 May 1857 and for passengers 8 April 1858. At that time the goods traffic over the N&SWJ was worked by the L&SW, who, with the L&NW, guaranteed a minimum net revenue to the N&SWJ. This guarantee did not include the Hammersmith branch and therefore the N&SWJ purchased a locomotive to work the branch. This appears to be the only article of rolling stock possessed by the N&SWJ. This locomotive passed to the NLR in 1860 and was converted into a steam crane which survived until well after the NLR was absorbed by the LMS; it was broken up in 1951.

The NLR agreed to attach a first and second class brake composite carriage on the rear of trains running to and from Kew. This carriage was 'dropped' at the junction with the Hammersmith branch and taken forward by the N&SWJ Company's engine. On the down journey the train did not always stop but when the train slowed down the guard snatched the coupling; there were of course no continuous brakes. This practice, which was 'unofficial', gave rise to subsequent suggestions that the NLR at one time had slip carriages. In the up direction the coach was attached at the rear of the main train.

Through carriages to and from Hammersmith apparently ran up to the end of October 1865. Broad Street station was opened on 1 November 1865 and the NLR commenced a regular half-hourly service between that station and Kew, later known as Kew Bridge. The service to Hammersmith was from this date hourly with a few extra trains. The branch train ran from Acton, the engine pushing the one or two carriages to the junction; on the return journey the carriages were propelled from the junction to Acton station. From 1 January 1880 the branch train worked to and from South Acton and the service was made half-hourly.

For many years the receipts did not cover the cost of working the branch and serious consideration was given to withdrawing the service. Nothing was done, however, until 1908 when the carriages were nearly worn out and were (with those on the North Greenwich line) probably the only carriages in London lighted by oil. Towards the end of this year it was decided by the lessee companies, the L&NW, the Mid and the NL, to obtain an L&NW [steam] rail motor car. This car commenced running 4 January 1909 and on 8 April of the same year (the anniversary of the opening of the branch for passenger traffic) three halts, Rugby Road, Woodstock Road and Bath Road, were opened. The branch, however, continued to be worked at considerable loss and the service was discontinued on and from 1 January 1917.

It may be mentioned that the station was originally named Hammersmith although actually in the Parish of Chiswick. It was renamed Hammersmith & Chiswick on 1 July 1880. In early days it was often known locally as the North London station at Turnham Green and a timetable of this and other services printed in the *West London Observer* from time to time used this title, making no reference to Hammersmith.

The branch was originally worked by train staff and ticket, later by electric train staff. When the passenger service was withdrawn the branch was worked by 'one engine in steam'. For many years there was a signal cabin, known as Hammersmith Junction, in the angle where the branch diverged. Even after the branch line was extended to South Acton, the cabin at the junction remained owing to an engine shed and coal siding connected with the branch at this place. The Hammersmith Junction cabin was closed 1 September 1910 and an instrument provided in the engine shed from which drivers of light engines could obtain a staff by authority of the signalman at South Acton. The engine shed was demolished by a gale on 8 December 1954.

In 1868 a branch line connecting the Midland Railway with the North & South Western Junction Railway at Acton Wells was completed and a service of goods trains worked by the L&SW Company started on 1 October 1868.

On 3 August 1875 the Midland Railway commenced a service of passenger trains between Moorgate Street and Richmond. There were eleven trains each way on weekdays, six on Sundays. These were poorly patronized and were withdrawn at the end of January 1876.

The Midland commenced a service between St Pancras and Earl's Court on 1 May 1878. At first there were 15 trains each way, but these were reduced gradually to seven with two more as far as Acton. This service was withdrawn at the end of September 1880.

Commencing 1 January 1894 until the end of September 1902 there was a service of eleven trains between Child's Hill & Cricklewood and Gunnersbury. The Midland has not run any more local passenger trains over the N&SWJ Railway but some through express services between the Midlands and the L&SW Railway have been worked.

The curve from Acton GW to Acton Wells was opened for goods traffic on 1 January 1877, the trains being worked by the NLR. On 2 January 1888 the GWR commenced a service of 12 passenger trains each way between Southall and Willesden Junction High Level, later increased to 13, then gradually reduced to seven trains.

A service on Sundays commenced 12 July 1891; this consisted of a through train from Willesden in the morning with carriages for both Taplow and Windsor, returning in the evening. In addition there was a local each way between Southall and Willesden. This Sunday service ran only during the summer and did not operate after 1897.

The trains were replaced by steam rail-cars on 1 October 1904 and withdrawn on and from 10 March 1912.

In 1899 the District Railway constructed a branch to South Acton and this was connected with the N&SWJ line at the north end of South Acton station. A new signal cabin was installed called 'District Junction'. This junction was little used, never for passenger trains. It was disconnected in 1915 and together with the signal cabin later removed.

The passenger service to and from Kew Bridge was withdrawn on and from 12 September 1940 and the conductor rails subsequently removed. A fairly heavy goods traffic is worked both to Old Kew Junction and to New Kew Junction.

(A) *JRCHS* 7, 2, pp.21–27 (3/1961) and 8, 2, pp.19–22 (3/1962)

(v) On the Tottenham & Hampstead Junction Railway

The Early History of the Tottenham & Hampstead Junction Railway

THE Tottenham & Hampstead Junction Railway Company was authorized by Act of 1862 to construct a line from a junction with the Great Eastern at Tottenham to a junction with the Hampstead Junction Railway at Gospel Oak. Work began at the eastern end and the line was completed to Highgate Road and opened on 21 July 1868, a passenger service being provided by the Great Eastern. The early history is rather obscure but apparently at first there were six trains each way between Fenchurch Street and Highgate Road, plus one to and from Stratford. On Sundays there were four trains each way. First, second and third class passengers were conveyed, the fares being 9d, 7d and 5d for the respective classes to each of the three stations, viz: Crouch Hill, Upper Holloway, Highgate Road, with return tickets at fares of 1s 2d, 10d and 8d.

West of Highgate Road an embankment had been partially made and a substantial brick bridge over Gordon House Road erected, but funds were exhausted and the Company looked to its neighbours for financial help without success. The Hampstead Junction Railway was at that time under the management of the North London Railway and that Company did not want a junction at Gospel Oak as thereby through goods traffic would be diverted from its own system. The Great Eastern did not wish to become further involved and the London & North Western took no interest in the Tottenham & Hampstead Junction line. The L&NW had recently acquired the Hampstead Junction line but it remained under North London management for another few years.

There being no immediate prospect of the line being completed, some rails which had been laid to the west of Highgate Road station were removed and used elsewhere.

The resident population being very small, the passenger traffic fell far short of expectations and the train service was much reduced, probably from 1 December 1868. There were now only two trains each way weekdays and Sundays. The London terminal was Bishopsgate, but in some cases passengers had to change at Tottenham. The fares, already low, were reduced, the third class being 4d single, 6d return from Bishopsgate.

The financial position of the Tottenham & Hampstead Company was now very serious, but this time the Midland Railway came to the rescue. Meanwhile the Great Eastern passenger service was withdrawn at the end of January 1870, but it is not clear from existing records on which day the last train ran.

The Midland constructed a curve on a rather steep gradient to the T&HJ line at Highgate Road and by means of a curve at Tottenham, probably constructed in 1868, the Midland began a regular goods service to Great Eastern depots in East London on 3 January 1870. From 1 July 1870 the Great Eastern ran some of its main line trains to and from St Pancras using the original curve which became known as Tottenham North Junction. From 1 October 1870 the Midland commenced a passenger service to Crouch Hill, the trains being extended to South Tottenham when that station was opened on 1 May 1871.

Nothing was done at the Gospel Oak end until 1887 when the GE decided to extend their Chingford–Highgate Road service to that place. The Midland then completed the line to Gospel Oak and constructed a station with a single platform forming a convenient exchange with the trains of the L&NW and NL Railways. A turntable was constructed* as the GE intended to run some through trains to Southend in the summer. The extension was ready for opening on 27 May 1888 and from 4 June of that year the Chingford service, which had run to Highgate Road from 1 August 1885, was extended to Gospel Oak.

There was no physical junction at Gospel Oak until 1916 and, although plans were drawn and it has been stated in one or two historical articles written many years afterwards that a junction was made in 1868, there is no contemporary evidence to support this; in fact, as stated above, there is ample evidence that no junction existed until 1916.

(A) *JRCHS* 18, 4, pp.93–94 (10/1972)

* [Although some brickwork had been constructed in 1868, no turntable was in fact installed. The Southend trains were worked by tank engines – Editor]

(vi) On the Great Northern Railway and its Predecessors

A Defunct Railway Station: Mill Hill (The Hale) – 1

THE Edgware, Highgate & London Railway was opened on 11 August 1867 from Finsbury Park (then called Seven Sisters Road) to Edgware with intermediate stations at Crouch End, Highgate, East End Finchley, Finchley & Hendon and Mill Hill. The line was single between Highgate and Edgware, but the Dollis viaduct was constructed for a double line. The High Barnet line was opened 1 April 1872, and from that date the Edgware section was (with some exceptions) worked by a short train from and to Finchley. This train was replaced by a steam railcar on and from 19 February 1906.

The station at Mill Hill, situated at the foot of Bittacy Hill, was fairly convenient for the village, Mill Hill Broadway at that time being just a country lane. Some time after the opening of the Midland Railway in 1868 the village gradually extended towards the Midland station (now called Mill Hill Broadway) and the Great Northern constructed a halt nearby with entrance from Bunns Lane. This halt consisted of a wooden platform with a small shelter and booking office on the platform. It was opened on 11 June 1906, and at first named The Hale, but renamed Mill Hill (The Hale) 1 March 1928, Mill Hill station being renamed Mill Hill East at the same time. For a time the booking office at The Hale was not in use, tickets to a limited number of destinations being issued by the guard of the railcar. The latter, however, proved unsatisfactory, and the branch was again worked by a short train, and bookings generally put into operation, tickets being obtained at the office.

Under the London Railway Scheme 1935 [the 1935–40 New Works Programme – Editor], the line was to be doubled and electrified, and some engineering work was done, but soon after the out-

break of war operations were suspended. The passenger service was entirely withdrawn on and from 11 September 1939 and a bus service substituted. The booking offices at Mill Hill East, Mill Hill (The Hale) and Edgware remained open and only passengers holding rail tickets were permitted to travel on these buses. Work was, however, resumed on the section Finchley to Mill Hill East and the London Passenger Transport Board ran a service of trains to and from Mill Hill East as from 18 May 1941, the trains running on a single line from a point a short distance west of Finchley Central station. From this date the buses ran only between Mill Hill East and Edgware, and the booking office on the platform at Mill Hill (The Hale) was finally closed. The ticket stock was transferred to the LMS station and tickets issued as formerly to most London Transport stations as well as to many Great Northern stations. At Edgware the issue of tickets at the Great Northern station ceased as from 14 April 1940, all booking being transferred to the London Transport station from this date. Henceforth the tickets at both Edgware and Mill Hill East, although headed LNER were of London Transport type and supplied by the Board (except some main line, etc., bookings). The tickets from Mill Hill (The Hale) continued to be supplied by the London & North Eastern and were of the usual type issued by that railway. This continued until nationalization, when tickets at all three stations were supplied by the London Transport Executive.

A few years after the closing of the defunct station at The Hale, the wooden steps leading to the platform being in a dangerous condition, the whole structure was removed. Today, it is not easy to see where the station was, but nevertheless one can still purchase at Mill Hill Broadway tickets, printed as from Mill Hill (The Hale) and headed London Transport, to nearly all stations on that system,

43. Mill Hill for The Hale station, L&NER about 1936, looking east. The bridge under the LM&SR Midland main line out of St Pancras can be seen in the background (right). The wooden platform and building enjoy a mixture of gas and paraffin lighting. *Anon/Collection Nick Howell*

available by bus to Mill Hill East thence by train. In Mill Hill village one can still see signs made of iron and erected many years ago by the Hendon Urban District Council reading: 'To the Great Northern Station' or 'To the Midland Station'.

Except that Mill Hill (The Hale) is shown on the public list of fares, the facility of obtaining tickets at Mill Hill Broadway station is not advertised and is not widely known, but the facility was given in detail in the L&NER suburban time-tables until nationalization.

When the electric train service to Mill Hill East was started in 1941, the buses ceased to be restricted to holders of rail tickets, and passengers could also pay the fare to the conductor. As the bus route was longer than the railway it was cheaper (except of course for short stages) to buy a ticket at the railway booking office. The anomaly terminated when, on and from 16 September 1951, the buses took a shorter route by way of a road recently constructed by the Hendon Borough Council.

British Railways (Eastern Region) still run goods trains to Mill Hill and Edgware. The issue of tickets to Great Northern stations ceased when the section between Finsbury Park and Alexandra Palace was closed for passenger traffic on 5 July 1954.

(A) *JRCHS* 5, 2, pp.25–27 (3/1959)

Mill Hill (The Hale) – 2

ABOUT THE TIME that LT trains began to run to Mill Hill East, all passenger business, except parcels, was dealt with at the LT station at Edgware and rail tickets were available by any bus running thence to Mill Hill East. To save people going on to the platform at The Hale a hut was erected in Bunns Lane for the sale of tickets, but a few months later these were issued at the London Midland station, Mill Hill Broadway. The old buildings at The Hale were then removed. This facility was duly recorded in the L&NER timetables, but after nationalization no mention was made at Mill Hill that such tickets could be obtained and the number of people applying decreased year by year. In almost all cases a road-rail ticket represented a reduction compared with the separate fares. The range of bookings from The Hale was curtailed in 1968, and all road-rail tickets were withdrawn on and from Sunday 7 September 1969 after almost exactly thirty years.

In 1951 a new road had been opened which enabled the buses to take a shorter route. Edgware ceased to deal with parcels in 1961 and the old Great Northern station buildings were demolished in that year. The line was officially closed to all traffic on and from 1 June 1964, but tickets, still printed Mill Hill (The Hale), continued to be

44. The L&NER (ex GNR) terminus at Edgware, looking north, about 1937 with N2 0-6-2T 4742 on a Finchley Church End train. Staff are more conspicuous than paying customers, the adjacent station of the 1924 tube extension having drawn off virtually all the passenger traffic.
Anon. Collection Nick Howell

issued for another five years. Only very short notice of withdrawal was given, with the result that few people, if any, managed during the last week to secure tickets for retention.

(L) *U* 8, II, 171–172 (11/1969)

The Edgware Branch of the GNR

As there appears to be some doubt about the early history of the Edgware branch it might be as well to place the following information on record. This has been extracted from Reports of the Engineer of the Great Northern Railway. The line was intended to be double throughout and the tunnels, the Dollis viaduct and most of the bridges were so constructed. When opened the branch was double track to the west end of the west tunnel at Highgate, approximately on the site of Park Junction. Thence to Edgware the line was single, apparently without any passing place. Double line was extended to East Finchley on 1 December 1867, and to Finchley (now Finchley Central) on 1 November 1869. At first passengers to and from the down platform at East Finchley crossed on the level; a subway, the present one, was brought into use in 1873.

(L) *JRCHS* 16, 2, p.44 (4/1970)

The Hertford, Luton & Dunstable Railway

MANY MEMBERS will recollect that when there were passenger services between Hatfield and Hertford and between Hatfield and Dunstable the trains ran on independent single lines on the east and west sides respectively of the Great Northern main lines. This was not, however, always the case.

The Hertford & Welwyn Junction Railway was incorporated in 1854. It was opened on 1 March 1858 from a junction with the Eastern Counties at Hertford to a junction with the Great Northern at Welwyn Junction where two platforms had been erected. The Company were granted running powers to Ware and the line was worked by the EC and GN Railways. The terminal station of the EC was at that time to the east of the present Hertford East station and the single line to Welwyn Junction was a continuation of the Eastern Counties line. In addition to some goods trains the EC probably worked some passenger trains from their station. The GN station at Cowbridge, Hertford, was certainly in use in 1858 and may have been opened at the same time as the line. Cole Green and Hertingfordbury appear in the timetables for December 1858 but may have been opened earlier.

Meanwhile, in 1855 the Luton Dunstable &

45. Finchley Church End station L&NER (ex GNR), looking north, about 1938. An Edgware train is standing in the platform at the left whilst a King's Cross train ex High Barnet is entering the main Up platform. Curiously this station survives with very little alteration from what is seen here, but with tube trains, under the guise of Finchley Central, Northern Line. *Anon/Collection Nick Howell*

Welwyn Junction Railway obtained its Act and the section from the junction with the London & North Western Railway at Dunstable to Luton was opened for certain classes of goods on 22 March 1858, all classes on 5 April and for passengers 3 May 1858. This portion was worked temporarily by the L&NW. The section between Luton and Welwyn Junction was opened on 1 September 1860 and worked by the GN between Dunstable and Hatfield. Additional stations were opened at Dunstable, Church Street (later Dunstable Town) on 1 October 1860 and Ayot on 2 July 1877.

In 1858, however, an Act had been obtained to amalgamate the two local companies under the title of Hertford Luton & Dunstable Railway. The intention being to connect the two lines by an overbridge across the GN just north of Welwyn Junction station. This was abandoned after some earthworks had been commenced. An embankment can still be seen. All trains now run through to Hatfield and the platforms at Welwyn Junction closed and demolished. The EC officially gave up their right to run over the Hertford section as from 19 October 1860 and the GN purchased the HL&D in 1862 by authority of Act of 1861.

The GN main line was double track and the Luton branch rose sharply from the junction, which was approximately on the site of the present Welwyn Garden City station. To help them up the incline drivers frequently took the junction and curve at a speed rather too high for safety and it was therefore decided to make an independent single line on the west side and to remove the points at the junction. The new single line from Hatfield was brought into use in December 1868, and the points removed in January 1869. Distances for charging purposes, however, continued to be calculated via Welwyn Junction until 1875. A similar course was adopted in the case of the Hertford trains and a single line on the east side of the main line was brought into use on 3 July 1876 and the points removed in October 1876, the junction being closed entirely. It was soon found necessary to divide the block section Hatfield to Welwyn station (now Welwyn North) and a signal cabin was erected just by the 20th mile post and the cabin was so named. With the continuing increase of traffic another cabin was provided on the opposite side of the railway, one being for up trains and the other for down trains. These cabins also signalled the branch trains, but they were not train staff posts.

Further alterations soon became necessary and in order to provide an up slow line for main line trains the Hertford single line was reconstructed to the east and brought into service in October 1882; the line constructed in 1876 became the up slow line. As, however, the GN in common with some other railways did not like facing points in main lines the physical connexion was well to the south of Digswell viaduct by means of a back shunt. In October 1885 a facing junction at Digswell was opened just south of the viaduct.

Later a similar situation arose on the down side. The Dunstable single line was resited to the west and brought into service on 27 September 1896, when the former line became the down slow; it was extended to Digswell in 1897.

A platform was erected on the Dunstable branch at Welwyn Garden City and opened on 16 August 1920. The main line station was opened on 20 September 1926 and the platform on the branch removed. The branch services continued to run through to Hatfield but called at Welwyn Garden City station. There were no physical connexions but later a junction with the Hertford line was made north of the station and the branch trains terminated at Welwyn Garden City. The single line to Hatfield became the up goods line from September 1944. With the opening of the line from Cuffley to Hertford the trains were diverted to the new station and Cowbridge closed to passengers from 2 June 1924. The Hertford branch passenger service was withdrawn from 18 June 1951.

For many years there had been through passenger trains between Leighton Buzzard and Luton; these were L&NW trains. The passenger service between Hatfield and Dunstable was withdrawn from 26 April 1965. Goods traffic, however, continued on both branches and to facilitate working at Hertford East a facing junction was installed and brought into use on 18 May 1958. The curve from Hertford North to Cowbridge became disused in 1963 and the branch virtually ceased to be a through route in 1964. Portions were removed in 1965 and the branch was officially closed from 13 March 1967.

On the Dunstable branch through traffic ceased at the end of 1965. A new junction with the Mid-land at Luton was brought into use on 2 January 1966 to serve goods depots on the GN line. This enabled the centre of the branch to be closed from the same date. A physical junction at Welwyn Garden City was installed in May 1966 but the only regular trains were those conveying London house and factory refuse to Blackbridge sidings (between Ayot and Wheathampstead); these were withdrawn from 24 May 1971. Both branches are now closed, except a section at the Luton end, and most of the track, including the additional lines to Hatfield, has been removed.

Since this was set in type additional information has come to light from a contemporary OS map. It would appear that provision was made for two additional lines to the east of the main line, and when the line of 1876 was laid, space was left for the up slow line which was completed in 1882. If such was the case it would not have been necessary to resite the Hertford single line.

(A) *JRCHS* 19, 2, pp.48–50 (7/1973)

Hatfield and Stevenage Stations

WHEN THE Great Northern Main Line was constructed Hatfield, Welwyn (now Welwyn North) and Stevenage stations were ordinary road-side stations, with side platforms. Hitchin, however, had centre up and down tracks, the platforms being set back. Presumably this was because the Royston & Hitchin line was also under construction and a railway from Leicester to Hitchin was contemplated. Knebworth station was opened for goods in 1883 and passengers on 1 February 1884. There were level crossings at the north end of both Hatfield and Stevenage stations.

As stated in the *Journal* for July 1973 a branch to Hertford was opened in 1858 and one to Luton in 1860, the branch trains starting from Hatfield from 1860. It was soon found necessary to improve facilities at the latter place. A footbridge connecting the platforms was erected in 1859, and separate platforms were provided for the branch trains; this work was completed in 1862. When a branch to St Albans was under construction in 1864 it was decided to resite the down platform westwards as an island platform, the west face thereof, usually called the 'back platform', being for the branch trains. This work was virtually completed by the time of the opening of the St Albans branch on 16 October 1865. The level crossing mentioned above was abolished and a bridge erected in 1865 carrying the St Albans–Hertford Road. These alterations gave two up and one down line between the platforms, as at present. However at that time the GN had strong objections to facing points in main lines and up trains calling at Hatfield were obliged to shunt to the original up platform. To obviate this as far as possible a narrow platform was made in 1879 between the two up lines, this being connected to the original up platform by two movable gangways across the original up line.

An additional up line to Potters Bar was completed in 1872 and the Board of Trade authorized the use of this line for passenger trains in 1879 providing all level crossings between Hatfield and Potters Bar were replaced by bridges and the practice of backing up trains abolished. The bridges were duly erected and a road diverted to an existing bridge, but the GN still objected to facing points and setting back continued when it was necessary to clear the up main line. A bay at the south end of the station was brought into use about the same time.

An independent single line for Dunstable trains had been brought into use in 1868 and another for Hertford trains in 1876. A down goods line from Potters Bar was constructed 1883–7 and the portion Marshmoor to Hatfield was brought into service on 17 September 1883; this line passed to the west of the station clear of the platform. Another portion, Hawkshead to Marshmoor, was opened in 1886 and completed from Potters Bar 14 March 1887. The position on the down side remained static for many years; through trains from London to any of the branches had to shunt, but up branch trains could run through.

On the up side the GN eventually agreed on 1 April 1892 to provide a facing connexion from the up main to the up platform line and to the removal of the narrow platform mentioned above. I have not been able to trace when this work was actually carried into effect but it was probably completed by the end of 1892. For many years the canopy over the up platform extended over the up platform line; the extended portion was, however, removed about 1921.

On 5 October 1941 the western platform line was connected at the south end to the down goods line which became the down slow line; this gave through running on that line from Potters Bar to Welwyn Garden City and to the Dunstable and St Albans branches. The Hertford trains were curtailed at Welwyn Garden City with effect from 17 September 1944 and the single line became the up goods line. This line and the Dunstable single line were put out of action on 20 February 1966 by the collapse of the bridge carrying the Great North Road over the railway north of the station; this bridge is now available only for pedestrians.

For many years there were four signal boxes at Hatfield; the number was reduced to three in 1920 and to two in 1969.

The station was almost entirely rebuilt in 1972 on the same site. The two bays on the up side, one facing north, the other south, were abolished in 1970.

The original entrance to Stevenage station was on the level direct to the up platform. Passengers crossed to the down platform on the level; apparently there was no footbridge until 1882. A level crossing at the north end of the station was replaced by a bridge prior to 1881 as a bridge is shown on an OS map dated that year. This bridge was reconstructed in connexion with the rebuilding of the station. There were also several road and footpath crossings to the south of the station.

Stevenage station was rebuilt in 1898 practically on the same site with two island platforms and the entrance at the north end, with stairways to the platforms. (The original entrance had been towards the south end.) The down side was completed and the down slow line through the station was brought into service on 28 March 1898. The up side, including the up slow line through the station, together with the main station buildings were completed later in 1898.

All the level crossings were abolished by 1906 and replaced by bridges, or road or footpath diverted to existing bridges.

A new station, about one mile south of the old, was completed in 1973. The last train to call at the old station was the 1.10 down train in the early morning of Monday, 23 July 1973, the new station being opened for the 5.40 up train that day.

(A) *JRCHS* 20, 1, pp.13–15 (3/1974)

Hitchin Station

Mr Hall is correct in suggesting that there is very little of the original building at Hitchin station still standing, but he would appear to be under a misapprehension regarding the widening of the line through the station as it is understood that there were always four tracks between the platforms. The station was probably so constructed to accommodate the Royston & Hitchin line trains which began running in the same year as the Great Northern. In 1859 the Great Northern Board authorized the construction of a footbridge connecting the platforms, and from the dimensions given it is obvious that there were then four tracks. Early photographs also show four tracks between the platforms.

The entrance buildings including the whole of the down side were reconstructed, and the footbridge replaced by a subway. The work began in 1910 and completed in 1911. Much of the up side has also been altered from time to time and there cannot be much of the original work remaining.

(L) *JRCHS* 18, 2, p.45 (4/1972)

Three Counties Station

On the Great Northern main line there was a station called Three Counties. This was in Arlesey parish but served a mental hospital (formerly called a lunatic asylum) in the adjoining parish of Stotfold, Bedfordshire. The asylum was jointly owned by Bedfordshire, Hertfordshire and Huntingdonshire, hence its name. Tickets to and from Three Counties also bore the word 'Station', presumably to indicate they did not include admission to the asylum!

(L) *JRCHS* 19, 4, p.89 (12/1973)

Sawbridgeworth

The Northern & Eastern Railway was opened from Harlow to a temporary terminus at Spelbrook on Monday 22 November 1841. (Some records give Tuesday 23 November, but it would appear to be most probable that passengers were first conveyed on the Monday.)

The intermediate station, Sawbridgeworth, was at a level (or surface) crossing and here was the boundary between Hertfordshire and Essex. The station buildings were on the down side and being south of the crossing were actually in the parish of Sheering, Essex. Early maps do not show a platform or buildings on the up side and so one cannot say where up trains actually stopped. In the early days platforms were not always provided at small stations. In 1846 the Company authorized the construction of platforms at this and certain other stations.

In 1883 the main passenger buildings were constructed on the down side north of the crossing and were therefore in Herts, and a short up platform is shown on the south side of the crossing in Essex. The old station buildings were used as goods offices. The goods station therefore remained in Essex until it was closed on 18 April 1966.

In 1960 in connexion with electrification a new up platform of full length was erected opposite the down platform. The passenger station is now entirely in Herts. Recently the buildings of 1883 were demolished and replaced by modern buildings on the same site. The work was begun on 1 May 1972, and a new ticket office was brought into use on 13 December 1972.

(L) *JRCHS* 19, 4, p.89 (12/1973)

Welwyn's Railways *

The above book was reviewed in the January *RO*. If D.F.C. had spent a little more time in reviewing this publication I think he would have found a considerable number of rather important errors, not just one which he does not name. I was much disappointed.

Several years ago in connexion with another book, I spent several days examining many London, Hertfordshire and Peterborough papers as well as GN official records. These definitely state that all the trains including the expresses ran on the opening day, Wednesday 7th August 1850. The single line for the Hertford trains was in use from 3rd July 1876. Additional tracks were in use from: Hatfield to 20th mile, 27th September 1896; Digswell, 1897 goods; Woolmer Green to Knebworth, 7th May 1894; Knebworth to Woolmer Green, 1869, remodelled 1876; Digswell to Hatfield, 1882 with back-shunt;

facing connexion at Digswell, 1885; passenger to Welwyn Garden City, 1926.

Welwyn station footbridge, 1882. Oakleigh Park station opened Monday 1st December 1873. Dates of some other stations appear to need rechecking. I am asking the authors to issue a list of amendments and additions which I shall be pleased to help; the results may be 100% accurate or nearly so.

(L) *RO* 58, 710, p.197 (4/1988)

* Gladwin, T W; Neville, Peter W; White, Douglas E, *Welwyn's Railways: A History of the Great Northern Line from 1850 to 1986*, Castlemead Publications, 1986.

The History of the Great Northern Railway, Grinling, Edition of 1966 †

MEMBERS may like to note the amendments and additions set out below which have come to notice since this edition was published.

Page 86, line 5. There was no regular passenger traffic between Clarborough and Sykes Junction until 7 August 1850.

Page 91, line 16: 'nine days' to read 'ten days'.
It may be added that the booked time London to Peterborough in August 1850 was 2½ hours, and for a stopping train 4 hours. The trains were accelerated from 1 September 1850.

Page 97, line 10: 'and Shepreth' to read 'at Shepreth'.
line 11: delete 'March 1850'; insert 'opened to Royston 21 October 1850, extended to Shepreth 1 August 1851'.

Page 232, line 7: '1865' to read '1864'.

Page 345, line 9 from foot: 'Norway' to read 'Florida'.

Page 350, line 2: 'about 8.25' to read 'about 8.52'.
bottom line: 'a' to read 'the'.

Page 352. The official report gives four passengers and a guard killed, fifteen passengers and two servants injured...

It was the practice on the NLR at that time when a junction was occupied and a train could not be accepted to return seven beats known in North London code as 'Line obstructed, Permissive block' which meant the junction was occupied or obstructed by permission and the occupation would not be for long. Even if the Great Northern man did consider the seven beats had the same interpret-

ation of Permissive block as in the GN code, he should have stopped the train and cautioned the driver verbally as well as exhibiting a green flag. The Canonbury Junction distant was at clear probably because the derailed vehicles had tightened the wire from the Junction box. The sequel to this accident was the deletion of the words 'Permissive block' from the NL signal of seven beats and the provision of two additional signal boxes, one at each end of the tunnel, that at the north end being named Drayton Park, and the other Highbury Crescent. The latter remained for about thirty years; Drayton Park for about another ten years. With improved signalling these two signal boxes became redundant and were removed.

Page 460, line 5: '1892' to read '1902'.
Page 463, line 6 from foot: 'Nottingham and Leicester' to read 'Sheffield and Lincoln'.
Page 488: Opening Royston to Hitchin: page 86 to read page 97.

(L) *JRCHS* 17, 3, pp.55–56 (7/1971)

† This refers to Grinling, Charles H, *The History of the Great Northern Railway 1845–1922*, with supplementary chapters by H V Borley and C Hamilton Ellis, Allen & Unwin, 1966.

The Railway in Finchley ‡

THIS IS a most interesting book, but unfortunately a few errors have crept in, which will be rectified in the next edition. The date relating to the Canonbury line should presumably read 1872, as the line was opened for goods on 14 December 1874, and for passengers on 18 January 1875, from which date North London passenger trains commenced to run between Broad Street and High Barnet. Great Northern trains ran to Moorgate Street, and did not naturally terminate at Aldersgate Street. The subways at Finsbury Park are approximately in the centre of the platforms.

(L) *JRCHS* 8, 5, p.87 (9/1962)

‡Wilmot, G F A, *The Railway in Finchley*, Finchley Public Libraries Committee, 1962.

(vii) On the Great Central Railway, the Metropolitan & Great Central Joint Railway and the Great Western & Great Central Joint Railway

Metropolitan & Great Central Joint Line

UPON THE FORMATION of the Joint Committee in 1906 the management of the line was assumed for alternate periods of five years, each company supplying its own tickets. Later the Metropolitan and subsequently London Transport supplied all tickets.

As regards the maintenance of the stations and permanent way the Great Central took over permanently all beyond milepost 28½, leaving the London end to the Met. An exception was Aylesbury, which had always been under GW control for maintenance, but in 1907 this station also passed to the GC.

The full Sunday local service ran on 3 March 1963. The last train to Calvert, Finmere etc. therefore was on Sunday 3 March. Quainton Road has been closed on Sundays for the past few years.

(L) *U* 2, 5, p.53 (5/1963)

Princes Risborough

THE RECENT ALTERATIONS at Princes Risborough whereby all trains are dealt with at the up side of the station provide an opportunity to place on record some details of earlier reconstruction at that place. The existing station is the second one and, with the sidings until recently attached thereto, occupied much of the site of the first station. Whilst the work was in progress temporary arrangements had to be made and it is therefore impracticable to give a definite date for the closure of the original building but it took place in 1904 or very early in 1905. The present station was virtually complete early in that year except for the through running lines which had been laid by the time the Great Central main line goods trains started running in November 1905.

It may be added that the new up line was brought into use in September 1904 and worked at first as a single line to enable the old line to be relaid and brought up to main line standards. Double line working throughout between Princes Risborough and High Wycombe began early in 1905.

(L) *JRCHS* 15, 4, p.86 (10/1969)

Signal Boxes

THE NAME OF the signal box between Amersham and Great Missenden should read Mantles Wood.

There was a box on the GCR named Willesden; it was at the north end of Willesden Green station. This may have been a Great Central box and replaced Mapesbury. There was also one called Brent South, at the south end of Neasden sidings; this was probably a Metropolitan box, and was I think provided a little later than Brent North. Brent South was replaced by a GC box, Neasden Junction South, when the High Wycombe line was opened.

During construction of the GCR there were small temporary Met boxes at West Hampstead and St John's Wood Road.

Quainton Road Junction box was abolished

and the points worked electrically from the Station box with effect from 27 November 1921. This was the first British example of remote operation of points. The installation is fully described in *The Railway Gazette*, 8 September 1922.

On the District Railway, Sion College*, although not dismantled, was not in general use in more recent years. After extension east from Mansion House trains cleared quicker than previously.

As regards the working conditions in the signal boxes, I believe the men worked 10 hours a day in some boxes and eight hours in others. The atmospheric conditions were not too bad; the worst was probably the Midland Railway box on the curve towards Camden Road. The access to this box was by a spiral staircase at the west side of St Pancras Station.

(L) *U* 14, 3, p.70 (6/1976)

* [Just east of Blackfriars station – Editor]

Brent North Junction S.B.

THE LINE from Harrow South Junction to Canfield Place was constructed by the Metropolitan Railway for Great Central trains. The Metropolitan erected five signal boxes: Preston Road, Brent North, Brent South, Willesden, and Canfield Place. Except the first-named these boxes signalled only the lines used by the Great Central.

Preston Road was only a temporary structure pending completion of the widening north of that place; Brent South was replaced by a Great Central Box at the junction some little time before the opening of the High Wycombe line. Willesden Box was removed when automatic signalling was installed. Canfield Place was closed at the same time, but retained for emergency working.

The physical junction at Brent North was removed in November 1965.

(L) *U* 6, 5, p.70 (5/1967)

THIS SIGNAL BOX, constructed by the Metropolitan Railway for Great Central lines, is now definitely closed and will be dismantled. The up line junction home and distant signals of Neasden South Box have been resited further from the junction points. The effective date was I understand Sunday 21 May 1967.

(L) *U* 6, 8, p.126 (8/1967)

An Incident at Northwood Hills

THE Question and Answer on page 595 of *Underground News* 203 reminds me of an incident at Northwood Hills some years ago when BR main line trains were hauled by steam locomotives.

I had just missed a southbound Met train one evening when all lights suddenly went out, and the train I had just missed came to a stop. Fortunately, the tail lamp was lit by battery or oil. The station being in total darkness, the staff, apparently three, brought some oil lamps from the lamp room. A British Railways express was approaching at full speed and I began to expect a collision as the station staff took no action. Fortunately, however, the driver realised something was wrong and braked, bringing the train to a stand a short distance behind the Met train. The BR guard came back and spoke to the stationman and then rejoined his train. Lights came on again in about an hour.

(L) *UN* 205, p.11 (1/1979)

Great Central Coal Trains to Neasden

A TIMETABLE of coal trains to Neasden to operate from Monday 25 July 1898 was agreed between the Great Central and Metropolitan Railways, as follows:

	MX	MX		
Woodford	0110	0310	0450	1000
Quainton Road Junction (pass)	0227	0427	0606	1117
Neasden		0420	0620	0759	1310

Note 'MX' – Mondays excepted.

Times were also agreed for the return of empty trucks.

Although the first two trains were Mondays excepted, the GC most unwisely sent a train forward approximately in the times of the first train; whether the Met signalman at the junction actually accepted the train is not known. As stated in *Great*

Central by George Dow, it was refused admission on to the Metropolitan line and was hauled back to Calvert later, on the up line, by another engine which arrived, presumably with a wrong-line order.

It is improbable that the GC men had sufficient knowledge of the road to Neasden, but the Met would naturally want an Inspector or Pilotman on the first train and there was no such person at Quainton Road. It is improbable that the signal boxes were manned. Aylesbury was then under Great Western control.

Both GC and Met records state that the service began on Tuesday 26 July 1898. The engine carried one white light at the base of the chimney and one at the middle of the buffer beam. A speed limit of 5 mph was imposed at Quainton Road Junction as the layout was not favourable to the Great Central.

(L) *UN* 234, pp.143–144 (6/1981)

Marylebone and Chesham Service

THE Great Central Railway commenced a through service between Marylebone and Chesham on 1 March 1906 and for several years there was a small number of through trains on weekdays and Sundays. In later years the service was reduced and was temporarily suspended for a few months in 1951.

In the last few years the only train (weekdays only) was a passenger parcels train. This was withdrawn with effect from Monday 16 October 1967.

(L) *UN* 234, p.142 (6/1981)

LNER Platform at Neasden

I REMEMBER this platform at Neasden and used it on two occasions. For some little time during World War 2, all access to Marylebone station was blocked by enemy action. Great Central Aylesbury line trains and most main line trains terminated and returned from Harrow-on-the-Hill. High Wycombe line trains terminated at Neasden GC.

Newspapers were not permitted to give details of altered train services; passengers only knew when they reached the station. The ticket office at Marylebone continued to issue tickets. Passengers

for the Aylesbury line were told to go by Bakerloo Line to Baker Street (or walk); those for High Wycombe line for a few days were told to go to Sudbury Hill, Piccadilly Line, and join GC trains from the adjacent station. A temporary platform was quickly constructed by the up GC line at Neasden, access to which was by a temporary footpath from the Metropolitan Line northbound through line platform.

Great Central tickets could not be obtained at Baker Street, nor at Neasden. Passengers arriving at Baker Street without tickets had to buy one at Neasden, the GC fare being usually collected on the train. Many agreements on railways and elsewhere were temporarily set aside during the war.

(L) *UN* 278 p.18 (2/1985)

I CONFIRM that there was only one timber platform at Neasden for the LNER trains to the High Wycombe line. I travelled from Neasden to West Ruislip. The platform was on the 'up' side and the train crossed to the down line soon after leaving. Tickets were issued on the train.

(L) *UN* 302 p.22 (2/1987)

Great Central, George Dow*

I HAVE HAD some correspondence with Mr Dow, and members of the Society may like to note the following:

Vol. 2, p.281: Quainton Road station. This photograph was taken in 1899 or 1900. The road bridge in the background was constructed in 1898-9. Previously there had been a level crossing; this was finally closed by certificate of the Justices issued 11 October 1899.

Vol. 3, p.3: The tube entrance was opened as stated, but the Bakerloo station had been opened the previous day. At that time there was also an entrance direct from the street.

Vol. 3, p.201, line 11: 'three' to read 'two'.
      line 16: Delete 'and at Akeman Street'.

Vol. 3, p.345, para. 4: The installation at Quainton Road Junction was brought into use on 27 November 1921 (*Railway Gazette*, 8 September 1922). The words 'early part of 1923' relate to the information given in paragraph 3.

(L) *JRCHS* 12, 2, p.33 (4/1966)

MEMBERS who have copies of Mr Dow's volumes, *Great Central*, may like to note a small correction in connexion with the opening of the line for coal traffic to Quainton Road and Neasden. [Vol. 2, pp.305–306. – Editor]

The timetable agreed with the Metropolitan provided for four coal trains daily, but two of these timed to reach Quainton Road in the early morning were definitely 'Mondays excepted' and the Great Central certainly would not try to run these trains on 25 July 1898 which was a Monday.

The paragraph in Dow's book is correct except that he appears to be mistaken in the date and the train. The Great Central agreed with the Great Western to begin a goods and coal service to Aylesbury and the GW line on Saturday 30 July 1898

but as the Metropolitan declined to agree, it was this train that Mr Bell, the Metropolitan Manager, sent back in the early hours of that day, presumably the GC sent an engine with a 'wrong line order' to Quainton Road Junction.

Aylesbury was at that time under GW control, but owing to opposition by the Metropolitan, this service did not begin until 20th March 1899.

(L) *UN* 258, pp.118–119 (6/1983)

* Dow, George, *Great Central: Volume 2: Dominion of Watkin 1864–1899*, Ian Allan, *1962*, and *Great Central: Volume 3: Fay Sets The Pace 1900–1922*, Ian Allan, 1965.

[See also letter, 'Great Central Coal Trains to Neasden', p.106.]

(viii) On the Metropolitan, Metropolitan & St John's Wood, Metropolitan District, East London, and Whitechapel & Bow Joint Railways

The Broad Gauge on the Metropolitan Railway

THE Metropolitan Railway was constructed as a mixed gauge line from Paddington (Bishops Road) to Farringdon Street and opened for public traffic on 10 January 1863. The line was worked by Great Western broad gauge stock. The terminus at Farringdon Street was a little to the south-west of the present station, at the corner of Farringdon Road and Charles Street (now called Cowcross Street). Difficulties soon arose between the two companies, and the Great Western gave notice that they would withdraw their trains on the evening of 30 September 1863. The Metropolitan had already ordered some engines and carriages, and these were expected to arrive by the date given by the Great Western. The latter then advised the Metropolitan that their trains would be withdrawn on the evening of Monday 10 August 1863. A physical connexion with the Great Northern had recently been made, and the Metropolitan were able to borrow rolling stock from that railway, and the standard gauge trains started running on the morning of Tuesday 11 August 1863. There was therefore no interruption of the service except for some minor derailments at the terminal stations owing to the standard gauge rails, which had not previously been used, being slightly out of gauge.

On 5 August 1863 it was reported that arrangements had been made with the Great Western for taking over the staff, stores, etc., and for the use of

Bishops Road station. On 12 August it was reported that an indemnity had been signed with the Great Western for the continued use of that Company's tickets.

The extension of the railway to Moorgate Street was authorized as a four-track system from a point near Clerkenwell Road bridge, the northern pair of lines to be standard gauge and the southern pair (the present Widened lines) to be mixed gauge. Meanwhile, the Great Western, on 1 October 1863, commenced to run some through broad gauge trains between Windsor and other suburban stations and the City. These trains were discontinued at the end of December 1863, but were resumed on 2 May 1864. The Metropolitan standard gauge trains were extended to Moorgate Street on 23 December 1865, and the Widened lines (mixed gauge) were opened to Aldersgate Street on 1 March 1866, and to Moorgate Street on 1 July 1866, the Great Western trains being extended to those stations on the dates named.* Some accounts give the opening to Aldersgate Street as 6 March 1866, but the Metropolitan records state the Widened lines were to be opened for Great Western trains on 1 March, and there is no record of any postponement. Some records also state that the Great Western trains ran beyond Farringdon Street on dates prior to those given, but this was impracticable as the main lines east of Farringdon Street were not constructed to take the broad gauge. The error was probably due to the rather ambiguous way in which the trains were shown in the timetables.

The Hammersmith line was opened 13 June 1864, and the line to Kensington (Addison Road) on 1 July 1864, both being mixed gauge and trains

[* GWR broad gauge trains used Farringdon Street old Station until February 1866 – Editor]

being divided at Notting Hill (now Ladbroke Grove); the up trains being combined at that place. From 1 April 1865 the Metropolitan provided the Hammersmith service (standard gauge) and the Great Western the Kensington trains (broad gauge). These trains ran from and to Aldersgate Street and Moorgate Street at the respective dates given above.

It would appear that the last broad gauge train on the Metropolitan Railway ran on Sunday 14 March 1869, after which date the Great Western worked their services with standard gauge trains. From 1 June 1869 the Great Western normally used the main lines, leaving the Widened lines for the trains of the Great Northern and London, Chatham & Dover Railways. The Great Northern trains had commenced to run to Farringdon Street on 1 October 1863 and to Moorgate Street 1 June 1869. The London, Chatham & Dover trains started to run to King's Cross (GN) via the Metropolitan Railway on 1 January 1866. The Widened

lines (standard gauge) between King's Cross and Farringdon Street were opened for traffic on 17 February 1868.

The Metropolitan was extended to Liverpool Street Great Eastern Railway station on 1 February 1875. Only the Hammersmith trains ran to Liverpool Street where they had the use of one platform, apparently the present no.1 platform, the Great Eastern having laid only a single line through the connecting tunnel. When Bishopsgate Metropolitan station was opened on 12 July 1875 the Metropolitan trains ceased to run into the Great Eastern station and, although a double line was subsequently laid to the present platforms 1 and 2, the connecting line was never used for regular traffic, although from time to time consideration was given for through services from Hammersmith or Richmond to Forest Gate, Walthamstow, North Woolwich or the East London line. The junction was taken out in 1907 and the connecting line subsequently removed entirely. Bishopsgate Metropolitan station was renamed

46. Broad gauge trials late in 1861 with 'Fowler's Ghost', the unsuccessful 'smokeless' and condensing broad gauge prototype 2-4-0 loco for the new Metropolitan Railway, just east of Edgware Road station, looking east to what is now Cosway Street bridge. Trucks belonging to the contractor, Smith & Knight, are occupied by invited guests of both sexes, including at least two young boys. *RCHS/Spence*

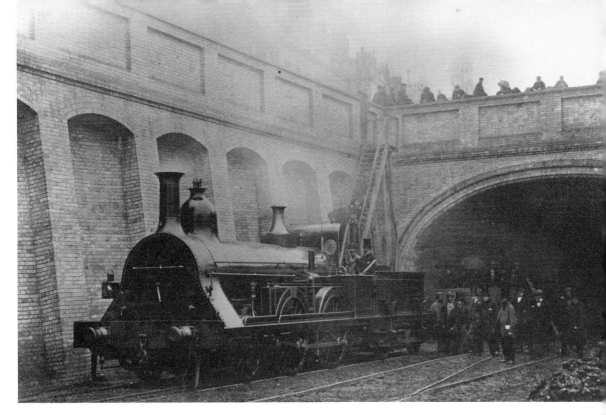

47. 'Fowler's Ghost', is again seen here at Stafford (now Cosway) Street bridge, just east of Edgware Road station, during trials late in 1861. *RCHS/Spence*

Liverpool Street 1 November 1909.

In 1876, the Metropolitan Railway was extended to Aldgate, where there were four terminal roads serving two island platforms. From 18 November 1876 a local service was provided from and to Bishopsgate. This must have resulted in considerable congestion at Bishopsgate where there were only three lines (as now), and it is not clear why this temporary method was adopted. On 4 December 1876, through working to and from Aldgate commenced, the Hammersmith, Inner Circle and Middle Circle trains running to and from that place. The Great Western Kensington trains had been extended to Mansion House on 1 August 1872, forming the Middle Circle.

The Great Western trains from Windsor, etc. ran to and from Bishopsgate from 12 July 1875, but when the line was extended to Aldgate the Great Western trains (other than the Middle Circle) were curtailed at Moorgate Street.

(A) *JRCHS* 4, 2, pp.23–25 (3/1958)

Metropolitan Railway Headcodes

ENGINES carried headlights denoting the service:

Inner Circle trains: One white light on buffer beam.
Hammersmith trains: One white and one blue light on buffer beam.
Richmond trains: Two white lights on buffer beam.
GW Main Line trains: One white and one blue light vertically, also a white disc with a blue cross.
Middle Circle trains: Two white lights vertically and a white disc.
District local trains to West Brompton: Two white lights on buffer beam and a blue disc.
Outer Circle L&NW trains: Two white lights diagonally and a loop on one side of funnel and a white diamond disc on other side.
GN and LC&D Ludgate Hill and Victoria trains: Two white lights on buffer beam and a red disc with a black cross.
GN Moorgate Street trains: One white and one blue light on buffer beam and a blue disc with a white cross.

48. The 'Clerkenwell Grid-Iron', looking north towards King's Cross, from Farringdon.
The top bridge carries Clerkenwell Road, the middle one the 1863 Metropolitan Railway and the tracks at the bottom are the 'City Widened Lines' of 1868, owned by the Metropolitan; the entrance to the Clerkenwell tunnel on these lines is seen just beyond the bridge carrying the Metropolitan Railway.
From a contemporary steel engraving

49. The King's Cross Junction of the Metropolitan Railway, looking west. At the extreme left are the
two mixed gauge tracks of the Metropolitan, with a westbound train; centre, the Midland Railway double line
tunnel from just north of St Pancras station – its Down line also giving access to the Down GNR tunnel
up to King's Cross surface station; and, right, the GNR Up line from York Road.
Steel engraving in 'The Illustrated London News', 8 February 1868

Midland and LC&D Ludgate Hill and Victoria trains:
Two white lights vertically and one white diamond
disc.

*Midland passenger trains to Moorgate Street, also Herne
Hill goods trains:* Two blue lights on buffer beam
and white disc with black cross.

Midland Battersea goods trains: Two blue lights on
buffer beam and one white disc.

Midland trains to Walworth coal sidings: Three blue
lights triangularly and two white discs.

LC&D trains Moorgate Street and Victoria: One white
light and one white disc.

LC&D Moorgate Street and Crystal Palace: Three white
lights triangularly, two white diamond discs
vertically.

All passenger trains carried destination boards on the
engine. Middle Circle trains carried 'Addison Road'
boards, being replaced by 'Aldgate' or 'Mansion
House' boards at Addison Road.

(L) *UN* 231, pp.77–78 (3/1981)

I REMEMBER many years ago an elderly Metropolitan man telling me about destination boards

for special excursions. I think he mentioned
Brighton, Clacton, Yarmouth, although as far as is
known Metropolitan locomotives never reached
those places.

(L) *UN* 292 p.52 (4/1986)

Metropolitan Station Entrances

T HE ENTRANCE to all the original stations Pinner
to Stoke Mandeville was on the street level to
the up platform, access to the down platform being
by footbridge or subway. Northwood had an
additional exit by a slope from the down platform
to Green Lane. However, Northwood was entirely
rebuilt in 1961–62 when the railway was widened.

Requests were made for exits from the down
side of some stations, but these were resisted for
many years. The first to be granted was, I believe,
Chalfont Road in about 1905, followed by Pinner
in about 1913. Chorley Wood was given an
additional exit in 1966 when the goods yard was

50. 0-4-4T no.1 on Ceremonial train, including the two six-wheeled 'Rothschild' saloons, for the opening of the Metropolitan Railway Uxbridge branch. A view at Ruislip station, looking east, 30 June 1904. *RCHS/Spence*

converted into a car park. Amersham was a little earlier, I think, but the down side and exit were reconstructed just prior to electrification. These exits were also entrances for ticket holders, but this was not usually enforced. Pinner was plainly marked 'Closed on Sundays' and this was always adhered to.

(L) *UN* 297, p.123 (9/1986)

Cromwell Curve – Outer Rail

ONE SUNDAY AFTERNOON about the year 1935, I entered South Kensington station intending to make a journey in an easterly direction, when I observed a notice directing passengers for High Street, Kensington, Paddington and Baker Street to the District westbound platform. I therefore decided to proceed westwards to reach the east and so travelled over the Cromwell Curve, thence over the north side of the Circle. The reason was

engineering work on the Metropolitan line between South Kensington and High Street, Kensington.

When the Metropolitan and the District were independent companies, during the period when their relations were not very harmonious, the Circle trains of the District Company used the Cromwell Curve. As the Met trains continued to use the Met lines, passengers were confused. The District Circle trains delayed westbound trains between Earl's Court and Gloucester Road.

(L) *U* 5, 12, pp.180–181 (12/1966)

Metropolitan Railway: Harrow–Uxbridge Line

SOME CONFUSION appears to exist about the opening of this branch. The ceremonial train with decorated engine illustrated in Mr C. E. Lee's book* ran on Thursday 30 June 1904. The branch was opened to the public on Monday 4 July 1904. The first train left Uxbridge at 05.30, while the first train from Harrow left at 06.05, calling at Ruislip (06.15), arriving at Uxbridge at 06.20. This information is clearly given in Metropolitan Railway Minute books, contemporary issues of Harrow and Uxbridge newspapers and *The Railway Magazine*, 1904.

(L) *UN* 234, pp.142–143 (6/1981)

[* This refers to Lee, Charles E, *The Metropolitan Line*, London Transport, 1972, plate 23, in which the wrong date is given in the caption – Editor]

Level Crossings: Aylesbury–Verney Junction

THE DATE of opening of the Aylesbury & Buckingham Railway was 23 September 1868. The road bridge at Quainton Road was brought into use in 1899 but I have not been able to trace the actual date. The level crossing was legally closed 11 October 1899, so the bridge was presumably in use a short time before that date. There are still a fair number of footpath crossings, some public, others existing but not dedicated as rights of way. The footpath crossing between Chalfont & Latimer and Amersham was replaced by a footbridge a short while before electrification.

(L) *UN* 250, p.224 (9/1982)

City Widened Lines

THE LAST OCCASION a full service was worked on a Bank Holiday on the City Widened Lines was on 26 December 1914. New Year's Day was not a Bank Holiday and the service was drastically reduced from 11 January 1915. There may have been a very few trains on some subsequent Bank Holidays.

(L) *UN* 263, p.197 (11/1983)

Ladbroke Grove Siding

LADBROKE GROVE siding was last in general use in 1910. It was used by Great Western steam trains between Ladbroke Grove and Richmond. These were withdrawn wef 1 January 1911. From this date

passengers had to change at Hammersmith. Metropolitan trains to Richmond were withdrawn wef 1 January 1907. The connecting curve at Hammersmith was never electrified.

(L) *UN* 263, p.197 (11/1983)

Quainton Road

FURTHER INFORMATION has recently been traced in the Bucks County Library and the County Council records. The Aylesbury & Buckingham Railway station had only one platform but the line was reconstructed and doubled by the Metropolitan and brought into use as a double line between Aylesbury and Granborough Road on 30 November 1896; it is, therefore, probable that the second station at Quainton Road was brought into use on or about that date. The doubling was completed to Verney Junction on 1 January 1897. The contract for a bridge to replace the level crossing was signed on 29 June 1898 and the certificate of completion was issued on 28 July 1899 and the bridge was probably brought into use the following day and the crossing closed.

Quainton Road station was closed to passenger traffic, the last train calling on Saturday 2 March 1963. The last trains to call on Sundays were: morning trains 14 September 1958; evening down 16 November 1958; evening up train 3 May 1959. These were all Great Central main line trains.

(L) *UN* 291, p.30 (3/1986)

Verney Junction and Brill Branches

THE Aylesbury & Buckingham Railway was worked by train staff and ticket, the only crossing place being Quainton Road. When the Metropolitan doubled the line, normal Metropolitan signalling applied. After the formation of the Joint Committee, the regulations of the Great Central Railway applied, possibly slightly modified. Following the withdrawal of the passenger service, the line between Quainton Road and Verney Junction was reduced to single track, worked by train staff and ticket.

The Brill branch was always 'one engine in

steam' with train staff. In the early years, this branch may have been worked without signalling or other security.

(L) *U* 5, 7, p.100 (7/1966)

Northwick Park

THE ORIGINAL station at Northwick Park consisted of an island platform nearer to the Great Central lines than the present platform is. At that time, the Metropolitan was only double track. The present platform was brought into use in 1931. The subway is a public footpath and was built when the railway was constructed. The original portion, also that under the GC lines, is narrow. The later extensions under the newer Metropolitan lines are considerably wider. If I remember correctly, the original entrance to the station led off this subway and tickets were issued and collected at ground level. For many years after resiting, the ticket barrier was at the foot of the stairs.

(L) *U* 5, 7 p.100 (7/1966)

The Wotton Tramway, by K Jones*

A FEW AMENDMENTS are necessary and the following have been agreed with the author. Members should alter their copies accordingly.

Page 3, line 21: '15 June 1939' to read 'Monday 10 June 1839'.

Page 5, line 7: delete '4 October'. Add 'The last broad gauge train ran on 13 October 1868 and the first standard gauge train ran on 23 October 1868; between these dates, passengers were conveyed by road service.'

Page 48, line 14 from foot: 'Gove House' to read 'Grove House'.

Page 50, penult. para.: The Metropolitan closed many level crossings (mainly farm crossings) but not all. Quainton Road crossing was closed and replaced by a bridge in 1899 (not 1897 as is sometimes stated). last line: '1923' to read '1 October 1922'

Page 51, line 11: The coal trains in 1898 ran only as far as Neasden, not Marylebone.

(L) *U* 13, 11, p.172 (11/1974)

* Jones, Ken, *The Wotton Tramway (Brill Branch),* Oakwood Press, 1974.

Trains to Southern Region via Metropolitan Widened Lines

THE REGULAR SERVICE over the Metropolitan Widened lines to the Southern Region was withdrawn on and from Monday 24 March 1969, the last train being an Eastern Region parcels train Holloway to London Bridge and back late on Sunday evening, 23 March 1969.

The ER freight service and the LM service ceased some time previously.

(L) *U* 9, 1, p.7 (1/1970)

Metropolitan Brake Vans

THE REAR of these vehicles was painted red for very many years, possibly from the opening of the railway. The brake-ends of North London Railway vans and those belonging to a few other railways, having 'train sets' were also red.

(L) *U* 5, 7, p.100 (7/1966)

I AM DEFINITELY of the opinion that the brake-ends of Metropolitan coaches were painted red, prior to electrification (see my previous letter; July issue). From Mr Reed's letter, it would appear that red was discarded in favour of brown and that later red was resumed.

(L) *U* 5, 10, p.147 (10/1966)

The Metropolitan & Saint John's Wood Railway

THE Metropolitan and Saint John's Wood Railway was incorporated by Act of 29 July 1864 to construct a railway from a junction with the Metropolitan at Baker Street to a junction with the Hampstead Junction Railway near Finchley Road Station. The line was opened on 13 April 1868 to Swiss Cottage, with intermediate stations at St John's Wood Road and Marlborough Road.

The Metropolitan station at Baker Street originally had separate entrances on the north and south sides of Marylebone Road at what is now known as Marylebone Circus. The staircases led to the west end of the platforms. There was no connexion between the two platforms, consequently, when the St John's Wood line was built, an overbridge had to be erected; this was placed at the east end of the station.

The St John's Wood line station, generally referred to as Baker Street East, consisted of two rather short platforms. The junction with the Metropolitan was an ordinary double line junction, and the double line continued through the station and for a short distance in the tunnel. There was a double line at each of the stations which extended for a short distance beyond each station and into the tunnel. Swiss Cottage station was mostly underground but the other stations were in open cuttings. About half the length of the tunnel between Baker Street and St John's Wood Road was constructed for a double line but only single track was laid, except at the entrance.

The railway was worked by block telegraph and pilotmen.* The pilotman for the section Baker Street to St John's Wood Road wore a red shoulder belt, and the man for the section thence to Swiss Cottage wore a blue shoulder belt. The only crossing place in normal use was St John's Wood Road, except for a few months in 1868 when it would appear that the trains crossed at Marlborough Road instead. Between Baker Street and St John's Wood Road, the original line is the present down or northbound line; between St John's Wood Road and Swiss Cottage, the up or southbound line is the original. Subsequently, the railway was widened by the construction of single line tunnels parallel to the original ones, and the railway was worked as a double line throughout on and from 10 July 1882.

The line was worked by the Metropolitan, the trains running every 20 minutes between Moorgate Street and Swiss Cottage. In addition, during the summer months, there were local trains Baker Street and Swiss Cottage also every 20 minutes. The through service from Moorgate Street was maintained during 1868 but in February 1869 it was decided to withdraw the through trains from 1 March 1869 and work a regular 10-minute service of local trains. In order that this could be done satisfactorily, certain engineering work at Baker Street was necessary. The work was not, however, completed by 1 March, so the through trains from Moorgate Street

continued to run up to and including 7 March 1869. Commencing 8 March, all passengers to or from the City had to change at Baker Street, the service thence to Swiss Cottage being every 10 minutes.

An Act of 5 August 1873 authorized the extension of the railway westwards to the river Brent, also a junction with the Midland Railway at Finchley Road and a junction with the Hampstead Junction near the Edgware Road (now Kilburn High Road), the section to West Hampstead being opened for traffic on 30 June 1879 and to Walm Lane, Willesden, (also called Willesden Green station) on 24 November 1879. The line from Swiss Cottage to Finchley Road was in tunnel and only the down line was ready when the railway to West Hampstead was opened, the trains being worked by pilotmen.†

The three intermediate stations, Finchley Road, West Hampstead and Kilburn–Brondesbury (renamed Kilburn in 1950), were of the ordinary two-platform type. Double line working commenced 24 November 1879 at the same time as the opening to Willesden Green. The platforms at West Hampstead have been resited twice: firstly at the time the Great Central was under construction, an island platform replacing the two side platforms on 13 June 1897; and this platform was resited northwards on 18 September 1938 in connexion with the extension of the Bakerloo trains.

The Metropolitan and Metropolitan & St John's Wood Companies were authorized by Act of 16 July 1874 to construct the Kingsbury and Harrow Railway. This railway together with the remaining portion of the Metropolitan & St John's Wood line was opened to the public on 2 August 1880 with one intermediate station, Kingsbury–Neasden. Wembley Park station was specially opened on 14 and 21 October 1893 and to regular traffic on 12 May 1894. Two additional platform lines (terminal) were provided but apparently seldom used. Dollis Hill was opened on 1 October 1909 (not 1 November erroneously given in Metropolitan Railway half-yearly report). Preston Road, originally two wooden platforms on the east side of the bridge at which trains stopped by signal, on 21 May 1908, the present station being brought into use on 3 January 1932. Northwick Park was opened 28 June 1923. The original entrance to Harrow-on-the-Hill station was on the south side and at first only the down platform was in use.

---

* See 5/1962 item p.119.   † See 5/1959 item p.119.

The junction with the Midland was brought into use for the exchange of merchandise from 1 October 1880. On 1 January 1894 the Metropolitan opened a small goods station at the point; this was closed on 1 July 1938. Finchley Road ceased to be used as an exchange point as from 6 March 1948. The connexion between the two systems was severed in June 1953 and the Metropolitan sidings removed in February 1955. Neither of the authorized junctions with the Hampstead Junction Railway was constructed.

From time to time the question of constructing a branch to Hendon was given careful consideration but the branch was never made.

The Metropolitan & St John's Wood Railway was absorbed by the Metropolitan by Act of 3 July 1882 when the doubling of the original section was practically complete. [The original section from Baker Street to St John's Wood Road became the down line, and the line thence to Swiss Cottage the up line. The double line was available throughout on 10 July 1882 – Editor] The final meeting of the Board was held on 25 May 1883 and notice was given in the *London Gazette* on 15 June 1883 that the Company was now dissolved. The tickets were headed Metropolitan Railway from the opening of the line; there is no trace of any tickets, labels, etc. headed Metropolitan & St John's Wood Railway.

In 1891–2 Baker Street (East) station was entirely reconstructed at platform level and the over-all roof removed. When completed there was only one through line connecting with the up or eastbound Circle line. There were also two terminal platform lines. There were three platforms connected at the south end by a movable bridge across the through line to facilitate passengers crossing from one platform to another. These arrangements were completed and operated from 14 November 1892.

The new layout at Baker Street made through working to the City difficult but when electrification was completed consideration was given to through working on a small scale. As an experiment a few up trains from Harrow worked through in the morning on weekdays commencing 28 January 1907, but these were withdrawn at the end of March 1907. In 1909 the single line was connected also with the down Circle line, and commencing 1 July 1909 a certain number of trains worked through over the single line in both directions

morning and evening on weekdays. The present double line for through trains with two terminal platform lines was completed and brought into use on 4 November 1912, from which date increased services of through trains were run.

During the period under review, the railway northwards from Baker Street was variously referred to in official records as the St John's Wood line, the Extension line or the Northern line. The railway from Aldgate to Paddington was the Main line.

(L) *JRCHS* 4, 6, pp.106–109 (11/1958)

[Note by C. F. Klapper on the above article, (L) *JRCHS* 5, 1, p.17 (1/1959) – The interesting article on the Metropolitan & Saint John's Wood Railway, in the November 1958 issue, nevertheless made no reference to the Act obtained by the Company on 26 May 1865. According to *Bradshaw's Manual*, this sanctioned an extension of one mile to Hampstead; the new capital was to be £200,000 in shares and £66,000 on loan. By Act of 28 June 1866, the company was authorized to raise £250,000 in shares and £83,000 on loan. Under a further Act (16 July 1868) powers to purchase lands in Hampstead under the original 1864 Act were extended until 1 November 1868, and those for land purchase under the 1865 Act until 1 October 1869. Completion of the Hampstead extension from Swiss Cottage was postponed until 26 July 1871. This Act also refers to contracts with the Midland in respect of a joint station at Finchley Road. Presumably it was difficult to raise the cash for the Hampstead extension on the strength of the early results of the line as far as Swiss Cottage; these do not seem to have provided proper coverage for the preference stock interest. Anyway, yet another Act, passed on 20 June 1870, authorized the abandonment of the extension to Hampstead.

Some work was done on the Hampstead line north of Swiss Cottage; according to Mr H. L. Cottell in *The Railway Magazine* of October 1917, there was a single-line tunnel parallel with Finchley Road which came into the open about the site of the present Finchley Road station. The two single-track tunnels made under the 1873 Act en route to Willesden Green were west of the abandoned one, which was at that time a source of fascination to boys playing in the fields near Swiss Cottage. He also states that the loop at Marlborough Road was taken out in 1874 until the line was doubled throughout in 1882. The change of purpose of this interesting underground line, from a short artery into the elegant suburbs of St John's Wood and Hampstead with connexions to an already successful suburban railway and to the Midland main line, then being built, into the country branch of the Metropolitan which later developed some main line characteristics, makes its early ambitions of particular interest.]

I WOULD LIKE to make it quite clear that when the portion of the railway from Swiss Cottage to West Hampstead was operated as a single line, it was worked as one section by a pilotman but I am unable to trace any reference as to what coloured shoulder belt or other distinctive badge or armlet this man wore.

(L) *JRCHS* 5, 3, p.61 (5/1959)

A DDITIONAL INFORMATION has now come to light, and the article in the *Journal* for November 1958 needs amplifying.
When first opened, the line was worked by train staff and ticket, the sections being:

Baker Street and St John's Wood Road:
round staff, red tickets;
St John's Wood Road and Marlborough Road:
square staff, blue tickets;
Marlborough Road and Swiss Cottage:
triangular staff, yellow tickets.

The colours of the staff, also the boxes in which the tickets were kept, were the same as the colours of the tickets. This method of working apparently only lasted a short while.

(L) *JRCHS* 8, 3, p.49 (5/1962)

[The round staff had a red band, the square a blue band, and the triangular a yellow band. It is probable that working by pilotmen began in 1874 – Editor]

Station Names

B LACKFRIARS was sometimes given as Blackfriars Bridge in early years, but not in *Bradshaw*. No other timetables were then available. Temple was often given as The Temple, as were The Monument and The Tower. No definite date can be given when

Temple lost 'The', but The Monument became Monument in 1902 according to *Bradshaw*.

(L) *UN* 210, p.142 (6/1979)

W HEN THE Central London Railway opened, the Metropolitan naturally lost passengers to the new line, so the Met added suffixes to the name of some stations, but whether these became the official names, is open to question.
In some cases, the names on the maps did not agree with the names in the pages of the timetable, or the name on the tickets, or that of the station nameboards. In such cases, it is difficult to decide the correct full name. I doubt if the correct name of Bayswater in certain years can be decided satisfactorily.
As regards Wood Lane, the suffix '(Exhibition Station)' or '(White City)' was frequently added in notices and on bills etc., as the name 'Wood Lane' conveyed nothing to visitors to London, or even to many Londoners.

(L) *UN* 221, p.170 (5/1980)

Earl's Court and Royal Oak Stations

A SEARCH through various London newspapers including the *Illustrated London News*, also the records of the Railway companies, reveals that both Earl's Court (first station) and Royal Oak were opened for public traffic on Monday 30 October 1871. At that time, Royal Oak had two side platforms. The down platform was removed and the up platform converted to an island platform in 1904 at the time the GWR were widening their line.

(L) *UN* 212, p.218 (8/1979)

Earl's Court Station

T HE DATE OF OPENING of the first station at Earl's Court is frequently given incorrectly. I have recently examined the Minute books of the District and Metropolitan Railways, also several contemporary newspapers, and have established beyond all reasonable doubt that the correct date is Monday 30 October 1871.

(L) *UN* 221, p.168 (5/1980)

T HE FIRST STATION at Earl's Court was opened 30 October 1871; this is in accordance with the Company's Minute books and local newspapers (31 October is sometimes given, but this is wrong). Little is known about this station; it was probably an ordinary District Railway station, constructed mainly of wood, with two side platforms. It is thought to have been on the other side of Earl's Court Road, but may have been just by the junction for Addison Road.

(L) *UN* 223, p.242 (7/1980)

[The above sequence of three letters demonstrates HVB's anxiety that accurate dates be recorded beyond dispute! – Editor]

The South Acton Branch

I HAVE KNOWN South Acton almost since the day the District station was opened and can assure you that there was never more than one platform. The line was doubled just before electrification when the passenger service began. At South Acton station, there was a facing crossover from the eastbound line to a long platform, much of which was overgrown with grass and weeds.

There was a small ticket office on ground floor level; this was closed about 1912 and a notice told passengers to obtain tickets from the signalman on the platform. There were no other staff on duty. On 14 February 1932 the branch was reduced to a single track with automatic signalling. The signalbox was closed and removed, and a small ticket office erected on the platform. The clerk also collected tickets. There were always runaway sidings into a field to prevent runaway vehicles getting on to the 'main line'.

When first opened, the branch was single. Both L&NW and Midland goods trains worked through, usually to Ealing Common; a District Railway pilotman joined the train at the junction. The 'goods' consisted of stores and material for the

District Railway and, except when the South Harrow line was under construction, the trains ran only about once a week. So far as is known, they always worked in the very early hours when there were no passenger trains. The date of the last goods train is not known, probably in 1914. The points at the junction were clipped out of use early in 1915 but retained for emergency use, being finally removed, together with the junction signalbox, in 1930.

(L) *UN* 240, p.315 (12/1981)

I N 1898–99 a sloping embankment was constructed for a double line from Mill Hill Park (later Acton Town) to a junction with the North & South Western Junction Railway, just north of South Acton station. Only one line was laid and there were facing and trailing junctions at each end. The N&SWJ erected a signal cabin named District Junction and the line was opened on 15 May 1899. It was used for materials and stores for the District Company, especially during the construction of the line to South Harrow. These trains were always worked at night (early morning), three trains a week by the L&NWR and three by the Midland Railway. A District Railway pilotman took charge of the train at District Junction. Empty wagons were taken back by the pilotman, from Ealing Common. A few years later, it was decided to run passenger trains. A second line of rails was laid and a long platform built on the south side of the westbound line. Access for passengers was by a short staircase from a small entrance hall with a ticket office. A signal cabin was erected on the platform and a facing crossover from the eastbound line to the platform. The line was electrified and a service began on 13 June 1905 with through trains to South Harrow and Hounslow. About 1913 the ticket office was closed and facilities made for passengers to obtain tickets from the signalman. The trains carrying materials and stores continued as required, becoming less and less frequent.

As passenger trains were short, a large part of the platform became overgrown with grass and weeds. There were runaway catch points, also much overgrown. The District Junction cabin had an additional duty in 1909 as the physical connexion with the Hammersmith branch N&SWJ was resited southwards and the Hammersmith

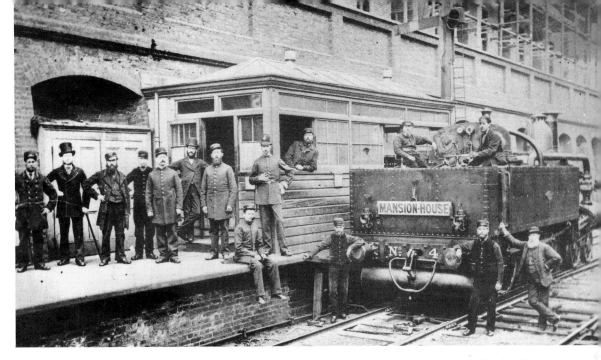

51. Metropolitan District Railway loco no.4 and railway staff at Earl's Court station (East Junction signal box) in May 1876. Wearing a top hat, second from the left, is Thomas Samuel Speck, the first MDR Locomotive Superintendent and Resident Engineer. The platform is that of the first Earl's Court station, opened on 30 October 1871 on the east side of the Earl's Court Road. Four months before this photo was taken, the station's timber building had been gutted by fire and was to be replaced by a new station on the west side of the road which was ready on 1 February 1878. Note the flat-bottomed rail, spiked direct into the sleepers, a feature of the early years of the MDR. *RCHS/Spence*

Junction cabin at Acton Lane closed. In 1915 the junction between the two railways was taken out of use, as was the signal cabin. However, everything remained for five years, so an emergency through traffic could be quickly restored. The instruments were then removed but signal cabin, signals, levers and points did not finally disappear until 1930.

From 14 February 1932 the line was reduced to single track with only a trailing connexion at Acton Town, the service being maintained by a shuttle to and from Acton Town. The signal cabin was abolished and a small ticket office erected on the platform. The Sunday service was withdrawn; the last Sunday trains ran on 8 June 1958. The line was closed with effect from 1 March 1959; the last trains ran on Saturday 28 February 1959.

(A) *UN* 302, pp.23–24 (2/1987)

IT MAY BE ADDED that the road bridge near South Acton station was removed in December 1963 – January 1964, and the one over Bollo Lane on 24–26 January 1964; the land eastwards was levelled.

(L) *UN* 304, p.65 (4/1987)

District and East London Railway Timetables

THE District Railway ceased to issue timetable books at the time of electrification. It is not, however, generally known that pocket-sized pamphlets were issued to the public free, but were rather difficult to obtain. Usually there were separate pamphlets for (a) Wimbledon, (b) Richmond, (c) Ealing, Hounslow, South Harrow, (d) Uxbridge, including connexions to Harrow-on-the-Hill via Rayners Lane. All trains were given in detail, and with the exception of the Uxbridge sheet, the stations were enumerated from and to Barking. It was not too easy to ascertain the complete service from Barking to Central London from these pamphlets but fortunately the LT&S time-book gave the complete service of District trains from and to the LT&S line.

The East London Railway issued a folded sheet timetable, price one halfpenny. When the District trains were withdrawn in 1905 and until electrification in 1913, the East London timetable carried the heading 'Provisional service of trains'. Both the District and the East London pamphlets ceased to be issued about 1915 and none appear to have survived.

(L) *U*14, 3, p.70 (6/1976)

The East London Railway

THE CENTENARY of the East London Railway took place in December 1969 almost without notice, but it is to be regretted that some factual errors were made in certain historical articles relating to the line. It would, therefore, be as well to place on record the following notes which have been compiled from the records of the various companies and from several London newspapers.

The line was opened formally on 6 December 1869 and to the public the following day from New Cross to Wapping (at first named Wapping & Shadwell station). The London Brighton & South Coast Railway undertook the working and maintenance and the line was extended to Liverpool Street (Great Eastern) without ceremony; public traffic began in the early hours of Monday 10 April 1876. A branch from Deptford Road Junction (just south of Surrey Docks station) to the South London line was opened 13 March 1871 with a service first from Wapping, later from Liverpool Street, to Old Kent Road. From 1 August 1877 the trains were extended to Peckham Rye.

In 1876 an additional up line from New Cross to Deptford Road Junction was constructed and this, together with an improved layout on the down side, enabled some trains to run through to and from New Croydon from 1 July 1876. On Sundays in the summer, from June 1876, one train had through carriages to and from Brighton, probably using the new connexions. Commencing 1 November 1876, there was a through service on weekdays, serving the same place. When the East London services began, the trains used a small station on the east side of the Brighton Company's station (sometimes referred to as the Low Level) at New Cross. The separate station was, however, closed [for the first time] with effect from 1 November 1876.

At the same time, it was agreed to make connexion with the South Eastern Railway and that Company began a service from Addiscombe Road to Liverpool Street on 1 April 1880; these trains were diverted to St Mary's on 3 March 1884 and ran for the last time on 30 September 1884.

From 1 November 1881, until the end of August 1882, there was a through service between the EL line and Crystal Palace (LBSCR).

A Joint Committee of management was formed by Act of 1882 consisting of the LBSC, the LC&D, the South Eastern, the Metropolitan and the District and commenced operations 1 October 1884 when connexion was made at St Mary's, Whitechapel Road, with the joint line of the Metropolitan and District Railways. [The New Cross ELR station alongside the LBSCR was reopened at the same date – Editor] As the LC&D was a member of the Joint Committee, it had to pay its share in the annual loss incurred, although not taking any active part in the running of the railway.

The inauguration of the services of the two newcomers has caused some confusion to historians. In order to give the trainmen an opportunity to become familiar with the new services, and as some of the stations were not quite ready, the Met trains, from 1 October 1884, detrained all passengers at Bishopsgate, ran empty to St Mary's and then conveyed passengers locally thence to New Cross (SE). Similarly, the District trains ran empty from Mansion House to St Mary's. On the return journey, passengers were detrained at St Mary's, taking up passengers again at Bishopsgate or Mansion House, as the case may be. From 6 October, however, both Companies conveyed passengers through from their respective systems to the East London Line. The service the various railways intended to operate, however, proved unworkable, with seven flat junctions (including three at Aldgate) and the entire service was revised from 10 November 1884 with Met trains every half-hour, District every half-hour and frequent LBSCR trains. The District used the East London station at New Cross until it was closed [for the second time] with effect from 1 September 1886; the trains

52. St Mary's (Whitechapel Road) station in 1930.
Photo Bancroft. London Borough of Tower Hamlets.

then ran to the LBSCR station. From 1 January 1886, the Met service was increased to three an hour on weekdays, but remained half-hourly on Sundays. All through working to Brighton ceased 1 October 1884, but an occasional excursion from Shoreditch was run. There were also occasional excursions Shoreditch to Ramsgate and other places by the South Eastern Railway.

In 1885, the Great Eastern joined the Committee and from 1 January 1886 that Company took over the service from Liverpool Street to New Cross LBSCR, but the LBSCR continued to run trains from Shoreditch to New Cross and to Peckham Rye. Through trains to Croydon were withdrawn, but from 1 February 1887 some of the Great Eastern trains were extended to New Croydon on weekdays (and to Central Croydon until closure in 1890). Various schemes were considered to run Met trains beyond the South Eastern station at New Cross but none was given effect to.

From about 1880 goods traffic was exchanged between the GE and the LBSC, the SE and the LC&D Railways via the East London line, the LBSCR working the trains from Liverpool Street. The GE took over this service from 1 January 1886 to New Cross LBSC. From 1 February 1886, GE goods trains ran also to New Cross (SE), extended to Hither Green in 1899. On 2 May 1904, the GE opened goods depot at New Cross. To facilitate the exchange of merchandise, a hoist was erected at Whitechapel sidings and brought into use in 1900, but some traffic continued to be worked via Liverpool Street.

Originally, the LBSCR had maintained the East London Railway but the South Eastern took over this work in 1885 and continued to do so until after electrification.

The services altered little until the electrification of the Met and District lines. This resulted in the District trains being withdrawn with effect from 1 August 1905, but additional LBSCR trains were provided. The Metropolitan service ceased on and from 3 December 1906 and was replaced by SE&C trains to Whitechapel from that date. The time sheets were headed 'Provisional service of trains on the East London Railway'.

Improvements were made at some stations; Shadwell and Wapping in 1892, Rotherhithe in 1905–6. On 1 August 1895, a direct stairway giving access to the Blackwall line station at Shadwell was brought into use. At Whitechapel, a joint entrance and booking office with the Whitechapel & Bow Railway was opened in 1904, and a suffix '(for London Hospital)' added to the name in 1910; this suffix was afterwards dropped.

All through services to Croydon, also those to Peckham Rye, were withdrawn with effect from 1 June 1911. The connecting link to the latter place was abandoned in 1913 and removed.

The question of electrification was considered from time to time but it was not until 1912 that an Act was obtained by the Great Eastern authorizing electrification between Shoreditch, St Mary's and New Cross. Meanwhile, Deptford Road had been re-named Surrey Docks from 17 July 1911.

Before continuing, it must be stated that the East London Railway did not have an independent line to Liverpool Street but joined the Great Eastern at Bishopsgate Junction. However, tickets headed

'East London Railway' were issued at Liverpool Street, but later, probably from 1886, the tickets were Great Eastern. The curve from Whitechapel Junction to St Mary's Junction was originally part of the ELR, but was transferred to the Met and District Joint Committee from 1 October 1884.

The Great Eastern having obtained the Act and raised the money to electrify the line, the South Eastern relaid the permanent way and renovated the stations. The District Company would supply the power from Lots Road and a sub-station would be erected at Surrey Docks. The pumping plant in the Thames Tunnel would be replaced by electrically driven pumps. Auto and semi-auto signalling would be installed with lower quadrant semaphores having two red and one green spectacles to ensure that the green light was shown only if the signal was properly in the 'off' position. The new signals were brought into use on Sunday 30 March 1913. In later years, however, normal colour-light signalling was installed. After various suggestions, it was decided that the Metropolitan would provide the whole of the passenger service.

Some trial electric trains ran during the last few days of March 1913, and in the early hours of Monday 31 March the Met took over the entire passenger service, and again one could travel from the Met line to the EL line without change of carriage. During the interim period, Met trains

53. East London Railway tracks at New Cross East London Down Junction signal box, looking into the Low Level ELR terminus alongside the LB&SCR (New Cross Gate) station, on 18 July 1898. After this two-platform terminal had finally been closed on 31 August 1886, ELR trains used the LB&SCR tracks beyond the box to reach the LB&SCR station but the ELR facility was not dismantled until 1900. *RCHS/Spence*

54. The unprepossessing surface station at Wapping ELR, in the 1920s, looking north east.
The circular building behind the ticket office contains the lift shaft. This wooden shed met a deserved fate in the
air attacks of 1940, only to be replaced with an even more modest structure, which in turn gave way to a
simple but elegant brick and concrete entrance building in 1960.
Photo Bancroft/London Borough of Tower Hamlets

had been running to Whitechapel (District line) where passengers for the EL line changed. The Met engine and carriage sheds at New Cross, which had apparently been disused since that Company's steam trains were withdrawn after traffic on the night of 2 December 1906, were again brought into service. (It has been stated that the SECR made some use of these sheds, but confirmation is lacking.) Four trains an hour were provided from South Kensington (via Edgware Road) to the New Cross stations alternately; from Shoreditch there were eight an hour (four on Sundays).

Starting 9 February 1914, the through trains ran from Hammersmith, those from South Kensington being withdrawn. The Hammersmith trains were composed of GW and Met Joint stock and on Sunday afternoons, until 1918, some of the trains came from Kensington Addison Road, but only in the eastbound direction. New Cross LBSCR was renamed New Cross Gate 9 July 1923.

The service was revised from 24 September 1928. There were eight trains an hour each way between Hammersmith and New Cross and New Cross Gate alternately (six an hour on Sundays). From Shoreditch, trains ran only in the peak hours and on Sunday mornings.

A more drastic alteration took place on 4 May 1936. The normal service was between Whitechapel and the two southern terminals. The Hammersmith trains, also Shoreditch trains, ran only during peak hours, Shoreditch also on Sunday mornings. The Hammersmith service was much reduced on 20 November 1939 and ceased entirely on and from 6 October 1941. The Shoreditch Sunday morning service ceased with effect from 5 October 1958.

The Great Eastern continued to work goods trains to Hither Green and goods and parcels trains to New Cross Gate (LBSCR). Regular booked services to Hither Green ceased with effect from 2 December 1940 but trips, as required, were arranged by the respective Control offices, but these had virtually ceased by 1945. The number of trains was gradually reduced and all regular services ceased 1 October 1962. Parcels trains and a few special goods trains to and from New Cross Gate (LBSCR) continued, the very last being a parcels train on Saturday 16 April 1966.

The Met took over the management of the line on behalf of the Joint Committee from 1 July 1921, and maintenance from 1 January 1924. The down line from near Canal Junction to New Cross (SER) had been worked as a single line by train staff and ticket, and repeated attempts had been made to adopt non-token working but Government sanction could not be obtained. In 1916, the electric train staff system was substituted for staff and ticket, and finally in 1925, a satisfactory method of non-token working was put into operation.

The East London Railway Company was extinguished in 1925 as by Act of that year the line was purchased by the Southern Railway. This made no practical difference to the running of the railway; the Joint Committee continued to function and management and maintenance by the Metropolitan continued.

When the through services were curtailed in 1936, direct stairways were provided at Whitechapel between the District line platforms and the East London line platforms. North of Whitechapel, a facing cross-over was provided, so that trains from Shoreditch could use either platform at Whitechapel; this cross-over was, however, later removed. Before this, the semaphore signals had been removed and normal colour-light signals installed.

With the gradual reduction of goods services, the sidings at Whitechapel, together with the hoist, ceased to be used in November 1955 and were removed. The up line from New Cross Gate (LBSCR) to Deptford Road Junction was severed by the Southern Railway at East London Up Junction on 1 November 1964 and the points at Deptford Road Junction were taken out on 20 February 1966; the track was subsequently removed. At the northern end of the line, Bishopsgate Junction was removed on 17 April 1966 and stop blocks erected. Both physical connexions with the former South Eastern Railway at New Cross were taken out and the up line removed in 1968.

The down platform at Shoreditch had been little used since 1913 and not at all from 1928. It was taken out of use and the footbridge removed. This station was closed on Sundays from 5 October 1958 and on Saturdays from 22 October 1966. St Mary's, Whitechapel Road, was closed entirely 1 May 1938. At Wapping, the question of providing lifts had been under consideration for many years. They were eventually constructed and brought into use on 4 October 1915. The entrance and booking office was reconstructed in 1960. Shadwell was closed on Sundays from 5 October 1958. The Great Eastern goods station at New Cross was transferred to the Southern Region soon after nationalization and at the time of writing a connexion exists at New Cross Gate (LBSCR) with some sidings, otherwise all physical connexions with British Railways have been removed.

In recent years, the East London line has been worked by former District Railway stock.

(A) *JRCHS* 16, 3, pp.62–64 (7/1970) and 16, 4, pp.85–87 (10/1970)

Train Services on the East London Railway and Inner Circle, 1884, 1885

AT THE BEGINNING of 1884, the services on the East London Railway were:

LB&SC trains Liverpool Street and New Cross LB&SC
LB&SC trains Liverpool Street and Peckham Rye
SE trains Liverpool Street and Croydon, Addiscombe Road

On weekdays, some of the New Cross trains ran to and from New Croydon. On 3 March 1884, the SE trains were diverted to St Mary's, Whitechapel.

The Inner Circle extended from Aldgate to Mansion House and was worked by both the Metropolitan and Metropolitan District Railways, the service most of the day (including Sundays) being six trains per hour in the ratio of five District trains consecutively to seven Metropolitan trains.

When the remaining portion of the Inner Circle and the extension to Whitechapel were nearing completion, the question of train service was considered by the Metropolitan and Metropolitan District Railways, and at a meeting held on 30 July

1884 the Metropolitan proposed that the Inner Circle service be increased to eight trains per hour. To this, the District agreed but apparently regretted having done so, as from 1 September 1884 that Company increased their local service, presumably with the idea of proving that it was impracticable to work eight Inner Circle trains in the hour. This action caused much confusion and delay, but it was hoped that the position would be eased when Mansion House ceased to be a terminus for all trains.

On and from 1 October 1884, the SE trains were withdrawn from the East London Railway and the New Cross (LB&SC) Liverpool Street service considerably reduced. On the same date, Metropolitan trains commenced to run to and from New Cross SE Railway and District trains to and from Whitechapel (Mile End) and New Cross EL Station. This station, sometimes referred to as the Low Level, was close to the LB&SC station. For the first few days, the Metropolitan and District trains did not convey passengers over the newly constructed portion of the railway but did convey passengers between St Mary's and the respective stations at New Cross. As regards the Inner Circle, it had been agreed that the trains on the Inner Rail (Mansion House, Aldgate, S. Kensington, Mansion House) should be provided by the District, and the trains on the Outer Rail by the Metropolitan, and this service should be worked by eleven trains on each Rail, averaging every 7½ minutes. On Sundays, the Metropolitan was to work the whole service on both Rails.

It proved quite impossible to work these services and serious delays took place, chiefly on the District Railway. However, the new lines and stations were opened to the public on and from Monday 6 October 1884. The District objected strongly to The Tower of London station, which had been constructed by the Metropolitan and opened 25 September 1882, and pressed for it to be closed. Under protest, the Metropolitan closed this station on and from 13 October 1884. In September 1884, the trains using The Tower of London station were the Metropolitan Hammersmith trains, which terminated there. It is not clear what trains actually called at The Tower during the first half of October, certainly the Metropolitan trains on the Outer Rail called and probably the District trains on the Inner Rail also. The *City Press*, reporting the public opening on 6 October of the

new lines, states that the first train left Mansion House at 5.35, called at Cannon Street, Eastcheap, Mark Lane, The Tower, and thence onwards from Aldgate. Starting from Mansion House, this must have been a District train and, as stated above, the District worked the service on the Inner Rail. The District trains to and from Whitechapel and New Cross did not call at The Tower and the District would not operate fares to that station.

The delays were made worse by the District Company running their Inner Rail trains over their own line from Kensington High Street (the Cromwell Curve) to South Kensington, thereby crossing the Outer Rail twice, at High Street and at South Kensington. The District tried to get the Metropolitan to agree a reduction in the number of trains on the Circle but without success, and the matter went to arbitration. The award being in favour of the Metropolitan, the District reduced their local services and agreed to run their Inner Rail trains on the Metropolitan lines between Kensington High Street and South Kensington. The revised services operated on and from 10 November 1884, from which day the Metropolitan provided some of the trains on the Inner Rail.

The services worked reasonably well but the District still wished to increase their local services and eventually persuaded the Metropolitan to agree a reduction in the number of Circle trains to six per hour. This service was to have started on 1 April but actually came into operation on 7 April 1885.

One of the suggestions put forward to relieve congestion was for the GW Middle Circle trains to complete the Circle, instead of terminating at Mansion House, but the Great Western would not agree.

The journey time around the Inner Circle in October 1884 was 81 to 84 minutes, the services being worked by eleven trains on each Rail, averaging every 7½ minutes. From 7 April 1885, there were six trains per hour, the journey time being 70 minutes, the District providing five trains and the Metropolitan two trains on the Inner Rail. On the Outer Rail, the Metropolitan provided seven trains.

A writer in the *City Press* suggested that Mark Lane and The Tower stations be combined by extending the platforms, with entrances at each end, the combined station to be named Mark Lane & Minories.

The East London station at New Cross had been closed since the night of 31 October 1876. It was reopened for the District trains but closed again on and from 1 September 1886.

St Mary's station and the connecting line from the East London Railway were built by the East London Railway and transferred to the Metropolitan and Metropolitan District jointly from 1 October 1884.

The East London Joint Committee was formed 1 October 1884, the Great Eastern joining 1 April 1885. The services on the EL line were:

Metropolitan

October 1884	Weekdays 4 trains per hour Sundays 2 or 3 trains per hour
10 November 1884	Weekdays and Sundays 2 trains per hour

District

October 1884	Weekdays 4 trains per hour Sundays 2 trains per hour
1 November 1884	Weekdays and Sundays 2 trains per hour

LB&SC

October 1884	Approximately 1 train per hour weekdays and Sundays: Liverpool Street and New Cross Liverpool Street and Peckham Rye since increased from 1 November 1884 from Whitechapel, and from 10 November 1884, from Liverpool Street, GER.

(A) *JRCHS* 4, 4, pp.74–76 (7/1958)

Connexion at New Cross Gate

I UNDERSTAND the physical connexion between the East London Line and the Southern Region main line situated at the south end of New Cross Gate station was taken out on Sunday 17 September 1972.

This was the last connexion between the East London Line and British Railways. At one time, there were six physical connexions, five suitable for through running, the sixth being a connexion by a hoist with Spitalfields Goods section.

I have been told that the connexion with BR at Ealing Broadway had been removed, but I am unable to confirm.

(L) *U* 12, 1, p.7 (1/1973)

East London Railway: Headcodes – October 1884

THE TRAIN SERVICE was provided by three companies; the engines carried the following headcodes:

London Brighton & South Coast trains:

New Croydon	Two discs diagonally, green with white rim. *At night:* Two green lights, same positions.
New Cross	Two discs vertically, green with white rim. *At night:* Two green lights, same positions.
Peckham Rye	One green disc top of smoke box. *At night:* One green light, same position.

District Railway trains:

Putney	Two white lights vertically, off-side end of buffer beam.
Richmond	Two white lights, one centre, one off-side buffer beam.
Hammersmith	Two white lights, one each end buffer beam.
Ealing	Two white lights, one on smoke box, one near-side buffer beam.

Metropolitan trains:

	One blue light near-side buffer beam, one white light off-side buffer beam.

(L) *UN* 234, p.143 (6/1981)

East London Railway to Liverpool Street

THE QUESTION of the opening of the East London Railway to the Great Eastern terminus at Liverpool Street has been raised again, owing to an ambiguous footnote in *The London, Brighton & South Coast Railway* by J. T. Howard-Turner.

The passenger service definitely began on Monday 10 April 1876; the first train arrived at 05.13 and left at 05.18. An official opening ceremony took place three days earlier when a special train conveying Directors and Officials ran to Brighton and back. All trains were LB&SC until the Great Eastern provided the service from 1 January 1886, but the LB&SC continued to run trains to and from Shoreditch.

(L) *UN* 272, p.92 (8/1984)

Rotherhithe and Shadwell

I WAS MUCH INTERESTED in the notes about the East London Line. There was also plenty of water at Rotherhithe, even during the very dry summers. There was, and still is, a spring at Shadwell, very cool and refreshing on a hot day. One drank the water for about ninety years, then it was declared unfit for drinking. I have never heard of it making anyone ill! When the Blackwall line station at Shadwell was open, it was a very long way up to the Blackwall platforms from the East London platforms.

(L) *UN* 260, p.150 (8/1983)

Train Destination Indicators, East London Line

I HAVE RECENTLY been asked what destination indicators were carried by the Metropolitan trains, when that company provided the whole of the passenger service on the East London electrified railway from 1913, and I think it would be well to put the following notes on record.

The indicators provided were 'New Cross LB& SC', 'New Cross SE&C' and, of course, 'Shoreditch'. The platform staff announced: 'Brighton line train' or 'South Eastern line train', as the case may be.

When the District and Metropolitan Companies ran steam trains over the East London line, as far as is known, the headboards read simply 'New Cross'. Regular passengers knew to which station the train would run, but others sometimes found themselves at the wrong station. Prior to electrification, two sets of tickets to New Cross were provided at each East London Railway station, but both singles and returns were inter-available.

(L) *JRCHS* 13, 1, p.18 (1/1967)

A S A RESULT of my letter in the *Journal* for January 1967, I have been shown a photograph of a District Railway engine bearing the headboard: 'NEW CROSS LBSC'. This photograph would appear to have been taken some time during the later period of steam operation and, of course, does not mean that headboards were equally precise during the whole period of steam working on the East London Railway.

(L) *JRCHS* 13, 2, p.33 (4/1967)

Whitechapel & Bow Railway

W HEN THE Whitechapel & Bow Railway was first opened to public traffic, trains ran through to East Ham, but some terminated at Bow Road where they reversed. As that station was not quite ready for opening, all passengers in such trains were required to alight at Mile End.

(L) *U* 8, 8, p.123 (8/1969)

55. Stockwell depot, City & South London Railway, with Mather & Platt locos, left to right, nos. 6, 11, and 1. Note the inscription 'City' to denote the King Willliam Street terminus. A photograph taken just before the opening of the railway in December 1890. *RCHS/Spence*

(ix) On the London Tube Railways

City & South London Railway

I RECENTLY examined the records of the City & South London Railway in order to settle the question of the original names of stations now known as Borough, Kennington and Oval.

During the construction, these stations were referred to as Great Dover Street, Kennington New Street (or simply New Street) and Kennington Oval (or The Oval) respectively.

At a Board meeting held on 29 July 1890, prior to the opening of the line, it was decided to name the stations:

BOROUGH, KENNINGTON, THE OVAL

and Borough was always so named subsequently. Kennington was sometimes so called, but at other times this station was given as New Street, the last occasion being in the Minutes of 29 January 1895. As regards the third station named, the word 'The' was soon dropped, but occasionally Kennington Oval appeared.

No early timetables or bills of the line are now available, and the earliest tickets bear the present names. *Bradshaw*, however, printed Great Dover Street, New Street, and Kennington Oval until the opening of the extension to Moorgate in 1900, probably having copied from an early announcement. It seems quite evident that the official names were the present ones from opening, but I have some recollection that, many years ago, a man told me that on the platforms 'New Street' appeared in smaller type under 'Kennington' and that on the platforms at Oval, the word 'Kennington' was also shown, but in much smaller letters.

(L) *JRCHS* 15, 1, pp.9 & 12 (1/1969)

A LTHOUGH it may have been decided to close the [tube railway surface] station buildings at Euston in August, they were actually closed on and from 1 October 1914, in accordance with a notice posted in mid-September. I may add that the 'interchange' entrance and lifts were staffed by the LNWR. The 'tube' booking office also issued L&NW tickets as far as Leighton Buzzard. This arrangement ceased about a year later when Underground staff took over and L&NW tickets ceased to be issued.

(L) *UN* 309, p.160 (9/1987)

Tube Railway Destination Indicators

E ARLY in the present century, the CSLR had small destination plates:

CITY, MOORGATE, ANGEL, EUSTON, STOCKWELL, CLAPHAM

I cannot recollect the colour. CITY originally applied to King William Street but was later used for a time for Moorgate. ANGEL and STOCKWELL continued to be necessary as a few trains terminated and were stabled there. It was at that time usual to refer to a terminal in the City of London as 'CITY'. The guards and station staff on the Central London Railway always announced 'City train' and many North London Railway stations carried a board outside reading, 'Frequent trains to the City' or 'Quickest route to the City'.

The Hampstead Tube had destination indicators:

CHARING CROSS, HIGHGATE, HAMPSTEAD, GOLDERS GREEN

In addition, on the side of some of the cars was a four-sided wooden indicator with a square end fixed into two sockets. This bore the four destinations and was turned by the guard or driver at the terminus. These were gradually abolished as they wore out and platform indicators were provided. For a few years from opening, only a quarter of the trains went through to Golders Green, the normal sequence being: Highgate, Hampstead (reverse), Highgate, Golders Green. I never remember a Mornington Crescent plate, and after the loop at Charing Cross was opened the Charing Cross plate continued to be used. However, whilst the extension to Kennington was under construction, 'Strand' plates were provided as Highgate trains terminated there. Trains carried headlights according to destination and large posters were exhibited at stations: 'Recognise your train by the headlights'.

(L) *UN* 173, p.207 (6/1976)

Tʜᴇ Hᴀᴍᴘꜱᴛᴇᴀᴅ Tᴜʙᴇ did have headlights and the code was made public by notices at the stations. I think the code was: Highgate – two white lights; Hampstead – one white light; and Golders Green – one white and one green light.

(L) *UN* 223, pp.242–243 (7/1980)

Hampstead and Marylebone Stations

Hᴀᴍᴘꜱᴛᴇᴀᴅ ꜱᴛᴀᴛɪᴏɴ was opened on 22 June 1907. It was intended to call this station Heath Street and this name was impressed on the tiles on the platforms which at that time was the normal way of showing the names of the stations. It was the practice then to name tube stations after streets rather than after districts, so Camden Town was to be called Camden Road, Chalk Farm was to be called Adelaide Road, and South Kentish Town, Castle Road. However, just prior to opening, it was decided to name the station Hampstead, and large enamel plates inscribed 'Hampstead Alight here for the Heath' covered the proposed name on the platforms on opening day.

Great Central station on the Bakerloo Line was opened on 27 March 1907. The entrance was on the west side of Harewood Avenue, the building being of the normal Bakerloo type. On the following day, a subway was opened from the Great Central Railway terminus. Passengers from the main line descended a short staircase, walked along the subway under Harewood Avenue and upstairs to the Bakerloo booking office and lifts. Holders of through tickets could go direct from the subway down the emergency stairs to the Bakerloo platforms. The station was renamed Marylebone on 15 April 1917. Escalators from Marylebone terminus were decided upon in 1937 and brought into use on 1 February 1943. The

building in Harewood Avenue, which had been damaged by enemy action, remained derelict, with the lifts, for many years. The building was demolished and the lift shafts were sealed off in February 1971.

(L) *UN* 204, p.614 (12/1978)

Heathrow Opening

I ᴡᴀꜱ ᴏɴ ᴛʜᴇ ᴘʟᴀᴛꜰᴏʀᴍ at Hatton Cross on opening day from 14.30 and walked along the platform several times speaking to friends and to the staff. I saw nothing in the way of 'disgraceful' behaviour.

When a westbound train arrived at 15.03, many people entered it in an orderly way, but immediately alighted when requested to do so by the station staff; I saw no disorder. About two minutes afterwards, another train arrived which the waiting passengers boarded, again, as far as I could see, in a perfectly orderly manner.

The indicators at stations showed 'Heathrow Central' all the morning, but were switched out in the early afternoon. This I consider to be a mistake and caused some confusion, especially as no announcement was made at Hammersmith, nor at Acton Town.

I was in the ticket hall from about 15.10 but did not observe passengers having to 'fight through' others waiting for tickets, as stated by Mr Hillier, who, if he does not wish to use 24-hour time, should, I submit, add pm to his times.

I think on the whole the opening arrangements were carried out satisfactorily.

(L) *UN* 191, p.416 (3/1978)

Tube Railway Lifts: Hampstead, Liverpool Street, Finsbury Park

I ᴅᴏ ɴᴏᴛ ᴛʜɪɴᴋ there ever was a lift in No.1 shaft at Hampstead. I knew this station from opening and I feel sure there were never more than five lifts. Liverpool Street, Central Line, had a lift to platform level at Broad Street, North London Line. This was taken out of use during the first World

War, but brought back into use for a few years afterwards. Through tickets were issued from Central Line stations to some North London stations but the service was never well patronized. One lift remained for many years and was used for taking stores and material to and from the Central Line. The entrance on Broad Street can still be seen. The lifts at Finsbury Park were never very popular. I was not acquainted with this station until 1915, I believe there was both stairs and lifts from the opening of the tubes, but most passengers used the stairs instead of waiting for the lifts. The lifts were taken out of use about 1916 but remained in place for several years, but only one until the construction of the Victoria Line. When the lifts were taken out of use, each of the staircases were made 'double' as now; but only one is in use at present, in each shaft.

(L) *UN* 223, p.241 (7/1980)

Finsbury Park Station

THE NEW TICKET OFFICE at Wells Terrace, Finsbury Park, is certainly convenient for passengers entering the station from that place but most inconvenient for those coming from Seven Sisters Road, which is, of course, the main road.

People from that entrance are obliged to walk the entire length of the subway to Wells Terrace, a distance according to the latest large scale Ordnance map of about 200 metres, buy a ticket, retrace their steps half way, 100 metres, turn left, another 50 metres, and eventually reach the platform, a total walk of 350 metres.

For nearly 70 years, ticket offices at the head of the staircases were convenient and most satisfactory; they are still in place and should, I submit, be re-opened. The present arrangements simply encourage people to travel without tickets. I find it quite impossible to understand why London Transport went to the expense of constructing an office at Wells Terrace.

(L) *UN* 160, p.44 (4/1975)

THE COMBINED [BR and LT Finsbury Park] ticket office was brought into use on Sunday morning 18 March 1984. There was a brief ceremony on 22 May of that year but the frontage and other work was not completed until the Summer of 1985.

(L) *UN* 298, p.145 (10/1986)

(x) On Some Other Railways

The First Railway to Aylesbury

ONCE A DATE is wrongly given, the error tends to be repeated many times, and the opening date of the first railway to Aylesbury is no exception. The event was fully reported in the newspapers of the day, and the correct dates are as follows: Ceremonial opening of the branch from Cheddington to Aylesbury took place on Monday 10 June 1839; after the ceremony, trains ran to and from Cheddington conveying ordinary passengers free of charge. The normal public service began the following day. There were three trains on weekdays and two on Sundays.

In 1889, the line was extended a short distance and a new station erected in High Street, Aylesbury. The old station was closed after traffic on 15 June and the new station opened on Sunday 16 June 1889. The Sunday service ran for the last time on 31 December 1916. The line was closed for passengers on and from 2 February 1953, and entirely on 2 December 1963.

(L) *JRCHS* 11, 2, p.15 (4/1965)

Alterations to Names of Stations

HATCH END: The suffix 'for Pinner' attached to the name of this station actually remained in the timetables until 1955, but it is within recollection that the suffix disappeared from the station nameboards a few years previously.

As regards the spelling of Perry Bar or Perry Barr, the L&NWR timetable used both at first, even in the same book, but settled for Perry Barr in October 1870, and *Bradshaw* soon followed. The RCH handbook of stations dated 1877 also gives Perry Barr. The RCH record of 1894 was probably issued to regularize the matter.

About the time of the opening of the London & Birmingham Railway, a 'ticket platform' was erected at Camden, at which passengers from up

trains could alight. Later this was converted into a station, at first named Camden. Owing to the proximity of the Chalk Farm station of the North London Railway, the L&NW station was shown in the timetable, as Camden (Chalk Farm) from December 1864, but on some pages simply as Chalk Farm. This continued until 1875 when the word Camden was dropped. However, as the signal boxes in the vicinity continued to be called Camden, this title was sometimes used by many railwaymen for many years afterwards.

[Station nameboards are not normally used as evidence for change of name, owing to the somewhat haphazard method of naming. One instance of this vagueness was on the M&GN at Hemsby, which was shown thus in all timetables. The main nameboards showed Hemsby, but the small blue-tinted glass plates in the flickering oil lamps bore the legend 'Hemsby for Winterton'. Also, Upper Warlingham on the Croydon & Oxted Joint was shown with a 'Warlingham' nameboard in a photograph at the time of opening, a name that was never used, as far as is known – Editor, *JRCHS*]

(L) *JRCHS* 16, 1, p.15 (1/1970)

The Aylesbury Railway by E. J. S. Gadsden*

THIS IS a useful book. It may be added that there was a service between Cheddington and Aylesbury, on Sundays, until the end of December 1916. A Sunday service was necessary on many branch lines for the conveyance of mails and perishables, as well as passengers. Letters were delivered every day in nearly all provincial towns and villages until 1921. The second L&NW station at Aylesbury was actually opened to the public on Sunday morning 16 June 1889.

(L) *JRCHS* 8, 6, p.109–110 (11/1962)

* Gadsden, E. J. S., *The Aylesbury Railway*, Bledlow Press, 1962.

56. LMSR Willesden Junction–Earl's Court electric train at the east side of Kensington (Addison Road) station (now Kensington (Olympia)) in the 1930s. This service was the emaciated relic of the original 'Outer Circle' (Broad Street–Willesden Junction–Kensington (Addison Road)–Earl's Court–Mansion House). *Anon/RCHME*

Bakerloo/LNWR Services

GEORGE AUGUSTUS NOKES (alias Sekon) did at one time live in Middlesex, but in later years he lived on the Kent coast, Broadstairs, I think.

At Hatch End, the Royston Park entrance was reopened late in 1919 for ticket holders [only], but this was not strictly enforced. The ticket office was open for Workmen's tickets, also for the morning peak. The only trains using the main line platforms were a few steam trains during the peak hours on weekdays.

In December 1962, the portion of the bridge over the main lines was in urgent need of repair and was closed, together with the Royston Park entrance, with effect from Monday 7 January 1963, according to public notice. The steam trains called for the last time on Saturday 5 January, but presumably the entrance was open on the Sunday. Despite strong protests, the portion of the bridge was soon removed.

(L) *UN* 297, p.123 (9/1986)

The LNWR Outer Circle Service

I REMEMBER the service, so perhaps I might add a few details. As the last Broad Street train arrived at Camden Town after the last up local had gone, the Outer Circle train ran No.1 line and called at all stations to Broad Street. The last train from Mansion House terminated at Hampstead Heath and returned as Servants' train to Willesden. I understand the crews were always Willesden men, the engines returning 'light' with the guards after working the last trains, the coaches remaining at the destination for the night.

As stated, the third class was always in front towards Mansion House, as the NLR had a rule that second class on all trains should be nearest the barrier at Broad Street. Many stations had boards on the platforms 'Wait here for ... class'. I cannot remember these on the District Railway but the North London and the Metropolitan had them at some stations. Platform porters, after announcing the destination of an approaching train, often followed this by, 'second forward, third behind,' or 'third forward, second behind.'

Through tickets were issued between Broad Street and Mansion House. Originally the third class fare was, I believe, 8d but was later reduced to 6d. As the fare from Broad Street to Willesden was 5d, one paid only one penny for the extra distance. Return tickets, available until the following day, were about a fare and a half. When the trains terminated at Earl's Court, second class tickets were endorsed 'Second class to Earl's Court, third class beyond'.

The side boards on the carriages read: 'Broad

Street, Willesden, Kensington and Mansion House'; later the latter was replaced by 'Earls Court'. The carriages were plainly marked 'L.& N.W. train'.

On Sundays in 1891, only a rather sparse service operated between Willesden Low Level [and] Addison Road, where passengers could proceed by GW Middle Circle trains. From February 1905, the latter terminated at Addison Road and the L&NW train ran to and from Earl's Court. From May 1906, there was a half-hourly service to Mansion House from Willesden Low Level on Sundays; this ran for the last time on 31 December 1916. As regards Kew Bridge, the last 20 chains or so, known as Kew Curve, was LSWR property. The LNWR rail-motor services commenced 1 October 1911 and ran from Willesden High Level. Prior to this date, the trains were all North London, some from Broad Street, others short locals from and to Acton.

(L) *UN* 249, p.189 (9/1982)

Kensington (Addison Road)

IT SEEMS DEFINITE that the words 'Addison Road'; were first used by the Metropolitan Railway from 1868, and the District Railway referred to the station as Addison Road when the Outer Circle train service began. The other interested railways, for many years afterwards, usually referred to the station as 'Kensington'. The timetables of the West London Railway in the latter part of the 19th Century gave the name as Kensington, except that occasionally it appeared as 'Kensington (Addison Road)'. The wording on the nameboards in the 19th Century is not known, but from about 1905 it was definitely 'Kensington (Addison Road)'. The wording on the tickets varied.

(L) *JRCHS* 8,5, p.87 (9/1962)

The Hampstead Junction Railway

ALTHOUGH the terminus of this railway was sometimes given as 'Acton Wells', the position of the junction with the North & South Western Junction Railway was not at the present Acton Wells Junction but at Old Oak Junction, in Acton parish, the actual point being about five chains

south of the bridge over the Grand Junction Canal. There was also a curve from the Harrow Road Bridge to the old Willesden station in Acton Lane, but this line was not used for passenger traffic. The original line to Old Oak Junction ceased to be used for passenger traffic in 1885 and was taken up in 1892. A considerable portion of the embankment remains, and the site of the bridge over the canal can be seen just to the west of the N&SWJ bridge. As regards the section between Old Oak Junction and the present Acton Wells Junction, the original lines of the N&SWJ are those on the west side and are now used only for goods traffic. The lines on the east side were constructed by the London & North Western and brought into use in 1885.

(L) *JRCHS* 6, 1, p.16 (1/1960)

Centenaries in 1970

THE SECTION of the Midland Railway, Kentish Town Junction to Highgate Road Junction, was opened for goods traffic, according to contemporary records, on Monday 3 January 1870. *The Railway News*, 8 January 1870, however, says the service began on Tuesday 4 January but this would appear to be wrong.

The initial service was nine Midland trains to and from Mint Street or Thames Lower Wharf. Previously the service had been worked by the North London Company from St Pancras Junction (Mid-NL) via Bow.

(L) *JRCHS* 16, 4, p.94 (10/1970)

Great Western London Suburban Services *

MEMBERS who have a copy of the 1970 edition of this book may like to note the following additions and amendments.

Page 16 (foot). An iron bridge over the N&SWJ Railway was erected and remained in place until 1915 or 1916.

Pages 42, 43. A level crossing at Ladbroke Road (Ladbroke Grove) would have been impracticable, but there was a level crossing just west of Westbourne Park station.

Page 100 etc. Aldgate East, St Mary's: First date to read 3/12/06 (same as Whitechapel). Bow Road, Stepney Green, West Ham: to read 30/3/36 (same as Mile End, East Ham).

The date of the last GW train at stations Charing Cross and west thereof is one day later than that given for Mansion House, Blackfriars and Temple, because the time was after midnight when the train reached Charing Cross.

Clapham Junction to read 16/4/05 (as given on p.60).

Gunnersbury. Change of name: date to read 1/11/71.

South Ruislip. Date of last train incorrect. Timetables show GW trains in July and October 1947 and after nationalization.

St Quintin Park & Wormwood Scrubs. First date to read 2/5/04 (from Company's Minute Books).

Beaconsfield Golf Links. Advertised date 1/1/15.
   Actually opened for public traffic 23/12/14.

Denham Golf Club. Opened July 1912.

(L) *JRCHS* 18, 1, p.20 (1/1972)

* Peacock, Thomas B. *Great Western London Suburban Services*, Oakwood Press, 1970.

The Last Midland Trains to King's Cross

AS SOME DOUBT appears to exist as to when Midland Railway trains ceased to run over the Great Northern Railway from Hitchin to King's Cross, I think it as well to put on record the facts as far as they can be ascertained.

The last passenger train left King's Cross on the evening of 30 September 1868; the last arrival was the up night mail from Leeds on the night of 30 September–1 October 1868 which was due at King's Cross at 4.15, and records of both the GN and the Midland say the mail duly arrived at King's Cross on the morning of 1 October. St Pancras passenger station was opened at 6 o'clock on that morning; the first departure was the 6.15 to Leeds and the first train to arrive was a local from Luton. As regards goods services, the evidence is not altogether clear. In 1862, the Midland built a separate goods depot, known as Agar Town, St Pancras, connected with the GN, also with the North London by way of the GN. This depot was enlarged and apparently from 2 January 1865, all Midland goods were dealt with thereat, arriving and departing by way of the GN, also through St Pancras Junction NLR and the London & North Western Railway.

The first train to use the new line from Bedford was a special on Saturday 7 September 1867; there was a return trip on Sunday and a regular service began on Monday 9 September 1867. A direct curve, known as the North London Incline, was brought into use in 1867. This enabled traffic to be exchanged with the L&NW and NL Railways. The physical connexion between the GN and St Pancras goods station was probably removed in 1868 but some merchandise continued to be exchanged between the two companies via the NLR sidings.

At first the Midland goods trains ran mainly at night in order to allow the contractors to complete the work and to construct passenger stations and goods sidings between Bedford and London.

The agreement with the GN did not expire until 30 June 1870 and legally the Midland were liable for payment for use of the railway from Hitchin and for the use of King's Cross station until that date. Eventually, an amicable settlement was arranged.

(L) *JRCHS* 20, 3, p.70 (11/1974)

Level Crossings at Peterborough

THERE WERE formerly two level crossings at Peterborough, one just south of the Great Northern Station and the other to the west of the Great Eastern Station. I think it might be of interest to place the following information on record.

As long ago as 1871, steps were taken to erect bridges in place of the crossings, but these attempts were abandoned owing to lack of funds. However, a bridge over the GN main line was constructed and brought into use on 16 April 1913 and the level crossing closed.

As regards the other crossing, near to the present East station and to the river, no definite action was taken until an Act was obtained in 1929. In conjunction with the Soke of Peterborough County Council and the Peterborough Town Council, it was decided to construct a viaduct over the river, and a bridge over the railway. This viaduct and bridge, half width only, was opened for traffic on Monday 23 October 1933 and an iron bridge which up to that time carried the road over the river was closed and removed. The railway crossing had to remain in use as well as the half-width of the bridge, in order to give access to the station and certain other places. The completed viaduct and bridge was officially opened on Thursday 20 September 1934 and the level crossing closed.

The details given above differ slightly from those stated in some publications but the dates set out here are from contemporary Peterborough newspapers and from the records of the Railway Companies.

(L) *JRCHS* 16,1, p.13 (1/1970)

[In a letter, *JRCHS* 16, 3, p.61 (7/1970), J. H. Boyes noted that agitation for replacement of level crossings by bridges at Peterborough had begun as early as February 1850 when Capt Simmons of the Railway Inspectorate carried out an inquiry into the problems of the crossing at the west end of the Eastern Counties Railway station, where the main London road crossed the railway. Evidence revealed a rail traffic of 15 passenger and 8 freight trains each way daily with an extra 6 cattle trains on Thursdays and Saturdays. In addition, the road was blocked for shunting movements. However, there was said to be insufficient justification for requiring the railway company to construct a bridge – Editor]

Opening of the L&SW Railway to Waterloo

WATERLOO STATION was opened to the public on the morning of 11 July 1848, the first train being the up night mail which arrived at 4.30am Vauxhall Station was opened the same day, Nine Elms being closed to passengers after the last train the previous evening. There is ample contemporary evidence to confirm this. The statement made in various publications within the last few years, to the effect that Waterloo Station was not opened to the public until 13 July, is entirely erroneous.

(L) *JRCHS* 6, 1, p.15 (1/1960)

Opening of Southampton West Station

SOME RECENT PUBLICATIONS give the opening date of this station as November 1892 but, after a thorough search of local papers, I can find no confirmation of this date. Contemporary issues of

the *Hampshire Independent* and the *Southampton Times*, definitely state that the new station at Southampton West was opened to the public on Friday 1 November 1895, and this date is also given in L&SW working timetables. The old station was closed the previous evening.

(L) *JRCHS* 12, 4, p.70 (10/1966)

Ascot & Sunninghill, L&SW Railway

THERE is no trace of an actual date when this station was renamed 'Ascot' but the L&SW timetables dropped the suffix as from 1 October 1922.

(L) *JRCHS* 12, 3, p.47 (7/1966)

Alderbury Junction and West Moors Line

THE DATE OF OPENING for public traffic of the line between Alderbury Junction and West Moors was 20 December 1866. A special train was, however, run on the previous day for Directors and Officers. Authority: *Salisbury & Winchester Journal* and *Wiltshire County Mirror*.

(L) *JRCHS* 13, 2, p.34 (4/1967)

L&SW Railway: Kensington & Richmond Line

AS I HAVE BEEN asked about signalling on the Richmond line, prior to the introduction of automatic signalling, I think it would be advisable to put the following on record.

The signal boxes were Turnham Green Junction, Acton Lane Junction, Gunnersbury East Junction, Gunnersbury West Junction, Kew Gardens and Richmond Junction. The block working was London & South Western Railway Lock & Block.

On the line used by the North London trains from South Acton Junction, the line was signalled by Preece's instruments to an intermediate box at Bollo Lane Junction level crossing, and Lock and Block thence to Gunnersbury East Junction.

57. Waterloo L&SWR 'throat' around 1870. Note how at this date the platform tracks still converged on to the four through lines of 1848. The London Necropolis Company's 1854 private York Street station for funeral trains to its Brookwood Cemetery is seen on the right. *RCHS/Spence*

Preece's instruments were used on some sections of the London & South Western Railway.

(L) *UN* 205, p.12 (1/1979)

Richmond Station Indicator

THE REBUILDING of Richmond station was completed early in 1938 and I feel sure that the indicator was installed in that year. St Mary's was closed 1 May 1938 and so just escaped inclusion. Kentish Town West was closed on 19 April 1971 – vandals usually work at weekends. Shoreditch and Haggerston were not included as the Richmond trains did not stop at these stations.

The original panel 'F' included stations on the Poplar line, change at Dalston Junction. This was later partly blocked out and marked 'Closed'. The new panel was provided about 1949 when it had been decided not to reopen the Poplar line. Additional numerals were provided to show 24-hour time when the railways adopted that method generally.

Prior to the installation of the present indicator, a rectangular sign was provided at each barrier. This had eight faces and was turned by hand. I think the indications were: two for South Western trains, three for District trains (Mansion House, New Cross, Barking) and one each for Great Western, Metropolitan and North London trains. The 'octagon' still had these indications long after some of the services had been withdrawn.

(L) *UN* 236, pp.192–193 (8/1981)

Howard Clayton's
The Atmospheric Railways *

MR CLAYTON would appear to be mistaken in saying that the Atmospheric Station at Carshalton was on the site of the present Carshalton Beeches station. It is generally understood it was at Wallington station.

(L) *U* 6, 8, p.127 (8/1967)

* Clayton, H., *The Atmospheric Railways*, Author, 1966.

Arundel & Littlehampton Station

THIS STATION was closed on and from Tuesday 1 September 1863; this is clearly stated in the *West Sussex Gazette*. Although the station on the new line is frequently referred to as 'New Arundel' in local newspapers, it seems to be rather improbable that this was the official name.

(L) *JRCHS* 8, 2, p.34 (3/1962)

The Mystery of East Grinstead

IN CONNEXION with the construction of a line northwards from Culver Junction, near Barcombe, it became necessary to resite East Grinstead station and to build a new one on two levels. The railway from Culver Junction to East Grinstead was opened on 1 August 1882, the trains using the low level platforms at the new station, but the construction thereof was far from completed.

The trains between Three Bridges and Tunbridge Wells continued to use the old station, but the timetables commencing with the November 1882 issue show certain trains calling at the new station in order to connect with trains arriving at or departing from the low level. The date this arrangement began cannot be traced, nor is it quite clear whether these trains called at the old station as well, but probably they did so.

The East Grinstead newspapers of 1882 and 1883 complain much about the inaccessibility and incomplete state of the new station, which was some little distance from the town. However, the matter was finalized by the closure to passenger traffic after the last train on Sunday 14 October 1883. The report in the *East Grinstead Observer* of Saturday 13 October 1883 read:

'The new station at East Grinstead will be fully opened on Monday morning and all business transacted there in future. The old passenger station will be permanently closed on Sunday night.'

(L) *JRCHS* 13, 1, pp.17–18 (1/1967)

Tunbridge Wells Central to Tunbridge Wells West

VARIOUS DATES have been given for the opening of the single line connexion between the South Eastern Railway and the London, Brighton & South Coast Railway at Tunbridge Wells.

The Brighton, Uckfield & Tunbridge Wells Railway was authorized by Act of 22 July 1861 to construct a line terminating at a junction with the Hastings branch of the South Eastern Railway by a certain public walk, called 'The Grove'. The line was completed between Groombridge and the SE Railway boundary in 1866, but whether the junction was

actually laid is not clear. The junction is, however, shown in RCH Junction Diagrams, 1867 edition, and RCH Distance Books dated January 1870.

The railway between Groombridge and Tunbridge Wells LB&SC station was opened for all traffic 1 October 1866 but at first little use seems to have been made of the connecting line to the SER. However, by 1870, the LB&SC worked a daily goods train to and from the SE station. On 1 February 1876, the SER commenced a service of local passenger trains and this company took over the goods working from the Brighton Company. In addition to the SE trains, the LB&SC worked some of their passenger trains through to Tunbridge Wells SER station, commencing 1 May 1886; this facility was withdrawn as from 1 January 1889, but the SE trains continued as heretofore.

(L) *JRCHS* 7, 1, pp.17–18 (1/1961)

The First Railway Bridge across the Medway

AS THERE APPEARS to be considerable doubt as to when the East Kent (later London Chatham & Dover) Railway bridge across the Medway was opened for public traffic, I think it desirable to place on record the actual date as given in the Minutes of the East Kent Railway and in local newspapers.

When the railway was ready for opening to Faversham in January 1858, the Board of Trade Inspector would not pass the bridge as being suitable for public traffic and certain alterations had to be made. In consequence, although the line from Chatham to Faversham was opened on 25 January 1858, the section from Strood to Chatham remained out of public use for more than another two months and normal passenger traffic did not begin until 29 March 1858.

(L) *JRCHS* 13, 3, p.48 (7/1967)

The Dartford Loop Line *

THOSE possessing a copy of this book may like to take note of a small error on p.17. Electric trains began to run over the second loop on 30 September 1935 and not in the same year as over the other loop.

(L) *JRCHS* 13, 4, p.70 (10/1967)

* Kidner, R. W., *The Dartford Loop Line 1866–1966*, Oakwood Press, 1966.

South Eastern Railway to Sevenoaks

WITH THE KIND HELP of two Borough Librarians, it now seems to be quite definite that the South Eastern Railway to Sevenoaks was opened for public passenger traffic from a temporary station at Chislehurst on Monday 2 March 1868. The misunderstanding arose because a Sevenoaks newspaper erroneously took a visit by the Directors and Officers on the Tuesday as the first day of operation. The temporary station at Chislehurst was at Old Station Hill, to the north of the present passenger station.

(L) *JRCHS* 17, 3, p.55 (7/1971)

Mid-Kent Railway to Addiscombe Road, Croydon

THE DATE OF OPENING of this branch is usually given as 4 April 1864, which was a Monday, but there is substantial evidence to suggest that 1 April is the correct date. An advertisement in the *Daily Telegraph* of Friday 1 April 1864 reads: 'South-Eastern Railway. Croydon Addiscombe Road Extension. Notice is hereby given that this line is opened for traffic this day and trains will run between Charing Cross, London Bridge and New Beckenham, Elmer's End and Croydon.' Advertisements in the *Daily Telegraph*, *The Times* and *Morning Post* for Saturday 2 April read: 'South-Eastern Railway. The Croydon Addiscombe Road Extension is now open for traffic.' *The Times* of 5 April prints a news item: 'South-Eastern Railway. The Extension to New Beckenham, Elmer's End, Addiscombe and Croydon has just been opened.' *The Observer* for Sunday 3 April does not mention the line, but that for Sunday 10 April prints a news item, similar to that in *The Times* of 5 April. If any

reader has any information, I shall be pleased to hear from them.

(L) *JRCHS* 5, 2, p.36 (3/1959)

RECORDS of the Mid-Kent Railway, which have recently been traced, definitely reveal that this line was opened for public traffic on 1 April 1864.

(L) *JRCHS* 8, 5, p.87 (9/1962)

The Middle Circle

I HAVE RECENTLY come across a note about the demise of the Middle Circle on the night of Saturday 30 June 1900. This service was worked by the Great Western Railway between Aldgate and Mansion House via Kensington, Addison Road, and on that Saturday the last train to Mansion House was hauled by engine No.1401, and the last train from Mansion House by No.3565. Engine 1401 later left Mansion House station for the Great Western sheds. The following day, the Great Western trains terminated at Earl's Court.

(L) *U* 7, 7, p.110 (7/1968)

Seven Sisters Station

I CONSIDER it should be recorded that the joint British Rail–London Transport entrance and ticket office at Seven Sisters was opened 1 December 1968. The original entrance to the BR station, in West Green Road, was closed the same day. The access to the BR down platform is now by way of a subway, which formed part of a supplementary entrance from Birstall Road which was closed in 1942.

(L) *U* 8, 2, p.30 (2/1969)

Epping–Ongar Branch

WHEN OPENED, the line from Loughton to Ongar was single throughout, with a passing place at Epping. An additional passing loop at Theydon Bois was made in 1885 and the line was doubled to Epping in 1892, being completed for the service given in the timetables for January 1893.

The loop at North Weald was constructed by British Railways in 1949 in anticipation of the transfer of the line to London Transport. In the same year, non-token working of the single line was introduced in two stages. In the early 1970s, London Transport remeasured their whole system in kilometres, based on Ongar.

(L) *UN* 226, p.327 (10/1980)

Level Crossings on the London Underground

THERE WERE a considerable number of 'occupation' (or 'accommodation') crossings, as well as footpath crossings, beyond Neasden. These have either been closed or replaced by bridges. There were no actual road crossings until Aylesbury, where a minor road crossed just north of the station. This was replaced by a footbridge when the Metropolitan assumed control of the Aylesbury & Buckingham Railway. However, the road was still available to landowners, who had to obtain keys from the station. A rather important road crossed the line by Quainton Road station; it was replaced by a bridge at the time the Great Central Railway opened. The legal date of closing

of the crossing was 11 October 1899. Crossings at Granborough Road, Winslow Road and Verney Junction remained.

There were two level crossings at Barking; these delayed electrification beyond East Ham for over two years. The crossings were replaced by bridges in 1906.

On the Central Line, both Eagle Lane and Snakes Lane (by Woodford station), also the crossing at Buckhurst Hill, were closed and walled off, but subways were provided for pedestrians. At Theydon Bois the level crossing was closed and the roadway diverted over the railway a little to the south.

(L) *UN* 229, p.27 (1/1981)

Upton Park Station, London Tilbury & Southend Railway

UPTON PARK station, London Tilbury & Southend Railway, was opened in 1877, as recorded in contemporary newspapers. It first appears in the timetables for October 1877. In 1895, the London & North Western Railway opened a goods station nearby and some writers have confused the two dates.

(L) *UN* 234, p.143 (6/1981)

58. An Ongar train about to take water at Epping GER, about 1906, looking south towards London.
Commercial postcard.
RCHS/Spence

(xi) On Tickets and Fares

Railway Season Tickets

SEASON or Periodical Tickets were issued by most railways from early days but the number was not very large until the latter part of the nineteenth century when people began to move further from their work.

A notice issued by the North London Railway to its employees has recently come to light. This gives interesting details, with illustrations of the types of season tickets issued in the late nineteenth century, with the shape and colour of the ticket which enabled examiners and collectors readily to identify each one. The practice of the NLR was probably typical of many other lines at the time.

The tickets had a leather background, the first class being rectangular; the second class were also rectangular but with corners removed (octagonal). The minimum period was three months, expiring on the last day of the month. They had to be ordered in advance from the Season Ticket Office, Broad Street, but would be sent to one of the stations concerned if the applicant so desired. A substantial deposit was required, and tickets had to be returned promptly on expiry, otherwise the deposit was liable to be forfeited. As stated, the shape denoted the class, and various colours were used to indicate the stations between which the ticket was available, covering the area Broad Street, Poplar and Richmond. Many were of two colours, some with stripes. There were also some oval tickets as well as some hexagonal. Through tickets to Great Eastern stations bore a diamond sign and those to Great Northern stations were also available by the Metropolitan Railway. It is improbable that third class passengers at that time could have found the money to pay fares three months in advance and the deposit. However, as a result of increased competition by omnibus and tramcar, third class tickets were introduced in 1902 with a small deposit. They were semi-elliptical. Deposits were abolished in 1909 and cloth tickets issued of uniform design. Monthly cardboard tickets were also introduced.

(L) *JRCHS* 19, 1, pp.25–26 (3/1973)

Tickets of the Great Eastern Railway

SOME TICKETS of the Great Eastern Railway have the letters 'BS' printed upon them and I think it may be of interest to place on record the meaning of these letters. 'BS' stands for Barrier Series, and the tickets were issued by the ticket examiner on the down platform at stations such as Bush Hill Park, Highams Park and Silvertown to enable passengers to go straight on to the down platform without first crossing to the booking office on the up side. Such tickets were, of course, only issued in the down direction. 'BS' tickets were also issued at Victoria Park by the ticket examiner in the passage connecting the North London and Great Eastern platforms.

(L) *JRCHS* 7, 3, p.58 (5/1961)

Tickets of the North London Railway

THE first tickets of the North London Railway were printed on stiff paper, square, about half the size of the present single ticket. Only one can be traced.

HACKNEY
TO
LONDON
SECOND CLASS
03

It is pale blue in colour, and the colour of the reverse side is light brown with date '26 SEPT'. No year is given but this is most probably 1850, the

59. A selection of North London Railway and London, Midland & Scottish Railway tickets.
The later NLR designs are similar to those which HVB would have issued during his spell as a booking
clerk, and the station code numbers mentioned by HVB can be clearly seen on three of the
tickets shown – *From the collection of Godfrey Croughton*

date of opening of the line. At this time the fares were 6d and 4d single, 9d and 6d return between any two stations. Parliamentary tickets were issued by one train each way at 1d per mile, where [this was] less than the second class fare of 4d.

Through tickets to other lines were presumably of standard size, and, a few years after opening of the railway, tickets of normal size were adopted for local journeys.

From 1 January 1864 the fares between any pair of adjacent stations were made 3d first, 2d second class, and these tickets bore a large number or letter front and back according to the station from which they were available. The stations were numbered consecutively from Hampstead Road, No.1, to Bow which was No.9. Similar tickets were issued on the Hampstead Junction and North & South Western Junction Railways and these bore a letter, Camden Road being 'A', Kentish Town (later renamed Gospel Oak) 'B', and so on – Hampstead Heath, Finchley Road, Edgeware Road, Kensal Green, Acton, Hammersmith which became 'H' – and finally Kew to which the latter 'K' was allocated.

Commencing 1 September 1870, the fares between adjacent stations were reduced to 2d first class, 1d second class. Additional passenger stations had been opened and given the following letters: Broad Street, 'L'; Shoreditch, 'S'; Dalston Junction, 'N'; Poplar, 'P'.

The normal colours of the tickets were: down direction, first class white, second class pink; up direction, yellow and blue respectively, but some were of two colours, such as Broad Street to Shoreditch which was of a dark pinkish mauve with a broad cream-coloured horizontal band. Return tickets were of two colours according to direction and bore number or letter corresponding to the station from which they were available.

Reduction in fares between adjacent stations to 2d and 1d respectively according to class necessitated modifications in other short distance fares.

In November 1873 an entirely new system was adopted. Down line tickets were first class white, second class pink (sometimes red), Parliamentary, where issued, green. Up line tickets were yellow, dark blue, and buff respectively. These tickets carried a large number according to destination station. The stations were numbered consecutively from Broad Street, No.1, to Chalk Farm, No.9, then Hackney,

No.10, to Blackwall, No.16. Kentish Town was No.17, thence to Hammersmith, No.25, Kew Bridge, No.26, Richmond, No.29. Return tickets were of two colours, according to direction, and tickets to stations on other railways bore the appropriate number of the NL station on the return half.

In 1875 third class tickets were issued between all stations and the colours were green, down line, buff, up line. Previously third class (or Parliamentary) tickets had been issued, first by one train, later by two trains, and such passengers travelled in second class carriages. Most of the second class fares were one penny or less per mile so the number of Parliamentary bookings was on a very limited scale. Upon the introduction of third class generally, for a few months between many adjacent stations both the second and third class fares were 1d (but later the second was raised to 1½d). With this exception the second class fares remained unaltered, the new third class fare being a little lower.

When additional stations were opened the new station took the number of the previous station plus 'A'; thus West End Lane became '20A'.

Tickets from stations on the Poplar line to stations west of Dalston were of the normal down line colours but locally on the Poplar line, as well as to and from Dalston, Broad Street and intermediately, the tickets carried a variety of vertical lines or stripes. NL tickets were issued from Blackwall, but very few survived and it would appear that at first these were of the usual up line colours, but later the down line colours were adopted. NL tickets were also issued from Fenchurch Street and Stepney until 1869. These were of normal down line colours, with a vertical band. Tickets to stations on the Blackwall line also carried a coloured band

Hampstead Junction Railway and North & South Western Junction Railway tickets were similar to those of the North London Railway. No Hampstead Junction tickets were supplied after 1874 but some remained until about 1912, chiefly first returns from Hampstead Heath and Finchley Road to some South Western Railway stations. Commencing in July 1874, tickets from Hampstead Junction line stations were standard London & North Western Railway type.

Tickets from NL and N&SWJ stations to L&NW main line stations north of Willesden were headed

London & North Western Railway and were supplied by that Company. Tickets to suburban stations on the Great Northern Railway were of the usual NL pattern, but Broad Street, Dalston, Hackney, Bow and Poplar had bookings to a large number of stations on the GN and NE Railways and tickets for these bookings were supplied by the GN Company. Most of these were withdrawn in 1916 as it was then impracticable to travel from the North London line, as very few long-distance trains called at Finsbury Park. Tickets to GN stations supplied subsequently were North London.

From an early date Workmen's tickets were issued between Chalk Farm, Broad Street and Poplar at a charge of 2d. Many stations had automatic machines, some of the first in existence. There were six different series, of different colours, one for each day of the week.

Privilege tickets were of the following colours, arranged horizontally:

Local tickets – first class white, yellow, white;
   second class blue, dark blue, blue;
   third class mauve, red, mauve;
Interchange privilege tickets – first class red, white, red;
   second class blue, white, blue;
   third class green, white, green.

Season tickets were issued for periods of 3, 6, 9 or 12 months. They were of leather and a substantial deposit was charged. The first class tickets were rectangular, the second class were rectangular with corners removed (octagonal). Third class season tickets were not issued until 1902; they were semicircular. Various colours and combinations of colours denoted the stations between which they were available. A few were oval or hexagonal in shape. All season tickets were issued from the Season Ticket Office at Broad Street but were sent to the station concerned if the applicant so desired. The Broad Street office supplied not only tickets with NL stations but also stations on the Hampstead Junction, Kew and Richmond lines. Commencing in 1909 deposits were abolished and season tickets of uniform design, on cloth, could be obtained on demand or at short notice at the stations. At the same time Monthly tickets were also issued which were of cardboard. Weekly tickets were obtainable between some stations.

Season tickets with Great Northern stations were always issued by that Company. Broad Street

tickets were also available at Moorgate; in 1904 they were made available at Bishopsgate Met (later Liverpool Street) and over the Great Northern & City Electric Railway. Third class tickets, and also Monthly tickets with certain stations, were introduced in 1904.

Through season tickets between NL and GE stations had a large diamond sign embossed upon them.

All distinctive types of Season tickets ceased to be issued in 1909, and from 1 July 1912 NL and N&SWJ tickets were printed by the L&NW Company in accordance with their standard designs, but with heading North London Railway or N&SWJ as the case may be.

N&SWJ tickets, also Hampstead Junction when issued, were, until 1912, identical with NLR tickets and all were printed by private firms.

N&SWJ tickets were issued from Richmond, Kew Gardens and Gunnersbury to South Acton, Acton and all places beyond, including L&NW main line, as for many years the South Western would not permit L&NW tickets at these three stations.

Ordinary return tickets were originally available on day of issue only, but from 1902 the return half was available the following day. Through tickets to other railways were, however, available for longer periods, with some exceptions.

(A) *JRCHS* 8, 3, pp.37–41 (5/1962)

Tickets of the Metropolitan District Railway

THE FIRST TICKETS issued by this railway were simple in design and were headed Metropolitan District Railway, but after a few years the title was shown as District Railway and the full name does not appear again on card tickets, although at times some paper tickets bore the full name, more particularly those printed from 1920 until the formation of the London Passenger Transport Board.

Few early tickets have survived, but the colours were: *First class –* white or pink; *Second class –* blue; *Third class* – purple or mauve.

Some of these tickets bore geometrical signs, such as a triangle or a circle, conspicuously overprinted, but the significance of these signs cannot now be traced. Return tickets were usually of one colour, but in some cases the return half was of a different colour.

Just prior to the opening of the extension to Hammersmith, which took place in 1874, it was decided to print a large initial letter representing the destination station on local tickets to assist ticket collectors. As the letter 'S' was allocated to Sloane Square, South Kensington was given 'K' and Kensington High Street 'H'. West Brompton was made 'X'. The only non-District station to be allocated a letter was Kensington Addison Road, to which station the letter 'A' was given. As extensions were opened other letters were used, in most cases arbitrary, the letter 'Z' being reached at Osterley. The original Hounslow terminus was the first station to be indicated by two letters, 'HW' being shown as a capital 'H' surmounted by a small 'w'. Hounslow Barracks when opened became 'HB' and when the old Hounslow terminus was closed the code letters 'HW' were transferred to the newly opened Heston-Hounslow station. Later the old Hounslow terminus was reopened as Hounslow Town and its code letters became 'HT'.

When the Inner Circle was completed in 1884 both the Metropolitan and the Metropolitan District considered it most important that the passenger travelled by the shortest route and all tickets partly or entirely on the Inner Circle bore a letter 'O' for Outer Rail, 'I' for Inner Rail, in large red type front and back. In a few cases, the distance being almost the same, the ticket was overprinted 'E' for Either Rail.

All stations east of Mansion House, also stations on the South Acton and South Harrow branches, had double letters printed, usually in skeleton form (black parallel lines) and, with a few exceptions, in the form of a monogram.

Once letters were allocated they were never changed. Thus Putney Bridge retained 'F' for Fulham; West Kensington 'N' (North End Fulham); Monument 'EP' (Eastcheap, which name it bore for only a month). Mile End was 'BT' for Burdett Road, the name usually given to this station when under construction.

In the case of return tickets to stations on other railways the return half bore the appropriate letter of the District Railway station. All return tickets were printed horizontally.

From about 1873 the colours of ordinary single and return tickets were standardized as under: *First class* – white; *Second class* – blue or bluish-grey; *Third class* – olive.

Some of the third class tickets were mauve and this colour was soon adopted generally for third class.

Second class was abolished in 1905 at the time of electrification and from that year the Ordinary Car (third class) tickets were green. The following year the railways attached less importance to the direction the passenger travelled round the Inner Circle and ceased to print the red 'O' or 'I' on the tickets, but the route was usually shown in small type. At the same time the black skeleton letter indicating the destination station ceased to be printed.

In 1917 a limited number of 'Scheme' or 'Zone' tickets were introduced for the lower fares, usually from automatic machines. The colour was green and the printing on the front was horizontal; on the back the destination stations were arranged vertically. The lay-out was the same as the tickets of the Bakerloo line of the London Electric Railway, where Scheme tickets (coloured blue) were issued as from 1 January 1911. All Scheme tickets issued from Charing Cross were blue. In 1925 the Underground Electric Railways Company decided on different colours for tickets of each line. That selected for the District Railway was pink and from this date tickets to all local stations, including Metropolitan, were Scheme tickets printed vertically with destinations on the front, continued on the back if necessary. Tickets to stations on other railways were also pink or light red, the singles printed horizontally, the returns usually printed vertically. Upon the formation of the London Passenger Transport Board green was adopted as the standard colour for ordinary tickets.

(A) *JRCHS* 6, 4, pp.61–63 (7/1960)

IT IS CORRECT that District Railway tickets did not normally carry the full title but some very early tickets bore the full name, Metropolitan District Railway, as did paper tickets in later years. These were used for bookings to stations on main lines where printed tickets were not held. For many years these were pink, but later were green.

The large destination letter was not changed if a station was renamed. Thus Putney Bridge & Fulham remained 'F', West Kensington, formerly North End Fulham, remained 'W', Monument (Eastcheap) was always 'EP'. Mile End was 'BT' as it was proposed to name the station Burdett Road.

Tickets to Ravenscourt Park and Turnham Green were not allowed letters as they were not District Railway stations; on the contrary, tickets to Addison Road bore letter 'A'. When the Tube railways were first opened there was a ticket office in the subway in nearly every case. These were soon found to be unnecessary and were gradually closed, but that in the Euston subway remained in place, unused, for very many years. Those at Baker Street, Charing Cross and Earl's Court were open until about 1950.

(L) *UN* 288, p.148 (12/1985)

Through Bookings, Central and Metropolitan Lines to Western Region Suburban Stations

IT IS UNDERSTOOD that all through bookings from the Central Line to WR stations via Ealing Broadway, as well as those from Metropolitan Line stations via Paddington, were withdrawn on and from 7 September 1969.

The bookings from Metropolitan stations had been in operation for over a century. When the Metropolitan Railway was an independent company through bookings operated to most Great Western stations. To places served also by the London & North Western Railway, such as Birmingham and Shrewsbury, the fares from Euston Square (Gower Street) were the same as from Paddington and Euston, thus giving passengers a free ride to Paddington.

(L) *U* 9, 1, p.7 (1/1970)

Through Fares via Richmond

AS MOST members will be aware, the line from Studland Road Junction, Hammersmith, to Turnham Green was originally the property of the London & South Western Railway and through fares to a considerable number of stations on that railway remained in operation from Ravenscourt Park, Stamford Brook and Turnham Green after London Transport took control. All through fares were, however, withdrawn in September 1969. This is to be regretted as passengers now have to pass through the exit barrier at Richmond and obtain another ticket.

(L) *U* 9, 4, p.58 (4/1970)

Through Fares, Metropolitan to Great Eastern stations

THROUGH FARES operated from Metropolitan Railway stations to Great Eastern suburban stations from about 1875. There were also through fares to and from suburban stations on most other lines: GN and Midland via King's Cross, GW via Paddington, L&SW via Hammersmith, LC&D via Aldersgate, South Eastern via Cannon Street or New Cross, LBSC via New Cross (now New Cross Gate), LT&S via Aldgate and Fenchurch Street or Mark Lane and Fenchurch Street or via Aldgate East and Bow Road. Tickets to New Cross (SE) and beyond were available either via Aldgate East or via Cannon Street.

The London Passenger Transport Board looked upon most through fares with disfavour and they were gradually faded out at very short notice, the reason given being that there was little demand, but as most stations had substantial printed stocks this remark was open to question.

(L) *U* 9, 9, p.150 (9/1970)

Toll Tickets: Earl's Court

FOR MANY YEARS Toll tickets (or Platform tickets) have been issued at Earl's Court to enable one to pass through the station from one entrance to the other. In addition, a double or return toll ticket could be obtained which enabled the holder to return without extra charge, the price of the double ticket being the same as the single, but the reason for this is not now clear. The original price of both the single and double tickets was 1d, later increased to

2d, then 3d and lastly 6d. From 14 February [1971], however, the price was slightly reduced to two new pence, but the double tickets are not now issued, so one must now pay 4p for the double journey.

(L) *U* 10, 4, p.58 (4/1971)

[This was one of the few published statements made by HVB to be challenged. In *U* 10, 5, pp.76–77, Mr G. Jasieniecki wrote as follows:

I HESITATE to rush forward and disagree with Mr Borley's note concerning Earl's Court Toll Tickets, published in the April *Journal*, but in the interests of the high standards of accuracy which he himself has always maintained, I feel that the record must be corrected.

For some days before Decimalisation, the two columns of 'platform tickets' in all the booking offices at Earl's Court had their price altered to 2p (although, of course, 6d tickets were issued). New 2p 'single' platform tickets were issued from Sunday 14 February but the Return Toll tickets were variously described by staff as 'not available,' 'not in yet,' 'withdrawn,' or simply 'haven't got any.' Enquiry at the Fares and Charges Office in late February revealed that the Return Tolls were 'delayed at the printers, definitely not withdrawn as there is a demand.' They have since appeared at the station, first noted 24 March, although none were *actually* sold from the main (A) office until the evening of 26 March. (Booking Office records may in the future suggest a different story, but that is what, in fact, happened.) They cost the same as platform tickets, 2p.

In amplification of the rest of Mr Borley's letter, may I say that from the later days of 1d platform tickets to date, the 'single' Toll tickets referred to have in fact been ordinary platform tickets in appearance and, presumably, in intention. The other tickets are the Toll tickets proper, permitting the holder to walk through the station from Earl's Court Road to Warwick Road (or Exhibition) and back, or vice versa. These tickets are sometimes erroneously called return platform tickets (surely an illogical term); unfortunately the Book of Routes does not state whether one is supposed to walk along the elevated footpath through the station or whether one is permitted to take the marginally longer route via the platforms!

I have heard tell that in the dim and distant past (well before 1948) there were such things as single toll tickets (as well as the returns) as distinct from the ordinary platform tickets.]

London Transport Tickets for BR Journeys

AT CERTAIN STATIONS London Transport supply and issue tickets for journeys which are actually local to British Railways. These tickets are all headed London Transport but the type varies and I consider it desirable to put on record the present position.

Tickets from Seven Sisters and Tottenham Hale to Great Eastern Line stations are normal size green tickets in the case of singles but only the fare is shown. Day returns are white and give both destination and fare. The passenger retains the whole of the ticket until he arrives back at the issuing station. Privilege tickets are green, of three separate categories: (a) single, (b) forward, (c) return. Each ticket is of normal size but destination is not shown.

From Moorgate and Old Street to Great Northern stations, all tickets are normal size. Singles are light green and destination and fare are shown. Day returns are brown, of standard type, and here also destination and fare are shown. The passenger surrenders the forward half at destination. Privilege tickets, singles only, are dark green and indicate only the fare, and are identical with those issued to stations outside the zone. King's Cross and Highbury & Islington have special yellow singles to GN stations showing destination station. For Day Returns, two separate tickets are issued, the forward one being yellow and the return red; destination is printed. Privilege tickets, single only, from Highbury are special green tickets giving destination and fare.

From Highbury & Islington to North London Line stations, ordinary station-of-origin yellow tickets are issued. Returns are not issued but the cross-town Broad Street – Richmond are normal size reddish-brown tickets which one retains complete until arrival back at Highbury. Privilege tickets are light green with destination and fare. Tickets for children are endorsed 'CHILD' in red and usually follow the same pattern as tickets for

60. London Transport
Automatic Ticket Machines
of late 1930s design at
Finchley Road in 1952. The
illuminated panels display
typical 'Scheme Ticket' fares.
RCHS/Spence

adults, except yellow tickets. As children may not use automatic barriers, green tickets are used in such cases. Child tickets Highbury to North London stations give destination.

(L) *UN* 212, pp.218–219 (8/1979)

Season Tickets: Great Northern Stations to the City of London

FROM 1875 Season Tickets from GNR stations to Moorgate were also available to Broad Street. Soon after the opening of the Great Northern & City Railway in 1904, these tickets were also available over that line, and to Bishopsgate (Liverpool Street) Met. These were the three-route Season Tickets. Until about 1915 season tickets were of various shapes and colours and with various markings to assist ticket examiners, but as a deposit was required very few have survived. The colours of the three-route Seasons were:

First Class: Red/Cream with gold lettering

Second Class: Blue/Green with black lettering
Third Class: (issued from 1904): Chocolate/Yellow
  with black lettering

These tickets ceased to be issued in 1964 when the section between Finsbury Park and Drayton Park was closed. See also *Railway Magazine*, December 1977, page 672, and February 1978, page 92.

(L) *UN* 250, p.224 (9/1982)

London Transport Scheme Tickets

IT WOULD APPEAR that London Transport have abolished Scheme tickets. These were last issued from the East London line to stations on the Southern Region but when fares were revised from 28 March 1971 new tickets were supplied and these were printed horizontally, with the destination station (or stations) prominently shown, the issuing station and fare in smaller type.

For the benefit of younger Members, I may add that Scheme tickets were printed vertically, with the issuing station and fare in large type top and bottom of the ticket, the destinations being in smaller type. At one time they were the normal issue on London Transport locally as well as for many through bookings.

(L) *U* 10, 9, p.141 (9/1971)

Some Early Forms of Ticket Identification

City & South London Railway

The C&SLR had different colour tickets for each destination, listed as under:

Clapham Common: Pink
Clapham Road: Pink with black diagonal line
Stockwell: Purple
Oval: Green
Kennington: Blue
Elephant & Castle: Yellow
Borough: Brown
London Bridge: Pale Blue
Bank: Buff
Moorgate: Orange
Old Street: Lilac
City Road: Red
Angel: White
King's Cross: White with red cross ✕
Euston: White with red U

District Railway

The list below is of letters indicating destination stations on District Railway tickets *circa* 1871 to *circa* 1905. Sometimes letters appeared in skeleton form, thus:

L

The letters were (and perhaps still are?) also shown on Season tickets to indicate station of issue. Mile End is unusual as it was only referred to as Burdett Road prior to opening.

Inner Circle tickets had 'O' to indicate Outer Rail, 'I' to indicate Inner Rail, and, very few, 'E' for Either Rail; these letters were sometimes in red. Ticket examiners at top or foot of stairs made sure the passenger went the correct way round the Circle.

(A) *UN* 302, p.23 (2/1987)

[Solid black letters were originally used (i.e. from about 1874), heavily serifed, with height, width and thickness varying greatly in the ensuing years culminating in thin sans serif. Large skeleton letters, apparently printed with the text rather than overprinted as before, replaced solid letters from about 1883, sometimes placed centrally, but mostly towards the left side of single tickets and centrally on each half of returns. Letter height varied from 21mm to 23mm, with width depending on the letter used – Editor, with acknowledgement to Godfrey Croughton]

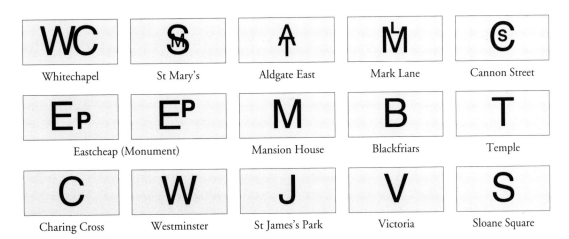

Whitechapel	St Mary's	Aldgate East	Mark Lane	Cannon Street
Eastcheap (Monument)		Mansion House	Blackfriars	Temple
Charing Cross	Westminster	St James's Park	Victoria	Sloane Square

K	**G**	**E**	**A**	**X**
South Kensington	Gloucester Road	Earl's Court	Addison Road	West Brompton
Q	**P**	**F**	**N**	**BC**
Walham Green	Parsons Green	Putney Bridge and Fulham	North End Fulham (West Kensington)	Barons Court
D	**U**	**I**	**L**	**O**
Hammersmith	Acton Green (Chiswick Park)	Mill Hill Park	Ealing Common	Ealing Broadway
SA	**R**	**NH**	**Y**	**Z**
South Acton	South Ealing	Northfield Halt	Boston Road	Osterley

WH	**TH**	**TH**
Hounslow Old Station Heston-Hounslow	Hounslow Town first station reopened	Hounslow Town second station

HB	**BH**	**BW**	**TB**	**PS**
Hounslow Barracks		Bow Road	Mile End (proposed name Burdett Road)	Stepney Green

ON	**PR**	**PA**	**RA**	**SS**
North Ealing	Park Royal	Perivale-Alperton		Sudbury Town

US	**HR**
Sudbury Hill	South Harrow

Books by H. V. Borley

London Transport Railways: A List of Opening, Closing and Renaming Dates of Lines and Stations (with A. E. Bennett), David & Charles, 1963; folding map, card covers, pp.32.

The West London Railway and the W.L.E.R. (with R. W. Kidner), Oakwood Press, 1969; card covers, pp.32.

Chronology of London Railways, Railway & Canal Historical Society, 1982; card covers, pp.94 (ISBN 0 901461 33 4).

H. V. Borley also contributed, with C. Hamilton Ellis, two supplementary chapters (XXVI and XXVII) to a new edition of Charles H. Grinling's *The History of the Great Northern Railway*, George Allen & Unwin, 1966; cased, pp.490.

The second enlarged edition of C. F. Dendy Marshall's *A History of the Southern Railway*, revised by R. W. Kidner, Ian Allan, 1963; cased, pp.563 (single volume reprint, Ian Allan, 1968) includes some, but by no means all, of the many corrections to the Marshall text identified and listed by H. V. Borley.

Index

Note:
There may be more than one reference
on the page given.
All maps and illustrations are included
in the index.